Heart in the Holy Quran

By
Dr. M. Adnan Raufi
MD FACP FACC FSCAI

Table of Contents

Dedication

To my parents

About the Author

Dr. M. Adnan Raufi, M.D., FACP, FACC, FSCAI, is a distinguished Interventional Cardiologist from Westchester Medical Center, New York. He has extensive experience in the field of cardiovascular medicine. With a career spanning multiple countries, he has served as a consultant Interventional Cardiologist in leading hospitals across the United States, the United Arab Emirates, and Pakistan.

Dr. Raufi holds board certifications in Cardiovascular Disease, and Interventional Cardiology from the American Board of Internal Medicine. He has been instrumental in introducing advanced interventional cardiology techniques in several healthcare institutions.

He has provided a leadership role in improving cardiac care standards and has initiated innovative treatment programs in various hospitals.

Dr. Raufi is a dedicated teacher and has played a key role in training young physicians at various institutions.

Beyond his clinical work, Dr. Raufi has contributed significantly to medical research, with various publications in peer-reviewed journals. He has presented at prestigious international conferences and actively participates in editorial and research committees. He is always inquisitive about new technology. He has great passion in developing new medical devices and has been working on such projects.
Dr. Raufi's commitment to patient care extends beyond hospital walls, as he is actively involved in charitable medical initiatives, providing interventional cardiology services to underserved

communities. His dedication to advancing cardiovascular medicine continues to make a lasting impact on the field.

DR MUHAMMAD AKRAM HURERI

796- Chicken Dozan Medan, Jandi Vehrrah Beroon Pak Gate Multan

mahurary@gmail.com

+92 321 7576 476

Visiting Faculty, The Knowledge University Riyadh, Ex Research Associate Malaya University Malaysia, Guest Anchor TVs, Columnist, Islamic Scholar.

Endorsement for **"Heart in the Holy Quran"**

It's my great pleasure that I present my endorsement for Dr. Adnan Raufi's insightful work, "Heart in the Holy Quran." This masterpiece in the shape of book serves as a remarkable exploration of the connections between the physiological functions of the human heart as it is considered in the field of cardiology.

In this book, Dr. Raufi organized a preface and seven comprehensive chapters. He explained functions of the human heart and prescribed it as expounded by modern cardiology. He compared between these scientific insights and the timeless verses of the Quran. Dr. Raufi illuminates the profound harmony between scientific knowledge and divine revelation.

As a researcher of Islamic and Quranic studies, I am deeply appreciated by the author's ability to navigate the intersection of faith and science in unique angle with such clarity and reverence. He underscores the spiritual significance attributed to this organ in Islamic teachings along with the physical attributes of the heart. I am feeling happy to read this book that presenting the functions of the human heart with Quranic verses. Author's intellectual analysis is according to the Islamic principals those will provide the readers and researchers a comprehensive exploration of this profound subject matter. Dr. Raufi's work is a specimen to his dedication to bridging the gap between disciplines and fostering a holistic appreciation of the human experience. In conclusion, I wholeheartedly endorse "Heart in the Holy Quran" as a thought-provoking and enlightening contribution to the fields of medical (cardiology), Islamic studies, and the intersection of science and spirituality. Hopefully, the book "**Heart in the Holy**

Quran" will be the useful for the readers, scholars and researchers and to inspire them the intricate design of the human heart and the profound wisdom narrated in the verses of the Holy Quran.

Sincerely,

Dr Muhammad Akram Hureri

Visiting Faculty, The Knowledge University Riyadh,
Ex Research Associate Malaya University Malaysia,
Guest Anchor TVs, Columnist, Islamic Scholar.

Mohammad Ali Jinnah University, Karachi

Dr. Mufti Muhammad Omer Rafique

3-21-2024

To Whom It May Concern,

I am writing to wholeheartedly endorse Dr. Adnan Raufi's book, "Heart in the Holy Quran." As a scholar deeply engaged in the study of Islamic texts and their implications, I have had the privilege of collaborating closely with Dr. Raufi on this remarkable work.

"Heart in the Holy Quran" stands as a testament to Dr. Raufi's dedication, scholarship, and profound understanding of the Quranic text. Throughout the process of editing and reviewing, I have witnessed Dr. Raufi's meticulous attention to detail, his commitment to accuracy, and his unwavering adherence to the principles of Shariah.

In "Heart in the Holy Quran," Dr. Raufi offers readers a profound exploration of the Quranic teachings concerning the heart. Drawing upon his deep knowledge of the Quranic text and its exegetical tradition, Dr. Raufi provides insightful interpretations and practical reflections that resonate with both scholars and laypersons alike. These interpretations can be observed as indications or possible connection between the spirituality of Quran and Cardiovascular systems created by Allah in our body. However, these connections are not the exact tafseer or meanings of Quran, as it is mentioned during the explanation of the verses in the book.

In conclusion, I wholeheartedly recommend "Heart in the Holy Quran" by Dr. Adnan Raufi to all -those interested in gaining a deeper insight into the spiritual dimensions of the Quran. Dr. Raufi's scholarly rigor, combined with his profound insights and commitment to excellence, make this book a significant contribution to the field of Quranic studies.

Sincerely,

Dr. Mufti Muhammad Omer Rafique

Assistant Professor, Muhammad Ali Jinnah University

Shariah Advisor UBM and qordata inc.

omerrafiq1@gmail.com

22-E, Block-6, P.E.C.H.S, Karachi-75400, Pakistan Tel: 021-111-87-87-87, 34314207-8, Fax: 92-21-34311327
URL: www.jinnah.edu E-mail: info@jinnah.edu,

Mohammad Ali Jinnah
University, Karachi

Commentary

The Holy Quran contains numerous references to the heart, both as a physical organ and a metaphorical symbol. The Quranic concept of the heart is multifaceted, encompassing spiritual, emotional, and moral dimensions. This book "Heart and the Holy Quran" delves into the significance of the heart in the Holy Quran, exploring its symbolism, functions, and the profound insights it offers into human nature and spiritual growth.

Physically, the heart is the vital organ that sustains life, pumping blood throughout the body. In the Quran, it is often mentioned alongside the brain, emphasizing the interconnectedness of reason and emotion (Quran 33:4). However, the Quranic concept of the heart transcends its physical function, representing the seat of consciousness, emotions, and spirituality.

The Quran describes the heart as a vessel that can be pure or impure, reflecting an individual's spiritual state (Quran 26:89). A pure heart is filled with faith, compassion, and kindness, while an impure heart is tainted by doubt, greed, and malice. The Quran encourages believers to cultivate a pure heart, warning that a corrupted heart can lead to spiritual blindness and moral decay (Quran 2:7).

The book "Heart in the Holy Quran" delves into various aspects of the heart and its function, drawing connections with Quranic verses. Across separate chapters, the author explores topics such as the heart's protective covering, maintaining a clean and robust heart, the autonomic nervous system's role in heart function, the impact of arterial hardening, valve health, muscle strength, and even heart anomalies like twisting. The commendable effort lies in expanding our understanding of cardiac anatomy while linking it to the teachings of the holy Quran.

Prof. Dr. M. Kamran Azim

Dean, Faculty of Life Sciences

Mohammad Ali Jinnah University

Karachi, Pakistan.

22-E, Block-6, P.E.C.H.S, Karachi-75400, Pakistan Tel: 021-111-87-87-87, 34314207-8, Fax:92-21-34311327
URL: www.jinnah.edu E-mail: info@jinnah.edu,

Diaa A. Hakim, MD, PhD,
FESC
Director of cardiac Imaging, Vascular Profiling Research Group
Director of Intravascular imaging core-lab-TIMI
group
Brigham & Women's Hospital
Cardiovascular Medicine Division
1620 Tremont Street,3-014PI
Boston, Massachusetts 02120
Phone: 347-839-1159
Email: dhakim1@bwh.harvard.edu

I am writing this letter to endorse Dr. M. Adnan Raufi for his elegant Book entitled "Heart in The Holy Quran". Firstly, I must congratulate Dr. Raufi on this piece of art that combine both science and faith.

The book combines in a charming way the science of heart disease, its anatomical, functional, and pathological characteristics, and the Qur'anic science, which supports scientific and medical theories with verses from the Qur'an.

This book can be considered a unique reference for clarifying the close connection between science and faith, and many will benefit from reading it.

Sincerely,
Diaa Hakim

DR. A. RASHID SEYAL
S.I

M. B. B. S. (Pb); Dip Card (UK); Dip Card (USA)
Ph.D (OIUCM), D Sc (OIUCM)
Chief Executive, Seyal Medical Centre (Pvt) Ltd

Author of:
- Glorious Qur'an in Poetic Stance with Scientific Philosophy (4 Volumes)
- Coronary Risk New Perspective. (Recommended by the American College of Physicians.)
- Enigma of Sudden Cardiac Death. Recommended for research oriented award (American College of Physicians.)
- Divine Philosophy of Modern Day • Faith in the Scientific Philosophy of Science.   Religion.
- Perception of Faith in Stress.   • Garments and Human Health.
- Smart Living.   • Living with The   • Morning Prayers.   • Faith in the Heart.   Unseen

• تغلیق کائنات وقت اور انسان قرآن اور جدید سائنس کے تناظر میں   • دل اور انسانی زندگی

The cadence and discipline of Dr. Adnan's writing gave medical reference rather cardiovascular reference of the Holy Quran besides its beautiful diagrammatic looks very imposing and inspiring within the fold of the Holy message of the text. Dr. Adnan was very kind to me and was sending me his hard earned knowledgeable manuscript that is virtually unique of its kind. His entire work is very conspicuous and convincing, as Lord Almighty has given him a special essence of this noble job to achieve. A lot can be said and written about this text but he seems to be motivated in the perpetuation of this prudent and prodigious work for the drill and direction of the people living in the West, in particular to affirm and embrace the ideology of the Holy Scripture based on logic and intellect.

20th April 2018

Preface

"Heart in The Holy Quran" was a concept, which I conceived many years ago. While reviewing various literatures regarding the scientific manifestations in the Holy Quran, I was always curious to learn whether there was any correlation between the heart as a vital organ in the body with its actual anatomical and physiological functions with respect to the Quranic verses. To elaborate on the importance of the heart as an organ in the body, we may say that a whole chapter, "Ya-seen," is mentioned as the "heart of Quran."

I have found it fascinating how beautifully the Holy Quran mentions about the "veil" or the "covering" around the heart and the concept of thickened covering (pericardium) and accumulation of excessive fluid around the heart, diseases which may explain how the otherwise normally existent external forces can affect the heart but the same effect may be blunted if there is a "thick covering" around it. Few other examples, like the concept of cardiac surgery, clean and pure heart and the turning or deviation of the hearts, etc., may draw the attention of the readers.

It is my sincere belief that the Holy Quran is a book of guidance for all human beings. Although it is not a book of science yet, one may find mention of a variety of topics including science and its further branches.

If its Holy verses are applied to a variety of topics, many more secrets inside this book will be unearthed.

When we read the Holy verses we find unimaginable information regarding the development of the earth and skies and heavenly bodies. In the same way, we learn that the human body, with its development

1

and all of its anatomical and physiological functions, is created in the most beautiful fashion.

A beautiful verse of the Holy Quran says:

$$\text{لَـقَـدْ خَـلَـقْـنَـا الْإِنْـسَـانَ فِـيّ أَحْـسَنِ تَـقْـوِيْـمٍ}$$

"We have created man in the best composition,"
(Al-Teen, The Fig, Chapter 95: Verse 4)

There are many Ahadees (Traditions/Narrations of the Holy Prophet Muhammad, Peace Be Upon Him) which indicate the importance of the most vital organ of the body and the problems which might incur on the whole human body should this organ suffer from a "disease."

عن الـنـعـمـان بـن بـشـيـر رضي الله عنـهـمـا قـال : سـمـعت رسـول الله صلـى الله عـلـيـه وسلم يـقـول : ألا وإن فـي الـجسد مضغة إذا صلـحت صلـح الـجسد كلـه ، وإذا فـسدت فـسد وهي الـقـلـب)) ؛ مـتـفـق الـجسد كلـه ، ألا عـلـيـه

Narrated An-Nu'man bin Bashir:

I heard ALLAH's Messenger[PBUH] saying, Beware! There is a piece of flesh in the body, if it becomes good (reformed), the whole body becomes good, but if it gets spoilt, the whole body gets spoilt, and that is the heart.

Before each chapter, a respective synopsis is given for a general reader to grasp the concept better without the use of any technical details. Later on a more detailed description is added for those who may be interested in more depth of these concepts. In this way, I

2

reckon that this book may be of some interest to people from many walks of life. I have tried to mention those Holy verses which I thought might be related to the anatomy, physiology and pathology of the heart as an organ. I have also tried to mention several heart diseases with their etiologies and possible treatments to help people get information which is easier to understand.

I would like to acknowledge that the interpretations used in this manuscript might be encompassed in what are called the "Motashabihaats" (verses that can have many meanings), and the exact meaning is only known to ALLAH (THE MOST EXALTED), yet it opens the door for tremendous academic research.

An important point also needs to be noted that the Holy Quran invites us to ponder upon its verses and ALLAH's signs that He has created around us. For example,

$$إِنَّ فِيْ خَلْقِ السَّمٰوٰتِ وَ الْأَرْضِ وَ اخْتِلَافِ الَّيْلِ وَ النَّهَارِ لَأٰيٰتٍ لِّأُولِي الْأَلْبَابِ$$

"Surely, in the creation of the heavens and the earth, and in the alternation of night and day, there are signs for the people of wisdom,"

(Aale-Imran, The Family of Imran, Chapter 3: Verse 190).

And also in the following verse:

$$حٰـمٌّ تَنْزِيْلُ الْكِتٰبِ مِنَ اللهِ الْعَزِيْزِ الْحَكِيْمِ إِنَّ فِي السَّمٰوٰتِ وَ الْأَرْضِ لَأٰيٰتٍ لِّلْمُؤْمِنِيْنَ وَفِيْ خَلْقِكُمْ وَمَا يَبُثُّ مِنْ دَآبَّةٍ أٰيٰتٌ لِّقَوْمٍ يُّوْقِنُوْنَ وَ اخْتِلَافِ الَّيْلِ وَ النَّهَارِ وَمَآ أَنْزَلَ اللهُ مِنَ السَّمَآءِ مِنْ$$

رِّزْقٍ فَأَحْيَا بِهِ الْأَرْضَ بَعْدَ مَوْتِهَا
وَتَصْرِيْفِ الـرِّيْـحِ أيْتٌ لِّقَوْمٍ يَّعْقِلُوْنَ

Ha Mim. This is revelation of the Book from ALLAH, the All-Mighty, the All-Wise. Surely, in the heavens and the earth, there are signs for those who have faith. And in your creation and in the living beings that He scatters on the earth, there are signs for people who believe. And in the alternation of the day and the night, and in the provision He has sent down from the sky, then has revived the earth after its death, and in changing of the winds, there are signs for a people who understand.

(Al-Jathiya, The crouching, verse: 1-5)

Also, one must look at the verses

الَّـذِيْ خَلَقَ سَبْعَ سَمٰوٰتٍ طِبَاقًا مَا تَـرٰى فِيْ
خَلْقِ الـرَّحْمٰنِ مِنْ تَفٰوُتٍ فَارْجِعِ الْبَصَرَ
هَلْ تَـرٰى مِنْ فُطُوْرٍ

"who has created seven skies, one over the other. You will see nothing out of proportion in the creation of the Rahman (the All-Merciful ALLAH). So, cast your eye again. Do you see any rifts?"
(Sura Al-Mulk67: verse No 03)

And

ثُـمَّ ارْجِعِ الْبَصَرَ كَرَّتَـيْنِ يَنْقَلِبْ إِلَـيْكَ
الْبَصَرُ خَاسِئًا وَّهُوَ حَسِيْرٌ

Then cast your eye again and again, and the eye will come back to you abased, in a state of weariness. (Sura Al-Mulk 67, The Kingdom, verse No 04)

4

I also think that it is the foremost duty of the believers to ponder upon these glorious verses, which actually become the easy pathways towards reaching ALLAH, their LORD and developing a direct connection. This can only happen when we first believe in the unseen, as elaborated in the first few verses of the Holy Quran in Al-Baqarah:

الَّذِيْنَ يُؤْمِنُوْنَ بِالْغَيْبِ وَ يُقِيْمُوْنَ الصَّلٰوةَ وَ مِمَّا رَزَقْنٰهُمْ يُنْفِقُوْنَ

who believe in the Unseen, and are steadfast in Salah (prayer), and spend out of what We have provided them.
(Al Baqarah, The Cow, verse 3).

Finally, I believe that the core essence of performing research in the signs of ALLAH should be to get closer to Him and nothing else. If one does so, science will be beneficial for the entire humanity and in the event of any deviation from this fact, there will be chaos in the world as we evidently manifest in our daily lives.

I humbly pray to ALLAH (THE MOST EXALTED) to accept this little endeavor and forgive all the mistakes.

The following few pictures depict the normal heart structures and normal blood flow pattern, which may be helpful in reading other chapters:

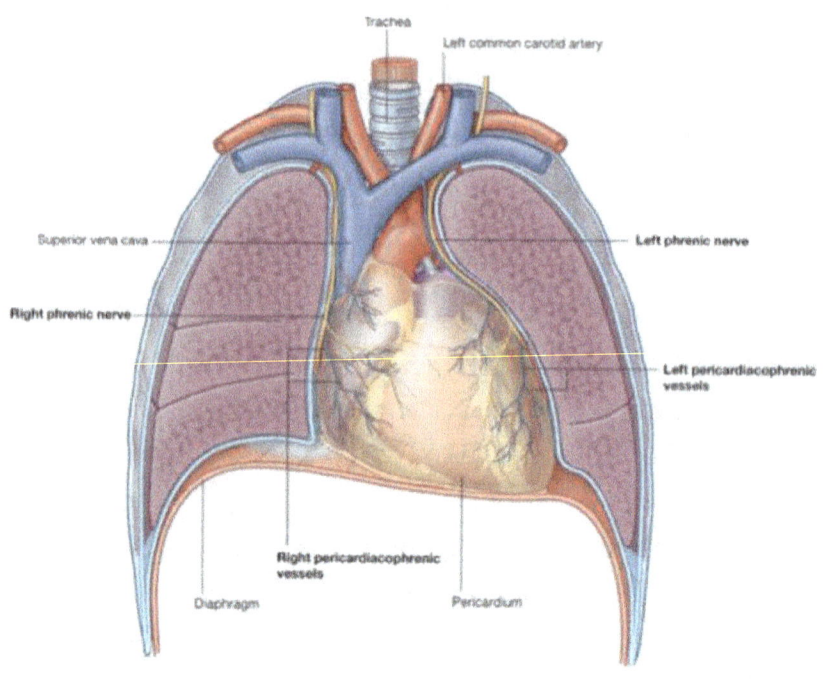

Trachea

Left common carotid artery

Superior vena cava

Left phrenic nerve

Right phrenic nerve

Left pericardiacophrenic vessels

Right pericardiacophrenic vessels

Diaphragm

Pericardium

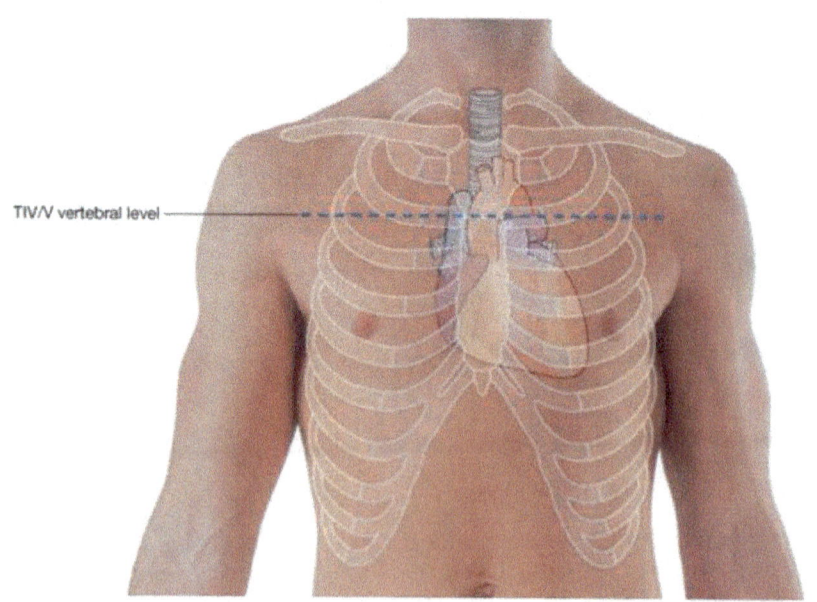

TIV/V vertebral level

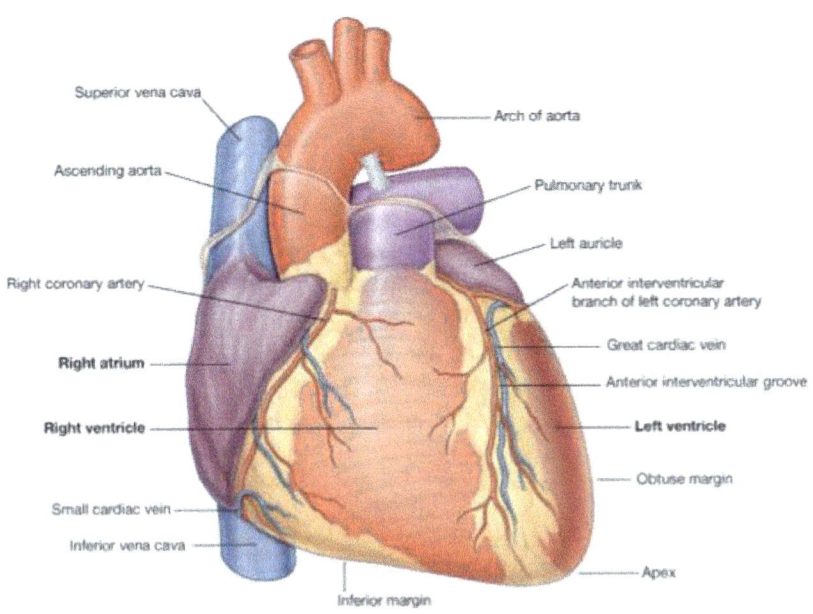

Superior vena cava

Ascending aorta

Right coronary artery

Right atrium

Right ventricle

Small cardiac vein

Inferior vena cava

Inferior margin

Arch of aorta

Pulmonary trunk

Left auricle

Anterior interventricular
branch of left coronary artery

Great cardiac vein

Anterior interventricular groove

Left ventricle

Obtuse margin

Apex

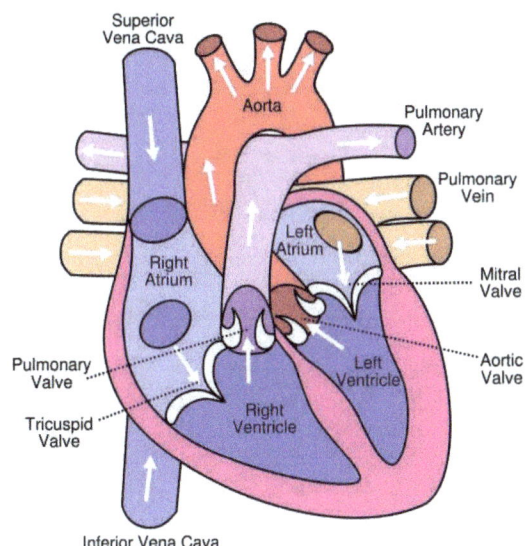

Superior
Vena Cava

Aorta

Pulmonary
Artery

Pulmonary
Vein

Left
Atrium

Mitral
Valve

Right
Atrium

Pulmonary
Valve

Aortic
Valve

Left
Ventricle

Tricuspid
Valve

Right
Ventricle

Inferior Vena Cava

7

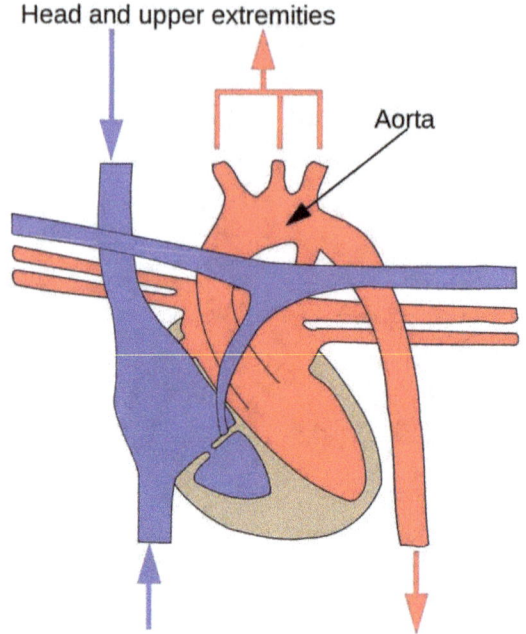

Head and upper extremities

Aorta

Abdomen and lower extermities

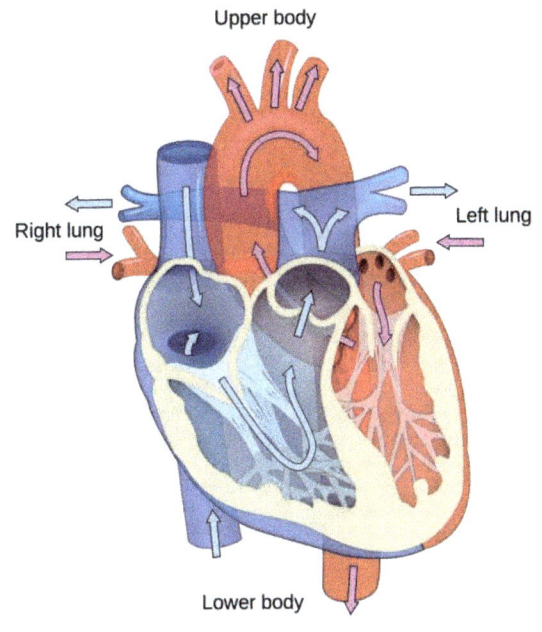

Upper body

Right lung

Left lung

Lower body

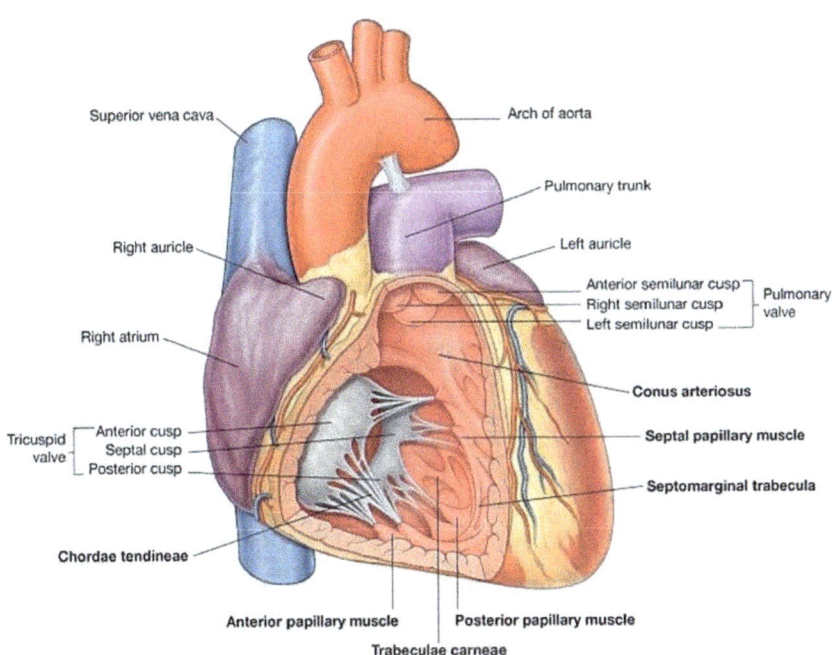

Superior vena cava

Arch of aorta

Pulmonary trunk

Right auricle

Left auricle

Anterior semilunar cusp
Right semilunar cusp — Pulmonary valve
Left semilunar cusp

Right atrium

Conus arteriosus

Tricuspid valve
Anterior cusp
Septal cusp
Posterior cusp

Septal papillary muscle

Septomarginal trabecula

Chordae tendineae

Anterior papillary muscle   Posterior papillary muscle

Trabeculae carneae

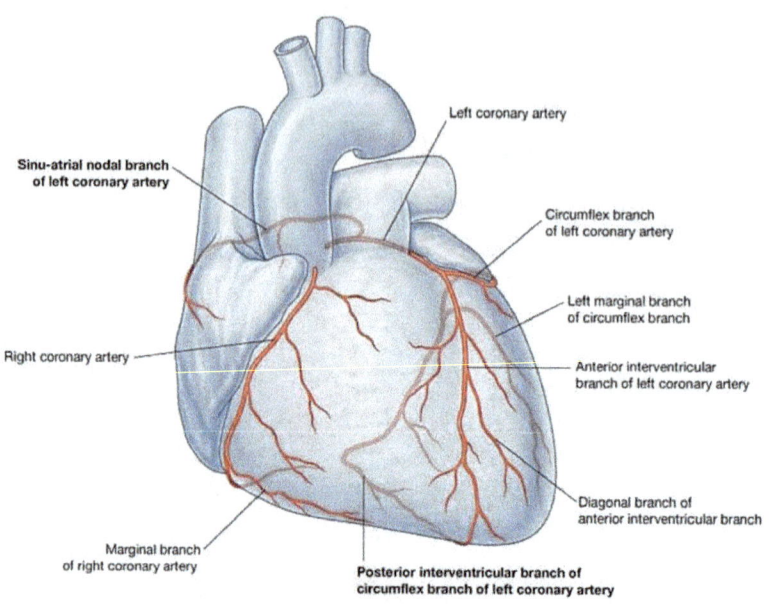

Sinu-atrial nodal branch
of left coronary artery

Left coronary artery

Circumflex branch
of left coronary artery

Left marginal branch
of circumflex branch

Right coronary artery

Anterior interventricular
branch of left coronary artery

Diagonal branch of
anterior interventricular branch

Marginal branch
of right coronary artery

Posterior interventricular branch of
circumflex branch of left coronary artery

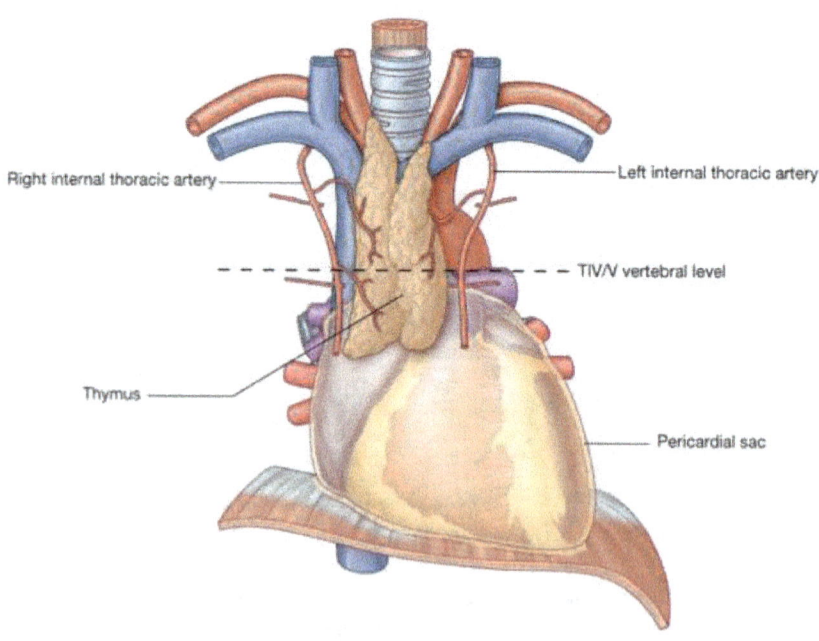

Right internal thoracic artery

Left internal thoracic artery

TIV/V vertebral level

Thymus

Pericardial sac

The following pictures depict the normal blood flow pattern.

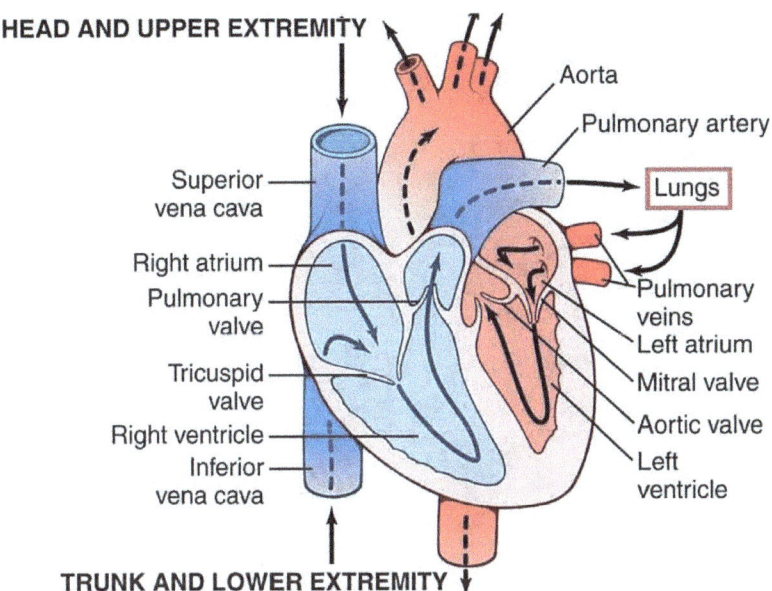

11

THE CIRCULATORY SYSTEM

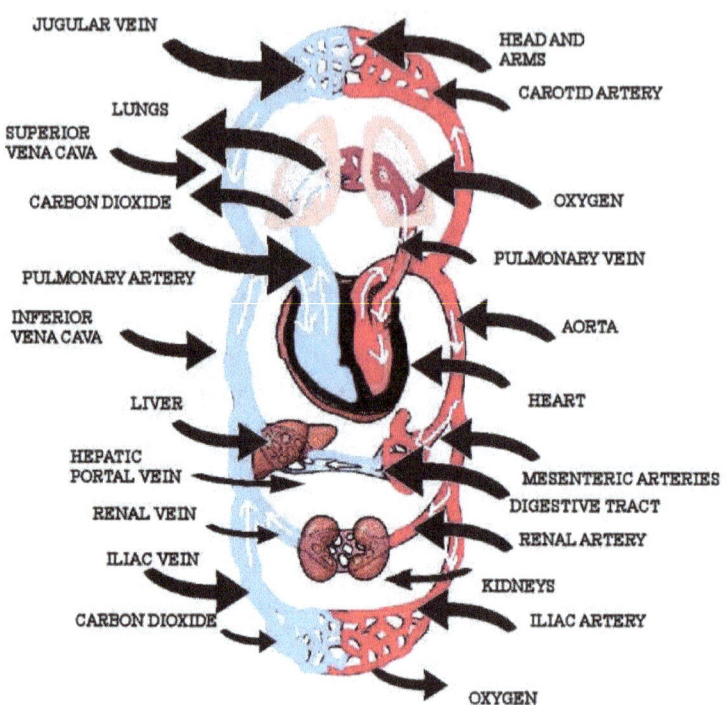

The picture above depicts the blood circulation to and from the heart. The red indicates pure, oxygenated blood from the heart, and the blue shows the impure and deoxygenated blood. It is worth noting that the heart "receives" pure blood (in red) from the lung, and then it pumps out. This is intuitively true as lungs are "cleaning machines" for the body and provide oxygenated blood to the heart in order to be distributed to the body.

Note: All the English translations of the verses of the Holy Quran in this manuscript are taken from "The Noble Quran," by Mufti Taqi Usmani.

Chapter 1 (Synopsis)

Stable Angina

Chest Pain during Exertion

In this chapter, we would like to focus on cardiac symptoms which occur upon exertion and the reason behind them along with treatment. It is a known fact that patients with significant blockages in their coronary arteries complain of chest pain of variable severity during physical exertion like walking, running, doing any manual chores like snow shoveling, climbing up the stairs or uphill, etc.

This is due to the fact that when plaque building crosses a limit, and the heart muscle cannot get enough blood and oxygen during times of extra demand, for instance, during the activities mentioned above, then the person starts to experience chest discomfort. This kind of discomfort typically gets relieved if the person takes rest or certain pain medicine like nitroglycerin (tablet or spray under the tongue).

Let us now try to ponder on the following beautiful Holy verse.

فَمَنْ يُرِدِ اللهُ أَنْ يَهْدِيَهُ يَشْرَحْ صَدْرَهُ
لِلْإِسْلَامِ وَمَنْ يُرِدْ أَنْ يُضِلَّهُ يَجْعَلْ صَدْرَهُ
ضَيِّقًا حَرَجًا كَأَنَّمَا يَصَّعَّدُ فِي السَّمَاءِ
كَذَلِكَ يَجْعَلُ اللهُ الرِّجْسَ عَلَي الَّذِيْنَ لَا
يُؤْمِنُوْنَ

"So, whomsoever ALLAH wills to guide, He makes his heart wide open for Islam, and whomsoever He wills to let go astray, He makes his heart strait and constricted, (and he feels embracing Islam as

difficult) as if he were climbing to the sky. In this way, ALLAH lays abomination on those who do not believe. "
(Chapter 6: Al- Anaam, The Cattle: Verse 125)

This analogy helps us understand, according to modern science, that if the heart arteries are narrowed, there is a sensation of a squeeze or heaviness in the chest, especially when the person is climbing uphill or upstairs, running or doing any extra hard work.

It is also noteworthy that some patients may explain the symptoms as if a heavy weight is sitting on their chests. These symptoms may also be combined with shortness of breath, sweating, fatigue, nausea, vomiting, or even fainting.

In patients, who develop stable angina (chest pain during exertion and related to significant blockage of the heart arteries), their disease process may be better studied by using several modalities. One of the most common is the treadmill stress test.

A simple analogy of this stress test is as if someone is walking fast and uphill (Quranic Verse reference as above, "climbing into the sky"). If someone has significant stenosis (blockage) in his/her coronary artery (ies), this test will be able to bring it out in several ways. Patients may complain of symptoms as depicted above, or there may be changes in their EKGs or vital signs (blood pressure or pulse rate) or all.

In order to specify which artery(ies) may be the culprit, one of the several tests may be used as a supplement. These may include the usage of imaging studies like radionuclides (thallium, or sestamibi, etc) or by echocardiogram.

On the other hand, a pharmacological stress test may be performed wherein either the heart rate is chemically increased (a medicine named dobutamine is used) or by creating what is referred to as the "steal phenomenon" (a medicine named adenosine or persantine is used). The sensitivity and the specificity of these tests are comparable, and the experience of the physician and the health care facility will finally dictate the choice of the test.

Treatment of Stable Angina:

Medical management

Angioplasty (PCI)

By-pass surgery (CABG)

Chapter 1:
Stable Angina

Chest Pain during Exertion

This chapter deals with chest pain upon exertion (stable angina or effort angina) related to stenosis or blockage of the coronary arteries secondary to plaque building.

This process of plaque building is called Atherosclerosis. The term Atherosclerosis *is* derived from the Greek "athero" and "sclerosis." The word "athero" means gruel or wax and corresponds to the necrotic core area at the base of the atherosclerotic plaque, and "sclerosis" is for hardening, referring to the fibrous cap of the plaque's luminal edge.

Atherosclerosis can affect any artery in the body, including arteries in the heart, brain, legs, etc., causing heart attack, stroke and peripheral vascular disease, respectively.

The figure below shows a comparison of a normal artery with the artery suffering from atherosclerosis resulting in reduced blood flow.

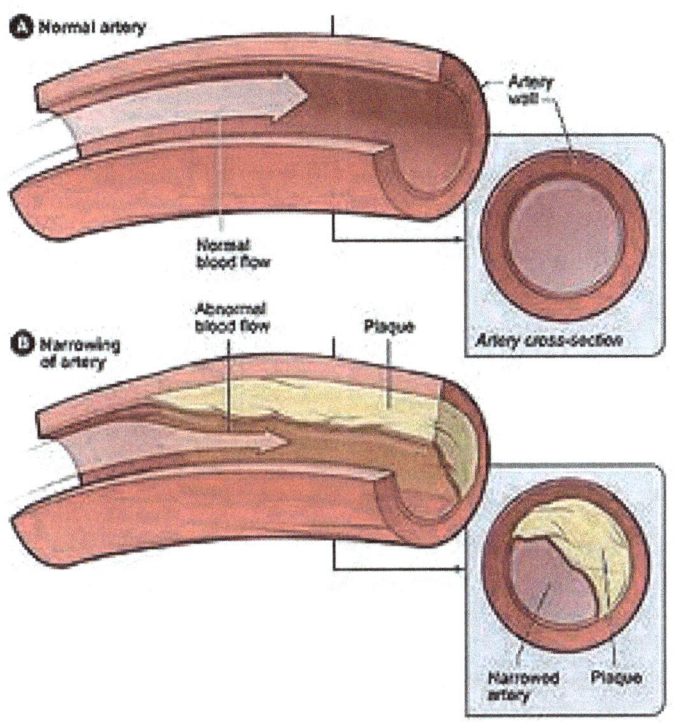

Figure A shows a normal artery with normal blood flow. The inset image shows a cross-section of a normal artery. Figure B shows an artery with plaque buildup. The inset image shows a cross-section of an artery with plaque buildup.

(Courtesy: National Heart, Lungs and Blood Institute)

Let's study this concept in the light of Holy Scripture.

فَمَنْ يُّرِدِ اللهُ اَنْ يَّهْدِيَهٗ يَشْرَحْ صَدْرَهٗ
لِلْاِسْلَامِ ۚ وَمَنْ يُّرِدْ اَنْ يُّضِلَّهٗ يَجْعَلْ صَدْرَهٗ
ضَيِّقًا حَرَجًا كَاَنَّمَا يَصَّعَّدُ فِي السَّمَآءِ

كَذَلِكَ يَجْعَلُ اللهُ الرِّجْسَ عَلَى الَّذِيْنَ لَا يُؤْمِنُوْنَ

"So, whomsoever ALLAH wills to guide, He makes his heart wide open for Islam, and whomsoever He wills to let go astray, He makes his heart strait and constricted, (and he feels embracing Islam as difficult) as if he were climbing to the sky. In this way, ALLAH lays abomination on those who do not believe."
(Chapter 6: Al- Anaam, The Cattle: Verse 125)

According to the *ATHEROSCLEROSIS TIMELINE,* plaque building starts from the early years of life as illustrated below in the diagram.

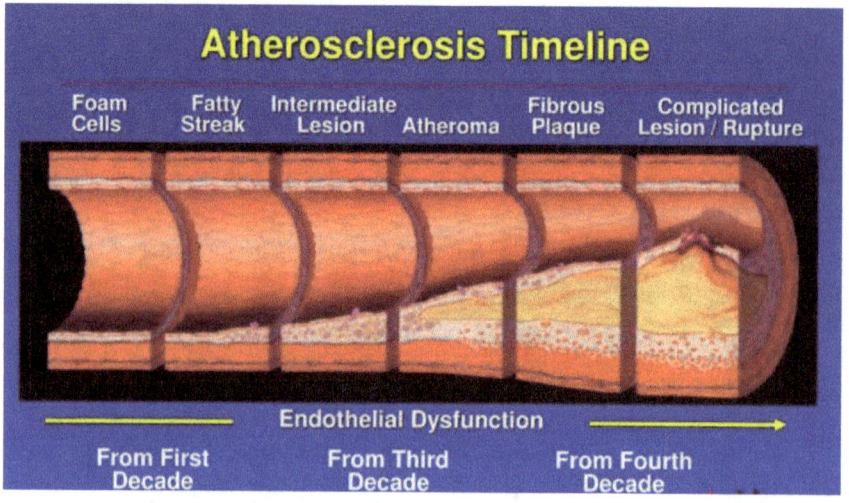

Adapted from Pepine CJ. Am J Cardiol. 1928; 82 (suppl 104)

With the passage of time and the involvement of risk factors, the process of plaque buildup progresses. According to Glagov's phenomenon, initially, there is positive remodeling in which plaque building grows outward with minimal effect on vessel diameter until it reaches a point when this plaque building undergoes inward

18

movement, resulting in the progression of stenosis and narrowing of vessel diameter.

This compromise of vessel lumen diameter, when it reaches a certain point, starts to cause an imbalance between oxygen demand and supply. Generally speaking, patients do not usually develop any symptoms while at rest, but during physical or emotional activity, this imbalance worsens (due to an increase in demand), and it results in the development of reduced blood supply to the myocardium or ischemia.

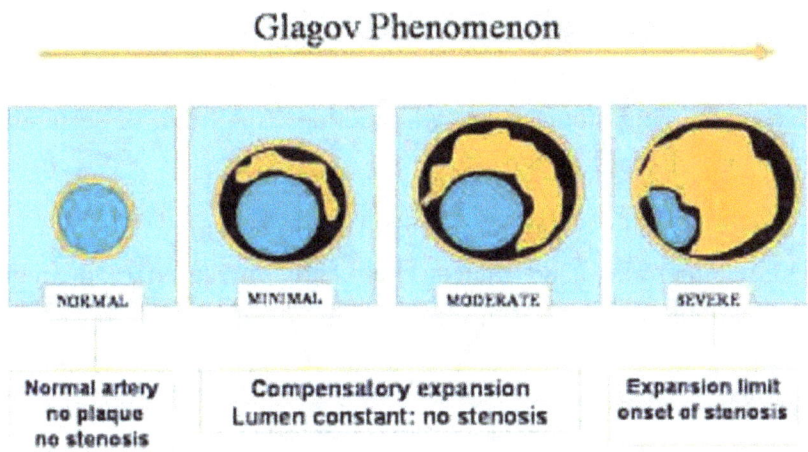

Glagov Phenomenon

This can be a beautiful depiction of the aforementioned Quranic Verse. The patients who experience this imbalance complain of chest pain, heaviness or choking sensation or symptoms described as if someone is *squeezing or constricting their* chest. Some patients explain the symptoms as if a heavy weight is placed on their chests. These symptoms may also be combined with shortness of breath, sweating, fatigue, nausea, vomiting, or even fainting. This type of discomfort is typically relieved by taking rest or using medicine like nitroglycerin.

In patients who develop chest pain during exertion (stable angina), several modalities can delineate their disease process, one of the most common being the treadmill stress test.

A simple analogy of this test is as if someone is walking fast and uphill (Quranic Verse reference as above, "climbing into the sky").

If someone has significant stenosis (blockage) in his/her coronary artery (ies), this test will be able to bring it out in several ways. Patients may complain of symptoms as depicted above, or there may be changes in their EKGs, vital signs or all.

In order to specify which artery (ies) may be the culprit, one of the several tests may be used as a supplement. These may include the usage of imaging studies like radionuclides (thallium, or sestamibi, etc.) or by echocardiogram.

On the other hand, a pharmacological stress test may be performed wherein either the heart rate is chemically increased (a medicine named Dobutamine is used) or by creating what is referred to as the "steal phenomenon" (a medicine named Adenosine or Persantine is used). The sensitivity and specificity of these tests are comparable, and the experience of the physician and the health care facility will finally dictate the choice of the test.

Following is an example of a positive stress EKG.

Positive stress EKG (above) in a middle-aged male patient of ours with typical chest pain and EKG changes as shown by blue arrows.

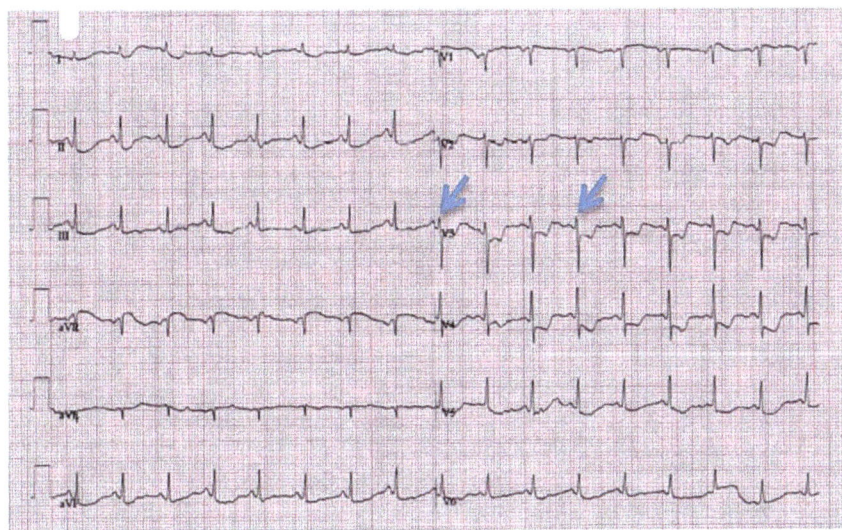

Duke Treadmill Scoring System (DTS):

The Duke Treadmill Score (DTS) is a point system to predict 5-year mortality based on treadmill EKG stress testing.

The Duke Treadmill Score is calculated as below:

DTS = Exercise time (minutes) - (5 x ST deviation in mm) - (4 x angina index)

The exercise time is based on using the standard Bruce protocol.

ST deviation refers to maximum ST change (elevation or depression) in any lead except lead aVR.

The angina index gives 0 points if no angina occurs, 1 point if non-limiting angina occurs, and 2 points if angina occurs, which limits exercise.

Patients are categorized as low-, intermediate- or high-risk.

Risk Group   Annual Mortality Rate

Low (>4)   0.25%

Intermediate   (-10-4) 125%

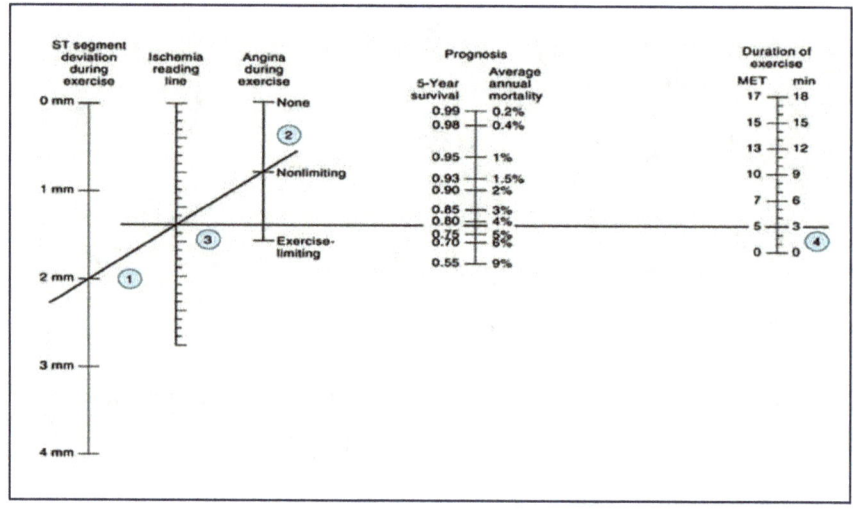

High (>10)   5.0%

Adapted from Mark DB, Shaw L, Harrell FE Jr, et al.: Prognostic value of a treadmill exercise score in outpatients with suspected coronary artery disease. *N Eng, J Med* 1991325: 849-853.

In high-risk patients, 74% had 3-vessel or left main occlusive 0 coronary disease on angiography.

Nomogram (above) of Prognostic Variables Using the Duke Treadmill Score

It incorporates the duration of exercise (in minutes) — (5 x maximal ST segment deviation during or after exercise) (in mm) — (4 x treadmill angina index). Treadmill angina index is 0 for no angina, 1 for non-limiting angina, and 2 for exercise-limiting angina. The marks on the ischemia reading line and duration of exercise line are connected, and the intersection on the prognosis line determines the five-year survival rate and average annual mortality rate for patients with these selected specific variables. MET = Metabolic Equivalent. (Adapted from Mark DE, Shaw L, Harrell FE Jr, et al.: Prognostic value of a treadmill exercise score in outpatients with suspected coronary artery disease. N Engl J Med 325: 849, 1991).

Heart Rate Recovery:

An interesting issue from the prognosis standpoint is the concept of what is called the heart rate recovery (HRR).

Heart rate recovery is the heart's ability to return to a normal rate after an activity within a specific amount of time. In general, a faster heart rate recovery from an activity is an indication of an improved fitness level.

Heart rate recovery has two decreasing phases. During the first minute after exercise, the heart rate drops sharply. After the first minute, during the resting plateau, the heart rate gradually decreases.

Heart rate recovery immediately after exercise is considered to be a function of reactivation of the parasympathetic drive and a decrease in the sympathetic drive that usually occurs during the first 30 seconds of recovery after exercise.

The prognostic value of slow heart rate recovery (HRR) after exercise in predicting cardiovascular disease and mortality has been established.

Abnormalities in parasympathetic activation and drive were suggested as a potential pathophysiological link to the observed association between reduced or impaired heart rate in early recovery after treadmill electrocardiographic exercise stress test and increased mortality during the follow-up period.

Initial increases in heart rate (HR) with exercise are due to parasympathetic withdrawal, while sympathetic activation is responsible for HRs greater than 100 beats/min. The slow HRR is associated with less autonomic nervous system responsiveness. It is possible that slow IIRR is associated with a higher susceptibility to atherosclerosis.

A delayed decrease in the heart rate during the first minute after graded exercise, which may be a reflection of decreased vagal activity, is considered a powerful predictor of overall mortality. This is independent of workload, the presence or absence of myocardial perfusion defects, and changes in heart rate during exercise.

Figure below depicts this concept.

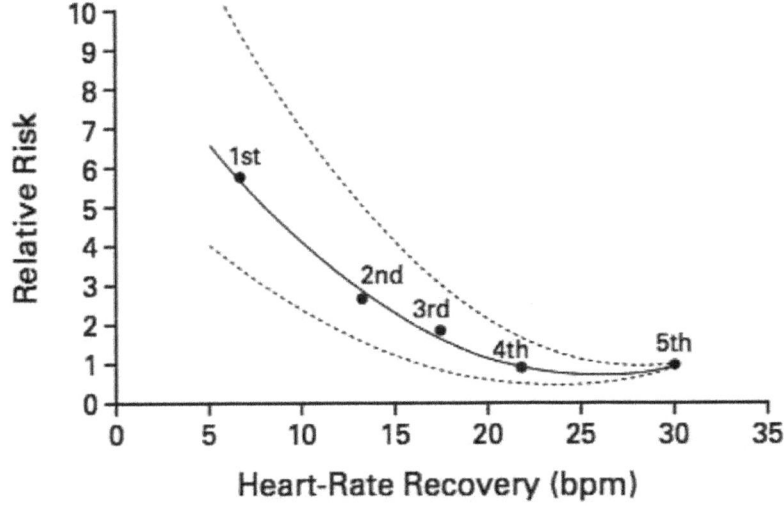

Estimates of the Relative Risk of Death within Six Years According to Heart-Rate Recovery One Minute after Cessation of Exercise. Circles represent the relative risk of death for each of the quintiles as compared with the quintile with the greatest reduction (5^{th,)} Dashed lines represent the 95 percent confidence interval. Bpm = beats per minute.

Let's now review some of the examples of positive stress tests using nuclear imaging techniques.

The figure above shows a large reversible cardiac perfusion defect in the territory of the left anterior descending artery (i.e. the anterior, septal, and apical walls) (arrows). Cross-hatching on the defect blackout map is indicative of a reversible perfusion defect (arrowhead).

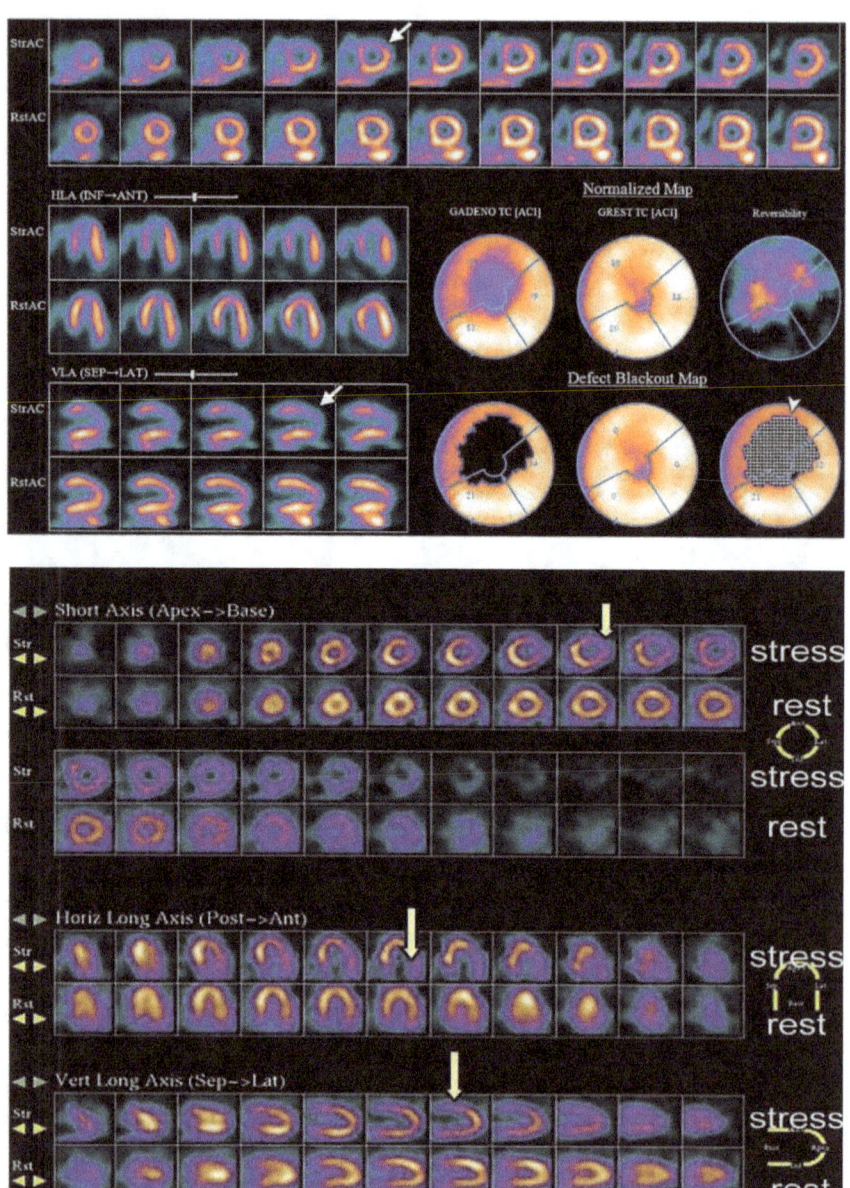

The figure above shows another example of ischemia during a stress test by nuclear study in the antero-lateral distribution (as evident by less uptake of radionuclide agent during stress as shown by arrows).

Following figure from one of our patients shows a severe lesion or stenosis in the mid-Right Coronary Artery (a) causing exertional chest pain or during walking on a treadmill. This was treated successfully by deploying a stent (b) resulting in relief of symptoms.

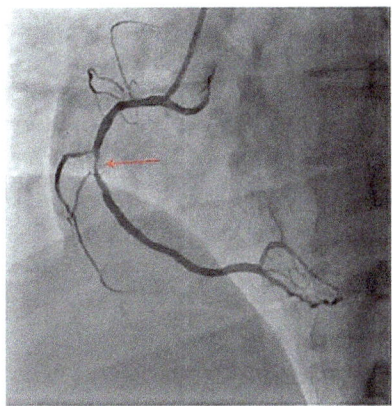

a:

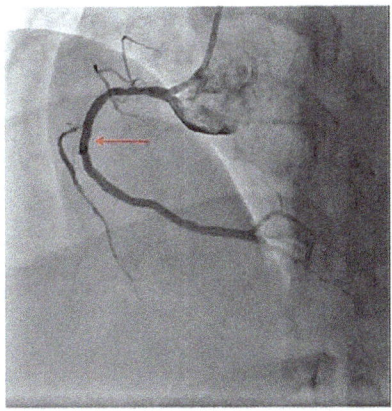

b:

It will be noted in the chapter *"Cardiac Surgery,"* *that* if these stenoses or blockages become too many, then a by-pass operation may be the last resort, which will result in relief of the symptoms.

Treatment of Stable Angina:

Medical management

Angioplasty (PCI)

By-pass surgery (CABG)

An Interesting Concept:

One of the beautiful Holy Verse says: "Say O Muhammad (PBUH):

"Who provides for you from the sky and from the earth? Or who owns hearing and sight? **And who brings out the living from the dead and brings out the dead from the living?** *And who disposes the affairs?" They will say: "ALLAH." Say: "Will you not then be afraid of ALLAH's Punishment (for setting up rivals in worship with ALLAH)?"*

(Chapter 10: Yunus, Jonah: verse 31)

This could be an analogy for what is referred to in modern science as "HIBERNATING" and "STUNNED" myocardium described below, and ALLAH knows the best.

Hibernating Myocardium:

This term explains the state of chronic myocardial dysfunction at rest that can be partially or completely restored to normal by creating an improvement in the blood flow. The underlying mechanism responsible for hibernating myocardium is believed to be due to a chronic reduction in resting coronary blood flow. The recovery of function has been shown to take up to 1 year after revascularization in myocardial hibernation.

An interesting example of this entity is presented here. One of our 55-year-old male patients with diabetes mellitus presented with shortness of breath. His ejection fraction was calculated to be only 10%-15%. An angiogram showed extensive coronary artery disease, as mentioned below. One year after a successful CABG, his ejection fraction increased to 40%. Below are the pictures of his initial coronary angiogram.

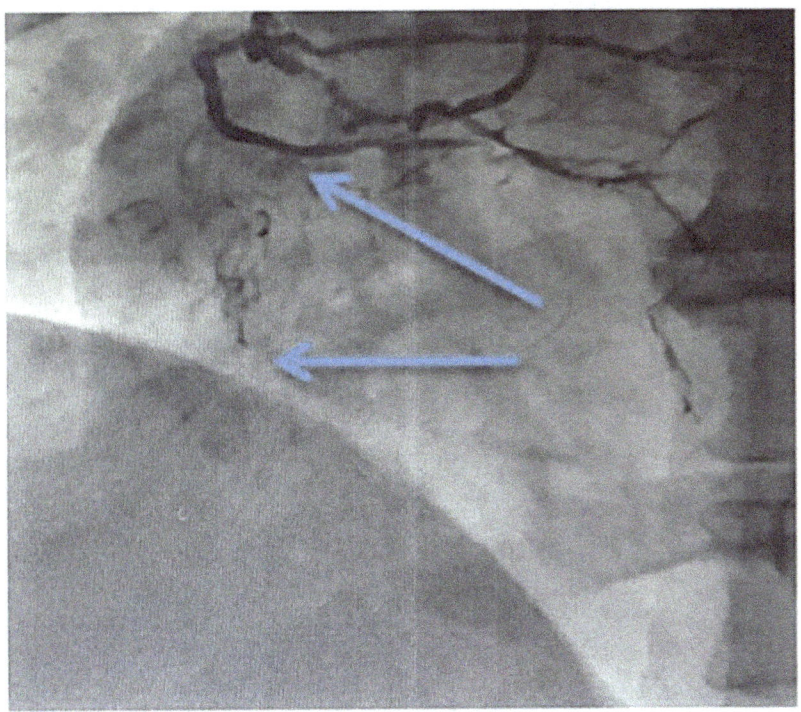

Figure above.
Right coronary artery (RCA) showing total occlusion (blue arrows).

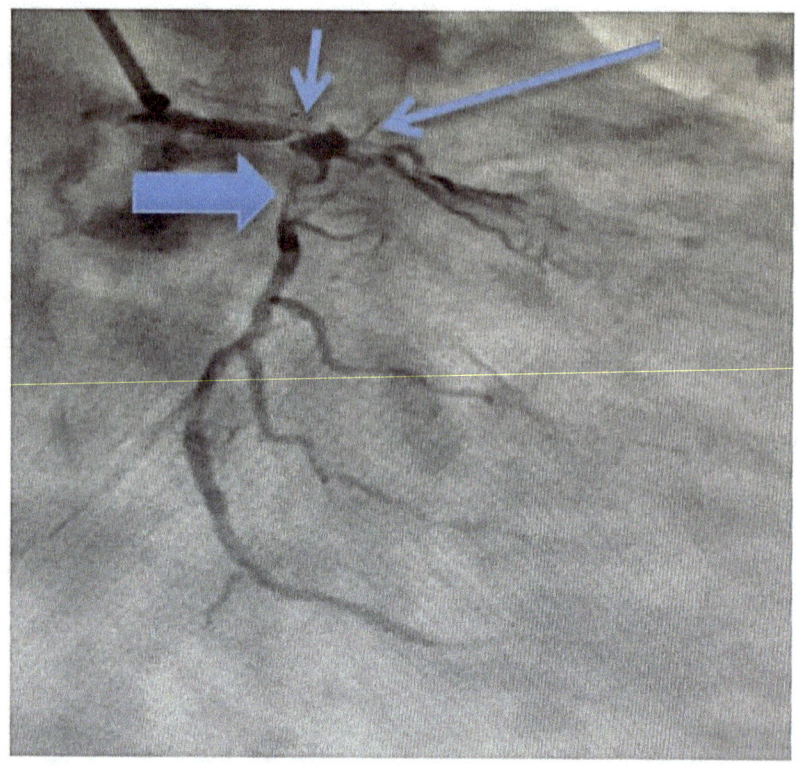

Figure above shows the severity of disease in the left system in the same patient.

There is a total occlusion of the left anterior descending artery (LAD), as shown by a long blue arrow. Severe stenosis of distal Left main coronary artery (short blue arrow). Severe stenosis of the Left Circumflex (LCX) artery (thick blue arrow).

Stunned Myocardium:

"Myocardial stunning" describes the state of post-ischemic myocardial dysfunction in the presence of relatively normal blood flow.

In general, stunned myocardium has been shown to recover function within hours to days, and recovery may take longer in cases of longer ischemic episodes prior to revascularization.

In this chapter we discussed the difference between normal and abnormal arteries, the implication of arterial blockages, the pathophysiology of plaque building, the symptoms related to arterial blockages and some of the tests which could be used for diagnosis.

References:

1. Ivana Antelmi; Eliseu Yung Chuang; Cesar Jose Grupi; Maria do Rosario Dias de Oliveira Latorre; Alfredo Jose Mansur Institut° do Coraclio - Faculdade de Medicina da Universidade de Sao Paulo, Sao Paulo, SP - Brazil

2. Nishime EO, Cole CR, Blackstone EH, Pashkow F, Lauer MS'. Heart rate recovery and treadmill exercise score as predictors of mortality in patients referred for exercise ECG. JAM4.2000; 284: 1392-8. [Links]end-ref

3. Shelter K, Marcus R, Frolicker VF, Vera S, Chalkiest D, Parakeet M et al. Heart rate recovery: validation and methodology issues. J Am Coll Cardiol. 2001; 38: 1980-7

4. Chaitman BR. Abnormal heart rate responses to exercise predict increased long-term mortality regardless of coronary disease extent: The question is why? J Am Coll Cardiol, 2003; 42: 839-841.

5. Morshedi-Meibodi A, Larson MG, Levy D, O'Donnell CJ, Vasan RS. Heart rate recovery after treadmill exercise testing and risk of cardiovascular disease events (The Framingham Heart Study). Am J Cardiol, 2002; 90: 848-852.

6. Nishime EO, Cole CR, Blackstone EH, Pashkow FJ, Lauer MS. Heart rate recovery and treadmill exercise score as predictors of mortality in patients referred for exercise ECG. JAMA, 2000; 284: 1392-1398.

7. Vivekananthan DP, Blackstone EH, Pothier CE, Lauer MS. Heart rate recovery after exercise is a predictor of mortality, independent of the angiographic severity of coronary disease. J Am Coll Cardiol, 2003; 42: 831-838.

8. Arai Y, Saul JP, Albrecht P et al. Modulation of cardiac autonomic activity during and immediately after exercise. Am J Physiol, 1989; 256: H132—H141.

9. Kizilbash MA, Carnethon MR, Chan C, Jacobs DR, Sidney S, Liu K The temporal relationship between heart rate recovery immediately after exercise and the metabolic syndrome: The CARDIA Study. Eur Heart J, 2006; 27: 1592-1596.

10. Myers J, Prakash M, Froelicher V, Do D, Partington S, Atwood JE. Exercise capacity and mortality among men referred for exercise testing. N Engl J Med 2002; 346: 793-801.

11. Kligfield P, Lauer MS'. Exercise electrocardiogram testing: beyond the ST segment. Circulation. 2006; 114: 2070 —2082.

12. Cole CR, Blackstone EH, Pashkow FJ, Snader CE, Lauer MS. Heart-rate recovery immediately after exercise as a predictor of mortality. N Engl J Med. 1999; 341: 1351-1357.

13. Ryan A. Dvorak; Richard KJ. Brown; James R. Corbett: RadioGraphics 2011, 31, 2041-2057.

14. Rahimtoola SH. The hibernating myocardium. Am Heart J 1989; 117: 211-21.

15. Macs A, Flameng W, Nuyts J, et al. Histological alterations in chronically hypoperfused myocardium. Correlation with PET findings. Circulation 1994; 90: 735-45.

16. Dakik HA, Howell JF, Lawrie GM et al. Assessment of myocardial viability with 99mTc-sestamibi tomography before coronary by-pass graft surgery: correlation with histopathology and postoperative improvement in cardiac function. Circulation 1997; 96: 2892-8.

17. Wijns W, Vatner SF, Camici PG. Hibernating myocardium. N Engl J Med 1998; 339: 173-81.

18. Braunwald E, Kloner RA. The stunned myocardium: prolonged, post-ischemic ventricular dysfunction. Circulation 1982; 66: 1146-9.

19. Kloner RA, Bolli R, Marban E, Reinlib L, Braurzwald E. Medical and cellular implications of stunning, hibernation, and preconditioning: an NHLBI workshop. Circulation 1998; 97: 1848-67.

20. Bax JJ, Visser FC, Poldermans D, et al. Time course of functional recovery of stunned and hibernating segments after surgical revascularization. Circulation 2001; 104(12 Suppl 1): 1314-8.

Chapter 2
(Synopsis)
"Pericardium" for GENERAL AUDIENCE

This chapter deals with the covering of the heart, called *THE PERICARDIUM* and this word is derived from the Greek περί, "around" and κάρδιον, "heart").

ALLAH (THE MOST EXALTED) has created the heart in such a fashion that it is covered from the outside by a layering which is called the pericardium. This layering is essentially a double-walled sac, which contains the heart itself and the roots of the great vessels.

The pericardial sac in itself is not just one layer but, in actuality, has two layers folded upon each other, with a small amount of fluid (the pericardial fluid) in between to avoid any friction.

The pericardium is supplied by several arteries and nerves. Pain due to inflammation of the pericardium is felt diffusely behind the sternum but may radiate.

Functions of the Pericardium

- Fixes heart in mediastinum and limits its motion
- Protects it from infections coming from other organs (such as lungs)
- Prevents excessive dilation of the heart in cases of acute volume overload
- Lubricates the heart

Clinical significance

Inflammation of the pericardium is called <u>pericarditis</u>. An excess of fluid in the cavity (Pericardial Effusion) can result in cardiac tamponade (compression of the heart within the pericardial sac). The fluid may be removed either percutaneously (Pericardiocentesis) or surgically (in which a pericardial window is created). A *Pericardiectomy* is sometimes needed, which is basically to remove the pericardium, surgically.

So the important point, as elaborated later in the script, that this fine layer called the Pericardium serves as a "covering or wrapping of the heart" and appears to have a "connection" to the outside "world" but when it gets "diseased," whether due to thickening, *(Constrictive Pericarditis)* or if the normal thin layer of fluid becomes enormous, *(Pericardial Effusion),* then this normal phenomenon is lost.

Let us now try to study these concepts in the light of the Holy Scripture.

Some of the Holy Verses which appear to be related to the Pericardium (or the "covering"/"veil"/"wrapping"/"seal" of the heart) are mentioned below.

(1)

وَقَــالُــوْا قُــلُــوْبُــنَــا غُــلْفٌ بَــلْ لَّــعَــنَــهُمُ اللهُ
بِــكُفْرِهِمْ فَــقَــلِــيْلًا مَّا يُــؤْمِــنُــوْنَ

And they said, our hearts are *veiled.* Rather, ALLAH has cast damnation upon them for their disbelief. So, they believe just in very little things
(Al-Baqara, The cow Chapter # 2, Verse #88)

(2)

وَإِذَا قَرَأْتَ الْقُرْآنَ جَعَلْنَا بَيْنَكَ وَبَيْنَ
الَّذِينَ لَا يُؤْمِنُونَ بِالْآخِرَةِ حِجَابًا مَّسْتُورًا
وَّجَعَلْنَا عَلَى قُلُوبِهِمْ أَكِنَّةً أَن يَّفْقَهُوهُ
وَفِيٓ أَذَانِهِمْ وَقْرًا وَإِذَا ذَكَرْتَ رَبَّكَ فِي
الْقُرْآنِ وَحْدَهُ وَلَّوْا عَلَى أَدْبَارِهِمْ نُفُورًا

When you recite the Qur'an, We place an invisible curtain between
you and those who do not believe in the Hereafter ,and We put *covers*
on their hearts barring them from understanding it, and (We put)
deafness in their ears; and when you refer to your Lord alone (without
referring to their presumed deities,) in the Qur'an, they turn their
backs in aversion.

(Al-Isr: ,The night journey, Chapter # 17, Verse #45 and 46)

(3)

وَمَنْ أَظْلَمُ مِمَّنْ ذُكِّرَ بِآيَاتِ رَبِّهِ فَأَعْرَضَ
عَنْهَا وَنَسِيَ مَا قَدَّمَتْ يَدَاهُ إِنَّا جَعَلْنَا
عَلَى قُلُوبِهِمْ أَكِنَّةً أَن يَّفْقَهُوهُ وَفِيٓ
أَذَانِهِمْ وَقْرًا وَإِن تَدْعُهُمْ إِلَى الْهُدَى
فَلَنْ يَّهْتَدُوٓا إِذًا أَبَدًا

Who is more unjust than the one who was reminded through the signs
of his Lord, but he turned away from them, and forgot what his own
hands sent ahead. Indeed, we have put *covers* on their hearts that bar
them from understanding it, and (We have created) deafness in their
ears. And if you call them to guidance, even then they will never adopt
the right path.

(Al-Kahf, The Cave, Chapter # 18, Verse #57)

(4)

كَذَلِكَ يَطْبَعُ اللهُ عَلَى قُلُوبِ الَّذِيْنَ لَا
يَعْلَمُوْنَ

Thus ALLAH *seals* up the hearts of those who do not believe.
(Ar-Room, The Romans, Chapter # 30, Verse #59)

(5)

الَّذِيْنَ يُجَادِلُوْنَ فِيْ أَيْتِ اللهِ بِغَيْرِ سُلْطٰنٍ
أَتْىهُمْ كَبُرَ مَقْتًا عِنْدَ اللهِ وَعِنْدَ الَّذِيْنَ
أَمَنُوْا كَذَلِكَ يَطْبَعُ اللهُ عَلَى كُلِّ قَلْبِ
مُتَكَبِّرٍ جَبَّارٍ

those who quarrel in ALLAH's verses without any authority having
reached them. It is terribly hateful with ALLAH and with those who
believe. That is how ALLAH stamps a *seal* on the entire heart of an
arrogant tyrant.
(Ghafir, The Forgiver, Chapter # 40, Verse #35)

(6)

وَقَالُوْا قُلُوْبُنَا فِيْ أَكِنَّةٍ مِّمَّا تَدْعُوْنَآ
إِلَيْهِ وَفِيْ أَذَانِنَا وَقْرٌ وَّمِنْ بَيْنِنَا
وَبَيْنِكَ حِجَابٌ فَاعْمَلْ إِنَّنَا عٰمِلُوْنَ

And they say, our hearts are *(wrapped)* in covers against that (faith)
to which you invite us, and there is deafness in our ears, and there is
a barrier between you and us. So, do (in your way). We too are doing
(in our own way.
(Fussilat, Explained in detail, Chapter # 41, Verse #5)

(7)

أَفَرَءَيْتَ مَنِ اتَّخَذَ اِلٰـهَهٗ هَوٰىهُ وَ اَضَلَّهُ اللّٰهُ عَلٰى عِلْمٍ وَّخَتَمَ عَلٰى سَمْعِهٖ وَقَلْبِهٖ وَجَعَلَ عَلٰى بَصَرِهٖ غِشٰوَةً فَمَنْ يَّهْدِيْهِ مِنْ بَعْدِ اللّٰهِ اَفَلَا تَذَكَّرُوْنَ

So, have you seen him who has taken his desires as his god, and ALLAH has let him go astray, despite having knowledge, and has *sealed* his ear and his heart, and put a cover on his eye? Now who will guide him after ALLAH? Still, do you not take lesson?
(Al-Jathiya The kneeling, , Chapter # 45, Verse #23)

(8)

وَمِنْهُمْ مَّنْ يَّسْتَمِعُ اِلَيْكَ حَتّٰى اِذَا خَرَجُوْا مِنْ عِنْدِكَ قَالُوْا لِلَّذِيْنَ أُوْتُوا الْعِلْمَ مَاذَا قَالَ اٰنِفًا أُولٰۤئِكَ الَّذِيْنَ طَبَعَ اللّٰهُ عَلٰى قُلُوْبِهِمْ وَاتَّبَعُوْۤا اَهْوَاءَهُمْ

Among them there are ones who (pretend to) give ear to you, until when they go out from your presence, they say to those who have been given knowledge, what did he say just now? Those are the ones on whose hearts ALLAH has put a *seal*, and they have followed their desires.
(Muhammad: Muhammad, chapter# 47, Verse #16)

(9)

ذٰلِكَ بِاَنَّهُمْ اٰمَنُوْا ثُمَّ كَفَرُوْا فَطُبِعَ عَلٰى قُلُوْبِهِمْ فَهُمْ لَا يَفْقَهُوْنَ

39

That is because they declared faith (in Islam apparently) , then disbelieved (secretly) . Therefore, a *seal* has been set on their hearts, and thus they do not understand.

(Al-Munafiqoon: The Hypocrites, Chapter # 63, Verse #3)

The above description is a synopsis of what this Pericardium is, its significance and functions and how beautifully there seems to be a plausible correlation with Quranic verses and ALLAH (THE MOST EXALTED) knows the best. A more detailed description of this topic is mentioned below.

Chapter 2:
The Pericardium

(The wall or covering around the heart)

Normal Anatomy of the Pericardium

The **pericardium** (from the Greek περί, "around" and κάρδιον, "heart") is a double-walled sac containing the heart and the roots of the great vessels. The pericardial sac has two layers,

- A serous layer, and

- A fibrous layer

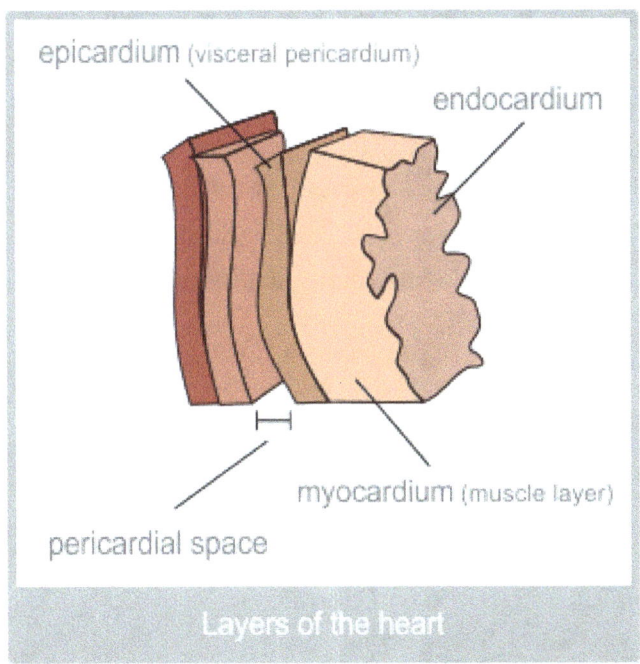

Layers of the heart

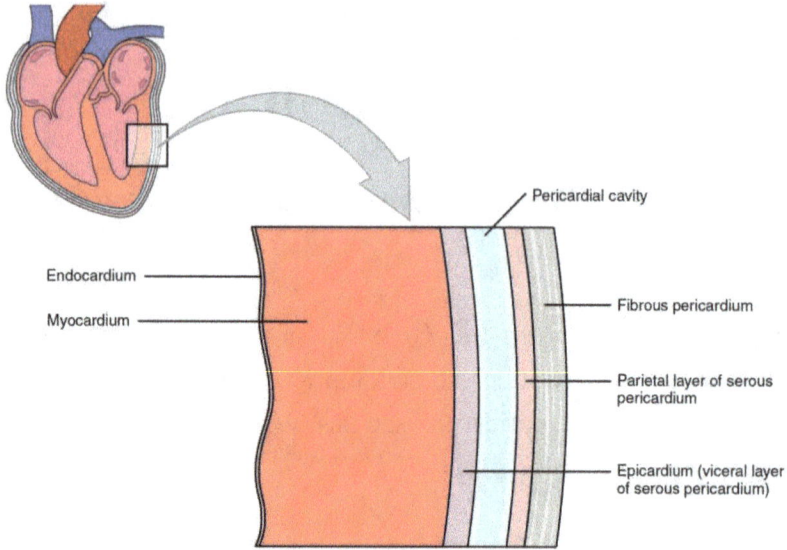

Endocardium

Myocardium

Pericardial cavity

Fibrous pericardium

Parietal layer of serous pericardium

Epicardium (viceral layer of serous pericardium)

The serous pericardium is a closed sac and consists of an inner visceral layer (close to the myocardium) and is also known as the *Epicardium*. The epicardium is largely made of connective tissue and functions as a protective layer. This layer is then reflected backwards as the *Parietal Layer,* with a potential space between these two layers, which is called *Pericardial Cavity*. This cavity is filled with a small amount (15 - 50 milliliters) of lubricating serous fluid called the *Pericardial Fluid.*

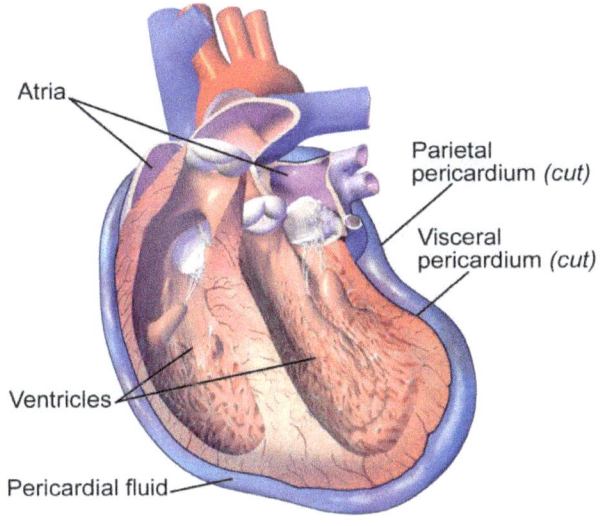

Pericardial Sac

Cutaway illustration of pericardial sac (above)

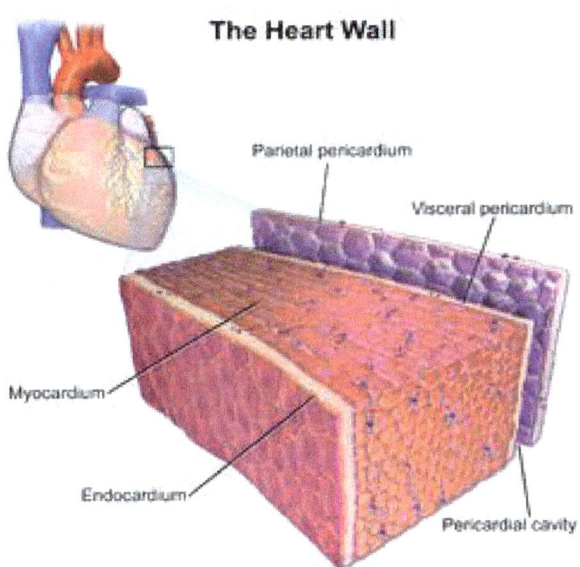

Walls of the heart above show a pericardium on the right

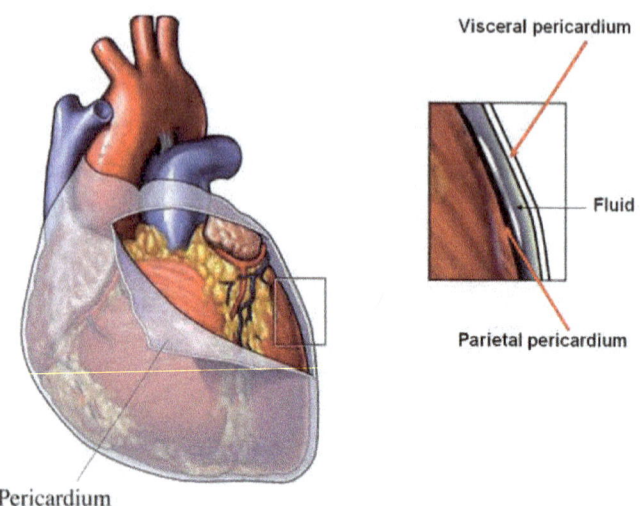

Visceral pericardium

Fluid

Parietal pericardium

Pericardium

Schematic sagittal section through the heart and pericardium. Note how the serous layer of the pericardium is reflected onto the heart and forms a double layer. (above)

The fibrous pericardium (picture below) is the outermost layer, and it is firmly bound to the central tendon of the diaphragm. It is a single connective tissue layer that is made up of collagen and elastin fibers. This layer is elastic but non-distensible. It is held in position with the tunica adventitia of the great vessels, to the central tendon of the diaphragm, to the sternum by superior and inferior pericardio-sternal ligaments, and to the esophagus and spine.

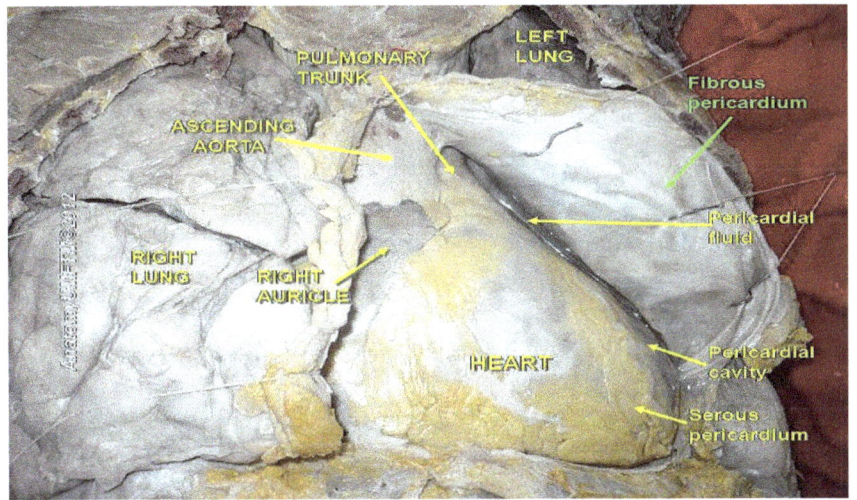

Extra pericardial fat, which may be visible radiographically, is often found in the angles between the pericardium and diaphragm on each side. The pericardium is adherent to the mediastinal pleura except where the two are separated by the phrenic nerves.

The pericardium is supplied by several arteries that are in the area (e.g., the internal thoracic) and by the phrenic nerves, which contain vasomotor and sensory fibers. Pericardial pain is felt diffusely behind the sternum but may radiate.

Anatomical relationships

- Surrounds the heart and bases of the pulmonary artery and aorta.

- The right phrenic nerve passes to the right of the pericardium.

- The left phrenic nerve passes over the pericardium of the left ventricle.

- Pericardial arteries supply blood to the dorsal portion of the pericardium.

Functions

- Fixes the heart in the mediastinum and limits its motion

- Provides mechanical protection for the heart and big vessels.

- Protects it from infections coming from other organs (such as lungs)

- Prevents excessive dilation of the heart in cases of acute volume overload

- Lubricates the heart to reduce friction between the heart and the surrounding structures.

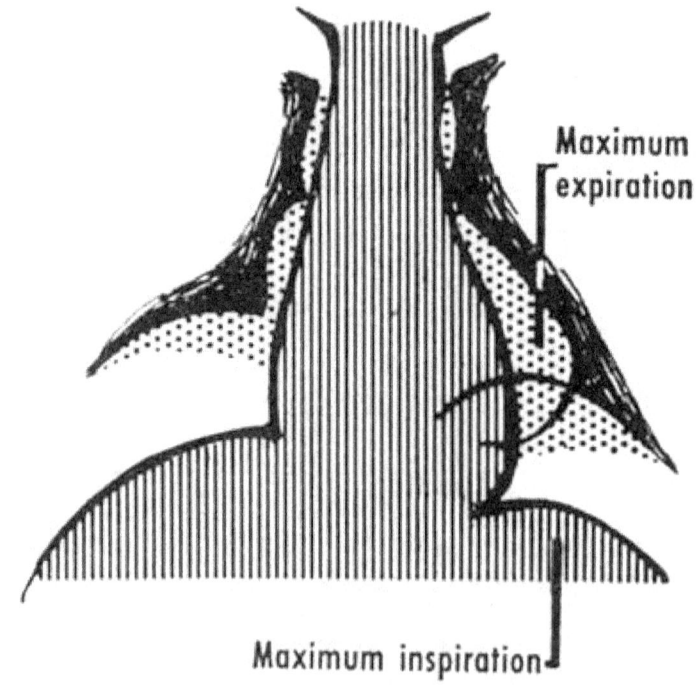

(above) The shape of the heart at maximum inspiration and maximum expiration

Clinical significance

Inflammation of the pericardium is called *Pericarditis* and may be detected by a stethoscope with a peculiar sound called the *Pericardial Rub*.

An excess of fluid in the cavity (such as in pericardial effusion) can result in cardiac tamponade (compression of the heart within the pericardial sac). The fluid may be removed either percutaneously (*Pericardiocentesis*) or surgically (in which a pericardial window is created). A *Pericardiectomy* is sometimes needed for Constrictive Pericarditis, which is basically to remove the pericardium, surgically.

The important point, as elaborated later in the script, is that this fine layer called the Pericardium serves as a "covering or wrapping of the heart" and appears to have a "connection" to the outside "world" but when it gets "diseased," whether due to thickening, *(Constrictive Pericarditis)* or if the normal thin layer of fluid becomes enormous, *(Pericardial Effusion),* then this normal phenomenon is lost.

Let us now try to study these concepts in the light of the Holy Scripture.

Holy Verses which appear to be related to the Pericardium (or the "covering"/"veil"/"wrapping"/"seal" of the heart) are mentioned below.

(1)

خَتَمَ اللهُ عَلَى قُلُوْبِهِمْ وَعَلَى سَمْعِهِمْ وَعَلَى أَبْصَارِهِمْ غِشَاوَةٌ وَّلَهُمْ عَذَابٌ عَظِيم

ALLAH has set a *seal* on their hearts and on their hearing; and on their eyes there is a covering, and for them awaits a mighty punishment.
(Al-Baqar: The Cow,, Chapter # 2, Verse #7)

(2)

وَقَـالُـوْا قُلُـوْبُـنَا غُلْفٌ بَـلْ لَّـعَنَهُمُ اللّٰهُ
بِـكُفْرِهِمْ فَقَـلِيْلًا مَّا يُـؤْمِـنُـوْنَ

And they said, Our hearts are *veiled*. Rather, ALLAH has cast damnation upon them for their disbelief. So, they believe just in very little things
(Al-Baqara: The Cow, Chapter #2, Verse #88)

(3)

فَبِمَا نَـقْـضِهِمْ مِّيْثَاقَـهُمْ وَكُـفْـرِهِمْ بِـاٰيٰتِ اللّٰهِ
وَقَـتْـلِـهِمُ الْاَنْـبِيَاۤءَ بِـغَيْـرِ حَقٍّ وَّقَـوْلِـهِمْ
قُـلُـوْبُـنَا غُلْفٌ بَـلْ طَبَـعَ اللّٰهُ عَلَيْهَا بِـكُفْرِهِمْ
فَلَا يُـؤْمِـنُـوْنَ اِلَّا قَـلِيْلًا

So, (they met their fate) for breaking their pledge, and for their disbelief in the verses of ALLAH, and for their slaying of the prophets unjustly, and for their saying, Our hearts are *sealed* - rather, ALLAH has set a seal over them for their disbelief, so they do not believe but a little
(An-Nisa: The Women, Chapter # 4, Verse # 155)

(4)

قُلْ اَرَءَيْـتُمْ اِنْ اَخَذَ اللّٰهُ سَمْعَكُمْ وَاَبْصَارَكُمْ
وَخَتَـمَ عَلٰى قُـلُـوْبِـكُمْ مَّنْ اِلٰـهٌ غَيْـرُ اللّٰهِ

يَـٰٓأَتِيْكُمْ بِهٖ أُنْظُرْ كَيْفَ نُصَرِّفُ الْأٰيٰتِ ثُمَّ هُمْ
يَصْدِفُوْنَ

Say, tell me, if ALLAH takes away your hearing and your sights and
sets a *seal* on your hearts, which god other than ALLAH can bring
these back to you? See how We put forth Our verses in various forms?
Yet, still they turn away.

(Al-Anaam: The Cattle, Chapter # 6, Verse # 46)

(5)

وَإِذَا قَرَأْتَ الْقُرْاٰنَ جَعَلْنَا بَيْنَكَ وَبَيْنَ
الَّذِيْنَ لَا يُؤْمِنُوْنَ بِالْاٰخِرَةِ حِجَابًا مَّسْتُوْرًا
وَّجَعَلْنَا عَلٰى قُلُوْبِهِمْ أَكِنَّةً أَنْ يَّفْقَهُوْهُ
وَفِيْٓ أٰذَانِهِمْ وَقْرًا ۖ وَإِذَا ذَكَرْتَ رَبَّكَ فِي
الْقُرْاٰنِ وَحْدَهٗ وَلَّوْا عَلٰى أَدْبَارِهِمْ نُفُوْرًا

When you recite the Qur'an, We place an invisible curtain between
you and those who do not believe in the Hereafter ,and We put *covers*
on their hearts barring them from understanding it, and (We put)
deafness in their ears; and when you refer to your Lord alone (without
referring to their presumed deities,) in the Qur'an, they turn their
backs in aversion.

(Al-Isra: The Night Journey, Chapter #17, Verse #45 and 46)

(6)

وَمَنْ أَظْلَمُ مِمَّنْ ذُكِّرَ بِاٰيٰتِ رَبِّهٖ فَأَعْرَضَ
عَنْهَا وَنَسِيَ مَا قَدَّمَتْ يَدَاهُ ۚ إِنَّا جَعَلْنَا
عَلٰى قُلُوْبِهِمْ أَكِنَّةً أَنْ يَّفْقَهُوْهُ وَفِيْٓ
أٰذَانِهِمْ وَقْرًا ۖ وَإِنْ تَدْعُهُمْ إِلَى الْهُدٰى
فَلَنْ يَّهْتَدُوْٓا إِذًا أَبَدًا

Who is more unjust than the one who was reminded through the signs of his Lord, but he turned away from them, and forgot what his own hands sent ahead. Indeed, we have put *covers* on their hearts that bar them from understanding it, and (We have created) deafness in their ears. And if you call them to guidance, even then they will never adopt the right path.

(Al-Kahf: The Cave, Chapter #18, Verse #57)

(7)

كَذَلِكَ يَطْبَعُ اللهُ عَلَى قُلُوْبِ الَّذِيْنَ لَا يَعْلَمُوْنَ

Thus ALLAH *seals* up the hearts of those who do not believe..

(Ar-Room: The Roman, Chapter # 30, Verse #59)

(8)

الَّذِيْنَ يُجَادِلُوْنَ فِيْ أَيْتِ اللهِ بِغَيْرِ سُلْطنٍ أَتٰىهُمْ كَبُرَ مَقْتًا عِنْدَ اللهِ وَعِنْدَ الَّذِيْنَ أَمَنُوْا كَذَلِكَ يَطْبَعُ اللهُ عَلَى كُلِّ قَلْبِ مُتَكَبِّرٍ جَبَّارٍ

those who quarrel in ALLAH's verses without any authority having reached them. It is terribly hateful with ALLAH and with those who believe. That is how ALLAH stamps a *seal* on the entire heart of an arrogant tyrant.

(Ghafir: The Forgiver, Chapter # 40, Verse #35)

(9)

وَقَـالُـوْا قُلُـوْبُـنَـا فِـيْ اَكِنَّةٍ مِّمَّا تَـدْعُوْنَـا
اِلَـيْهِ وَفِيْ اٰذَانِنَـا وَقَرٌ وَّمِنْ بَيْنِنَـا
وَبَـيْنِكَ حِجَابٌ فَـاعْمَلْ اِنَّـنَا عٰمِلُـوْنَ

And they say, Our hearts are *(wrapped) in covers* against that (faith)
to which you invite us, and there is deafness in our ears, and there is
a barrier between you and us. So, do (in your way). We too are doing
(in our own way.

(Fussilat: Explained in detail, Chapter # 41, Verse #5)

(10)

اَمْ يَقُـوْلُـوْنَ افْتَـرٰى عَلَـى اللّٰهِ كَـذِبًـاۚ فَـاِنْ
يَّشَـاِ اللّٰهُ يَـخْتِمْ عَلٰـى قَـلْبِكَ وَيَـمْحُ اللّٰهُ
الْـبَـاطِلَ وَيُـحِقُّ الْـحَقَّ بِكَلِمٰتِهٖۚ اِنَّـهٗ عَلِيْمٌۢ
بِـذَاتِ الـصُّدُوْرِ

Is it that they say: He has forged a lie against ALLAH? So, if ALLAH
wills, He may put a *seal* on your heart. And ALLAH blots out
falsehood and establishes truth with His words. Surely, He is fully
aware of what lies in the hearts.
(Ash-Shura: Council, Chapter # 42, Verse #24)

(11)

اَفَرَءَيْتَ مَنِ اتَّخَذَ اِلٰـهَهٗ هَوٰىهُ وَاَضَلَّهُ
اللّٰهُ عَلٰى عِلْمٍ وَّخَتَمَ عَلٰى سَمْعِهٖ وَقَـلْبِهٖ
وَجَعَلَ عَلٰى بَصَرِهٖ غِشٰوَةًۚ فَمَنْ يَّهْدِيْهِ مِنْ
بَـعْدِ اللّٰهِ اَفَلَا تَـذَكَّرُوْنَ

So, have you seen him who has taken his desires as his god, and
ALLAH has let him go astray, despite having knowledge, and has

51

sealed his ear and his heart, and put a cover on his eye? Now who will guide him after ALLAH? Still, do you not take lesson?
(Al-Jathiya: The Kneeling, Chapter # 45, Verse #23)

(12)

وَمِنْهُمْ مَّنْ يَّسْتَمِعُ إِلَيْكَ حَتَّىٰٓ إِذَا خَرَجُوْا مِنْ عِنْدِكَ قَالُوْا لِلَّذِيْنَ أُوْتُوا الْعِلْمَ مَاذَا قَالَ اٰنِفًا أُولَـٰٓئِكَ الَّذِيْنَ طَبَعَ اللّٰهُ عَلَىٰ قُلُوْبِهِمْ وَاتَّبَعُوْٓا أَهْوَاءَهُمْ

Among them there are ones who (pretend to) give ear to you, until when they go out from your presence, they say to those who have been given knowledge, what did he say just now? Those are the ones on whose hearts ALLAH has put a *seal*, and they have followed their desires.
(Muhammad: Muhammad, chapter#47, Verse #16)

(13)

ذٰلِكَ بِاَنَّهُمْ اٰمَنُوْا ثُمَّ كَفَرُوْا فَطُبِعَ عَلَىٰ قُلُوْبِهِمْ فَهُمْ لَا يَفْقَهُوْنَ

That is because they declared faith (in Islam apparently), then disbelieved (secretly). Therefore, a *seal* has been set on their hearts, and thus they do not understand.
(Al-Munafiqoon: The Hypocrites, Chapter # 63, Verse #3)

In the next session, two interesting phenomena, i.e. Constrictive Pericarditis and Pericardial Effusion will be elaborated in detail.

CONSTRICTIVE PERICARDITIS

It is a severe form of pericarditis in which granulation tissue forms in the pericardium. The layers of the pericardium get thickened and stiffened, thereby they develop scar tissue and finally stick together. The granulation tissue may get calcified. There is a loss of pericardial elasticity and the ventricular filling gets restricted. This usually happens after multiple episodes of acute pericarditis over time.

PERICARDIAL EFFUSION

A pericardial effusion refers to the accumulation of excess fluid in the pericardial cavity, which may be transudative, exudative, or sanguineous and may contain infectious organisms or malignant cells.

It can occur due to several reasons like infection, inflammation, or direct filling of the pericardial cavity by blood from a defect in the myocardium (iatrogenic or traumatic injury or cardiac wall rupture) or backfilling from an ascending aortic dissection that dissects into the pericardium.

Beck Triad:

Beck's triad was originally described in 1935 by the American cardio-thoracic surgeon Claude Beck. It consists of three classic clinical signs associated with cardiac tamponade, namely,

1. Increased venous pressure
2. Decreased arterial pressure
3. Muffled heart sounds

Although the presence of the complete triad is highly suggestive of cardiac tamponade, only a small number of cases present with all the elements of Beck's triad at diagnosis.

Grade	Pericardial Volume (ml)	Cardiac Index	MAP	CVP	HR	Beck's Triad
I	<200	Normal or ↑	Normal	↑	↑	usually not present
II	≥200	↓	Normal or ↓	↑ (≥12 cm H₂O)	↑	May or may not be present
III	>200	↓↓	↓↓	↑↑ (≤30–40 cm H₂O)	↓	usually present

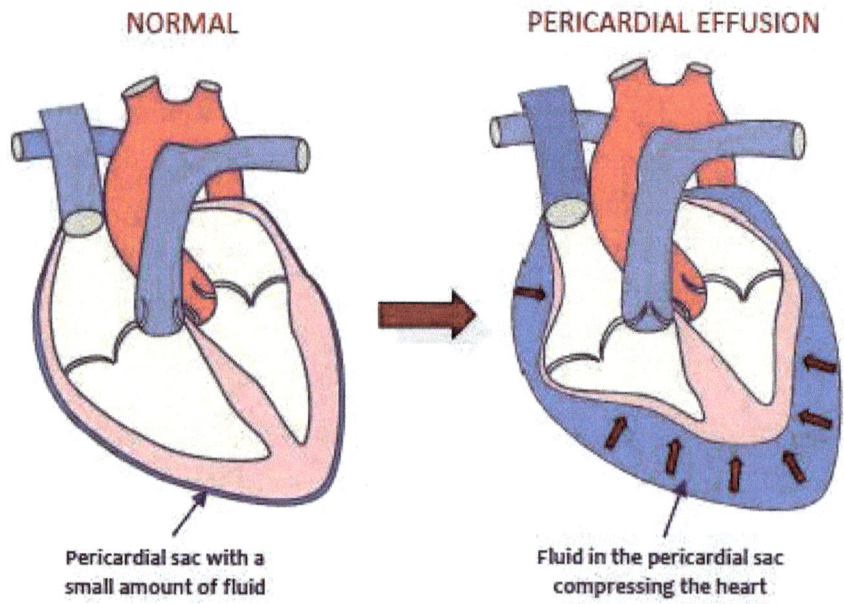

NORMAL

PERICARDIAL EFFUSION

Pericardial sac with a small amount of fluid

Fluid in the pericardial sac compressing the heart

This picture depicts the transformation of a thin fluid film to a large amount of fluid covering the heart with the exertion of external pressure onto the heart chambers, thus causing hypotension. This can be a medical emergency.

The underlying figure depicts how the heart can be "separated from the real world" if there is a thick covering around it. This thick covering could be due to an abnormal amount of fluid accumulation (effusion) or a thickened layer (of pericardium).

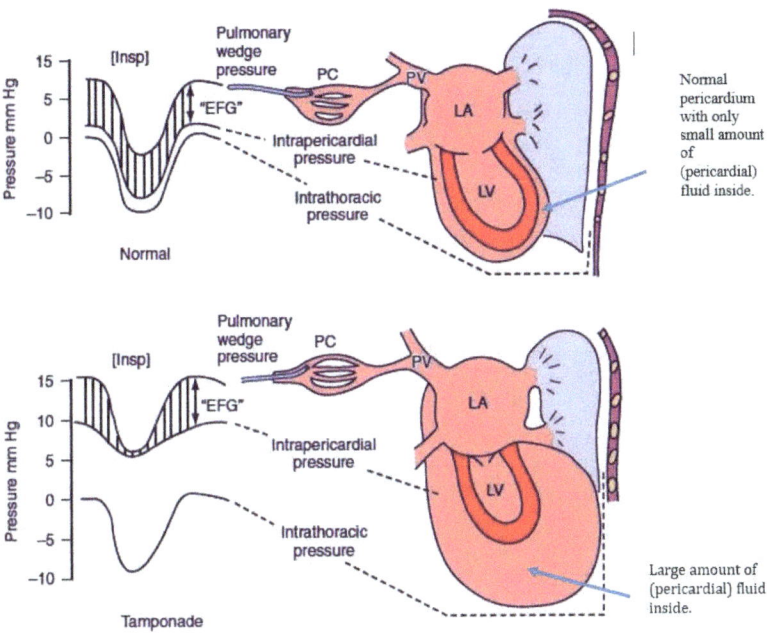

The top half of the figure (above) represents the normal situation in which changes in intra-thoracic pressure are transmitted to both the pericardial sac and the pulmonary veins. The effective filling gradient (EFG) changes only slightly during respiration.

The bottom half of the figure (above) represents cardiac tamponade in which changes in intra-thoracic pressure are transmitted to the pulmonary veins but not to the pericardial sac. The EFG falls during inspiration.

Insp, inspiration; LA, left atrium; LV, left ventricle; PC, pulmonary capillaries; PV, pulmonary veins.

Pericardial Effusion by Echocardiogram:

Let us review some of the images by echocardiogram showing Pericardial effusion.

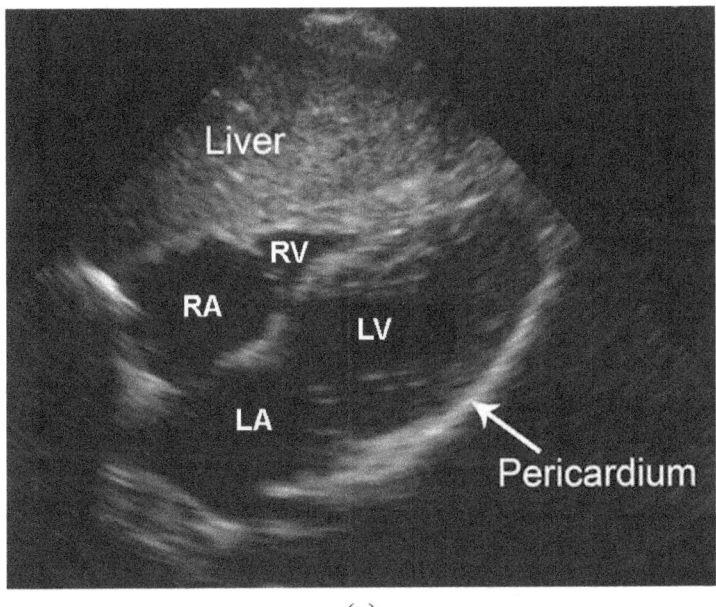

(a)

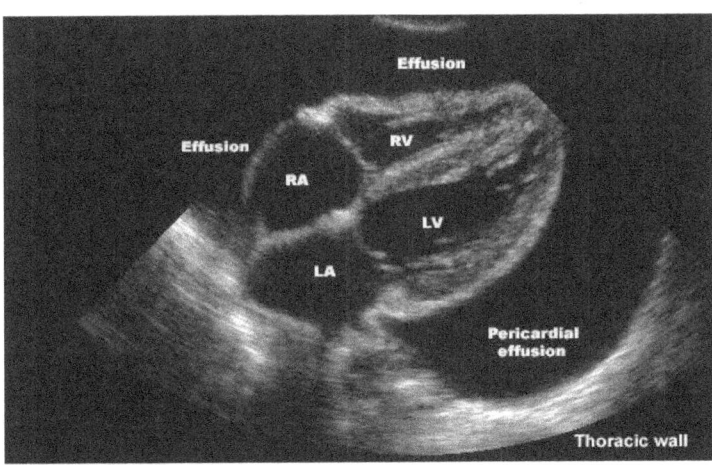

(b)

Sub-xiphoid view (above) of a normal echocardiogram (a) and the one with large pericardial effusion (b).

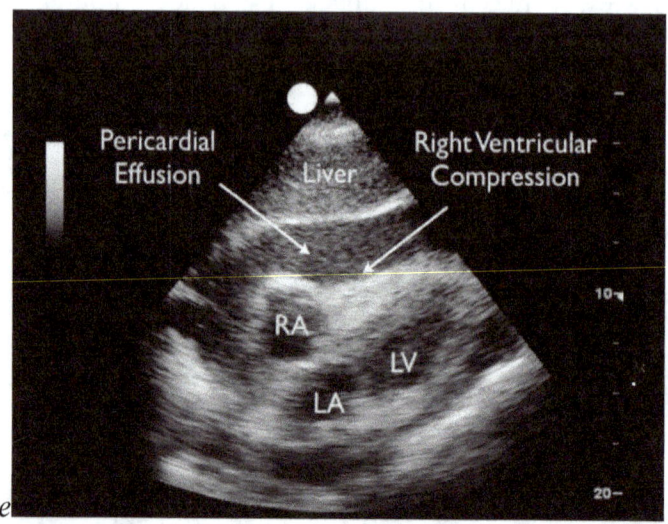

Another image (above) with large effusion resulting in collapse of the right ventricle, which will lead to hypotension

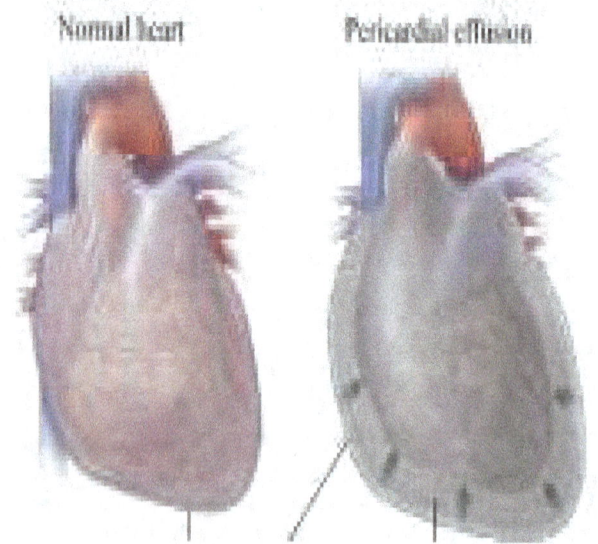

Pericardium Fluid accumulation

Another picture (above) shows the accumulation of excess amount of fluid around the heart which may cause symptoms.

The following pictures belong to one of our 28-year-old male patient who was admitted with a one-week history of feeling tired, upper abdominal pain, and fever and was found to have sinus tachycardia. His chest x-ray showed an enlarged cardiac silhouette. This was followed by an EKG, which showed low voltage and sinus tachycardia. An emergent echocardiogram revealed a large pericardial effusion with cardiac tamponade. This was successfully drained under echocardiographic and fluoroscopic guidance. Approximately 1600 cc of sanguinous fluid was drained, and all the cultures were negative. Patient was seen as a follow-up and found to be doing very well.

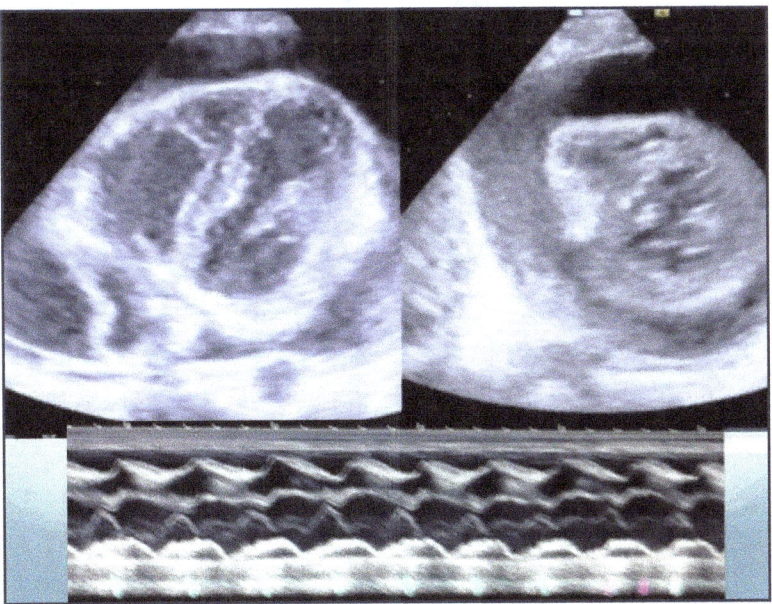

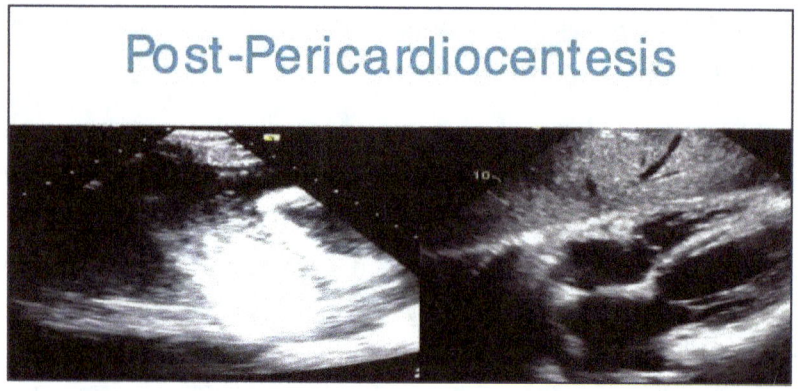

After the successful fluid drainage, there was no more fluid present (above)

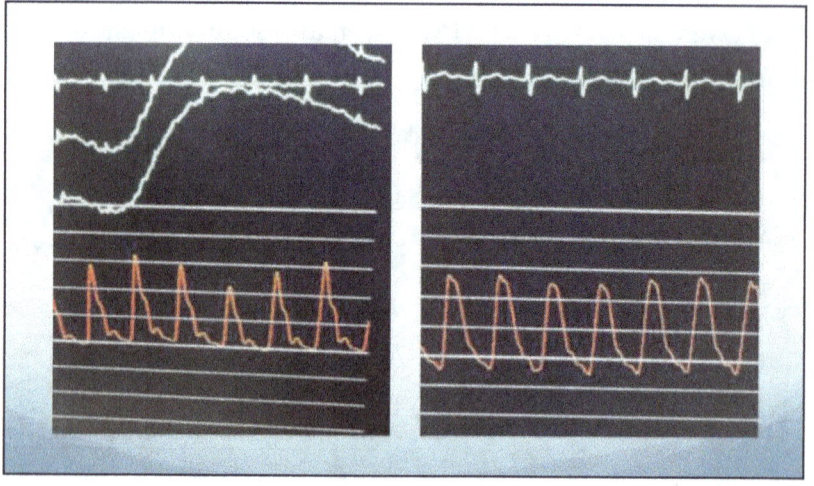

Picture above shows a comparison of abnormal hemodynamics (left) with resumption of normal hemodynamics (right).

PERICARDIAL EFFUSION, CONSTRICTIVE PERICARDITIS BY CXR:

In patients with a large pericardial effusion (at least 250 ml), the chest radiograph usually demonstrates

- Symmetrically enlarged cardio-pericardial silhouette.

- The appearance has been characterized as the flask or water bottle configuration.

- The normal great vessels contours are smoothed out and the hilar vessels are obliterated.

- The cardiophrenic angles show acute rather than obtuse angles.

- Another clue is the rapid change in heart size or presence of cardiomegaly without the radiographic findings of congestive heart failure (pulmonary edema, etc.)

- Pulmonary olegemia.

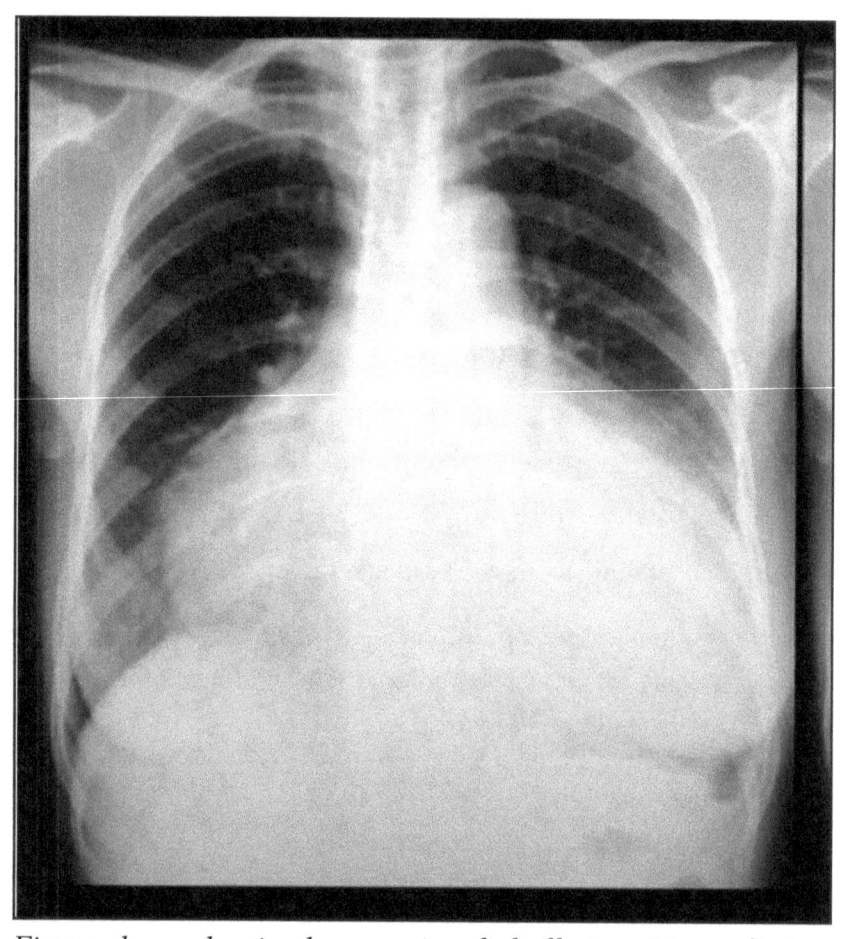

Figure above, showing large pericardial effusion giving a flask or water bottle configuration

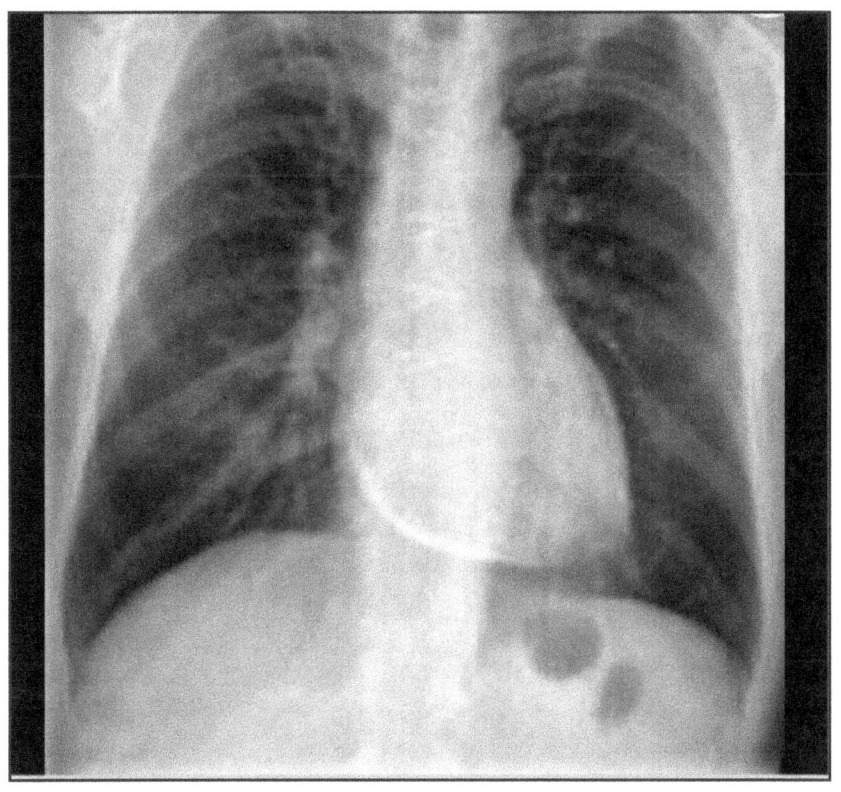

Figure above, showing Pericardial calcification (arrow)

PERICARDIAL EFFUSION BY CT:

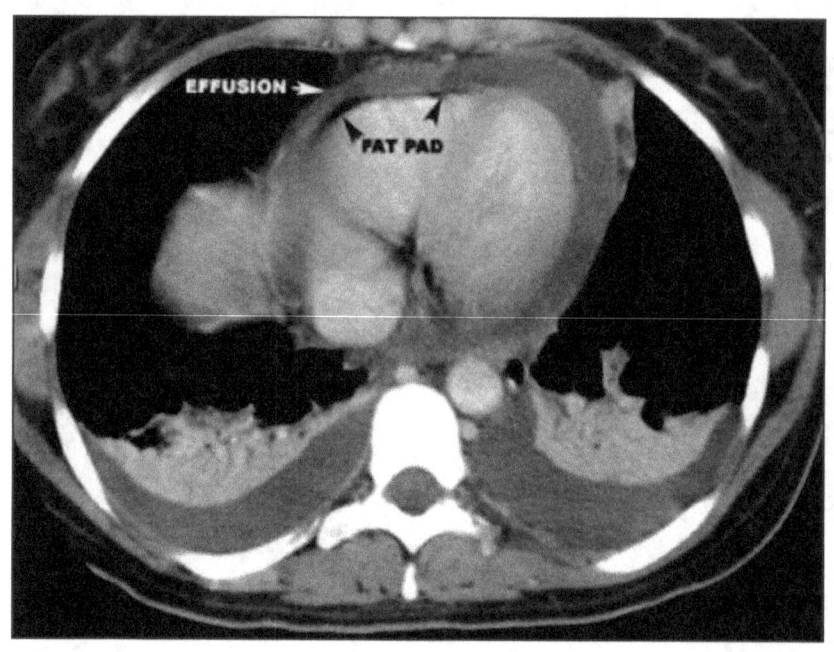

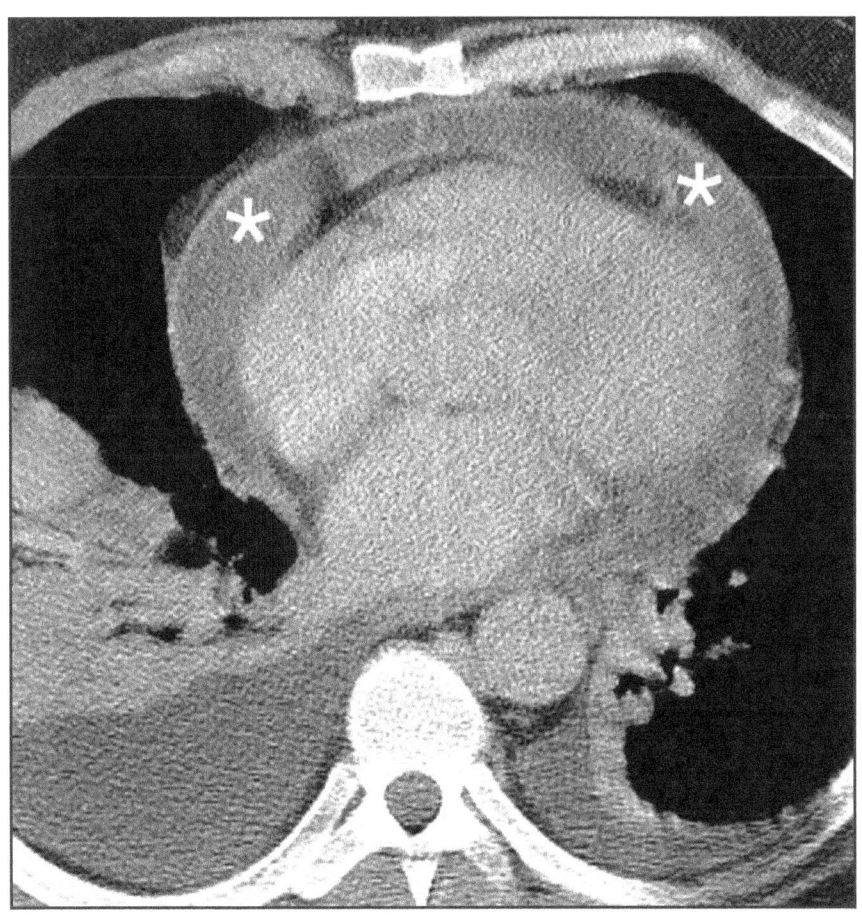

Figure above: Pericardial effusion (*) in a patient with shortness of breath.

The following diagram shows how a pericardiocentesis (drainage of fluid around the heart) is done:

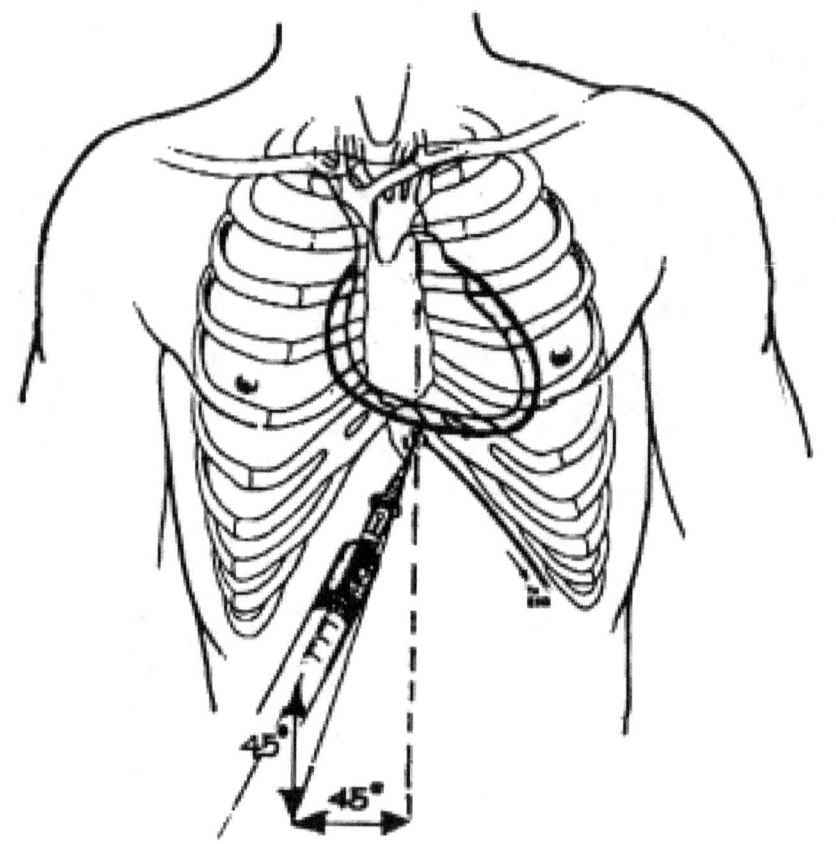

MRI scans of Normal Pericardium, Pericardial Effusion and Constrictive Pericarditis:

Below are a few examples of how thickened and calcified Pericardium and Pericardial effusion would appear on MRI scans in comparison to the normal.

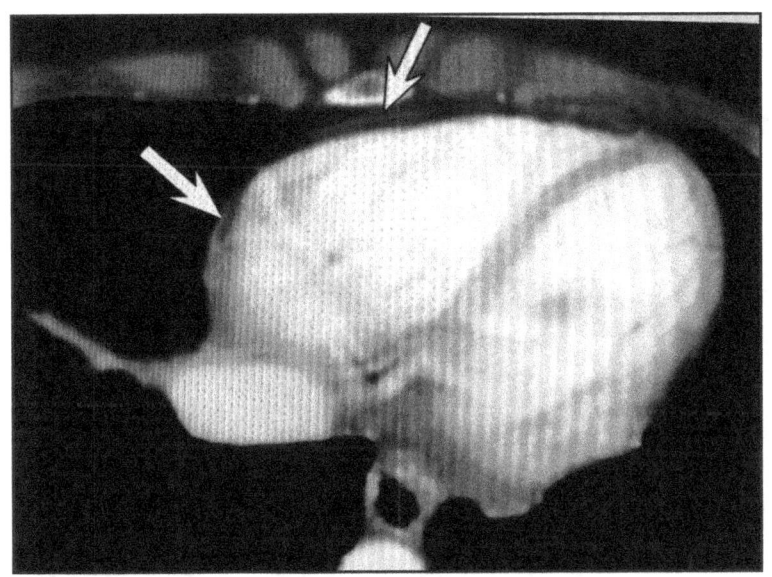

Figure above: A pericardium with normal thickness (arrows)

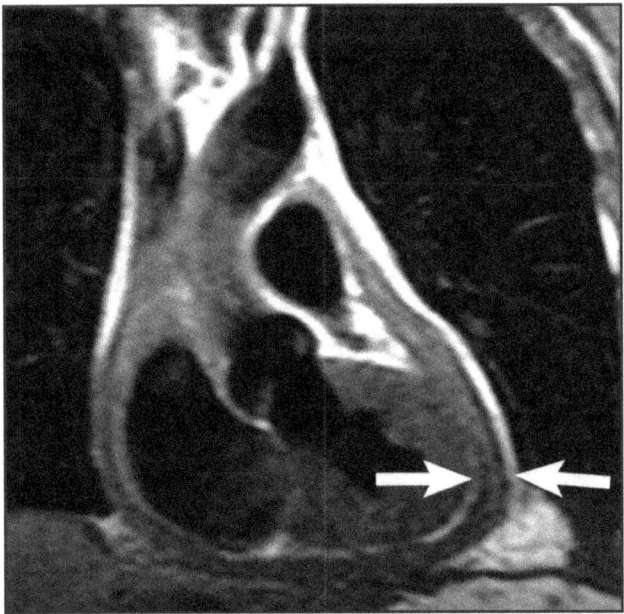

Figure above: Constrictive pericarditis. Abnormally thickened pericardium (arrows)

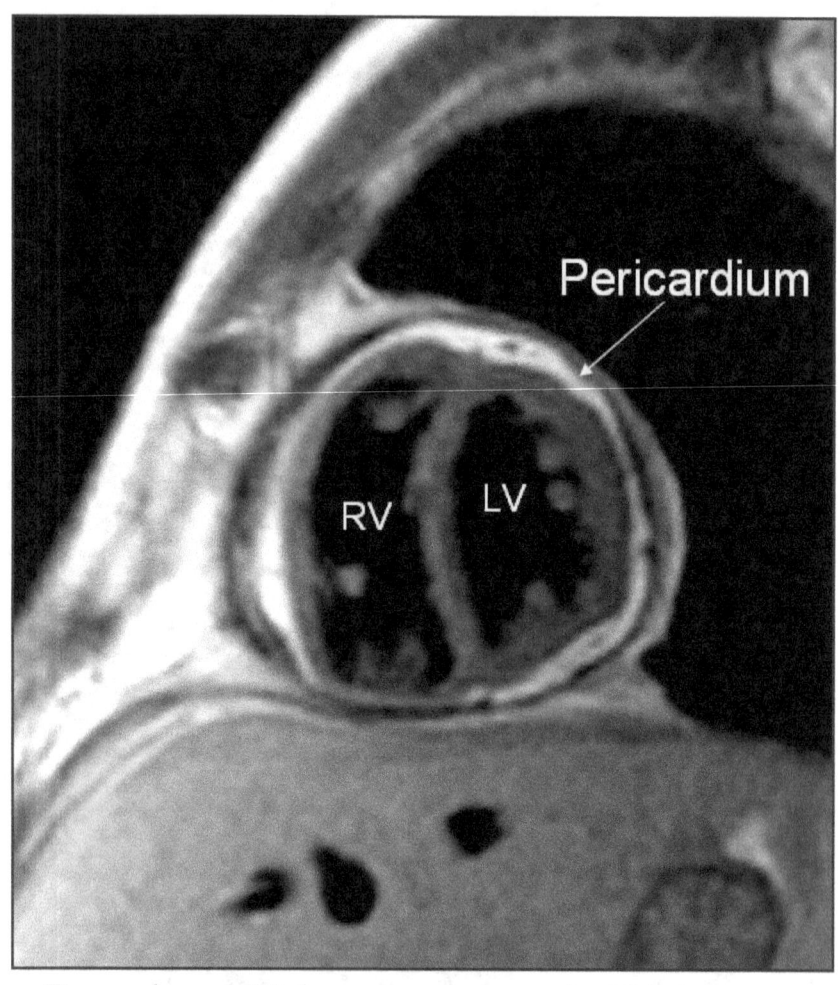

Figure above, MRI shows constrictive pericarditis in a young patient.

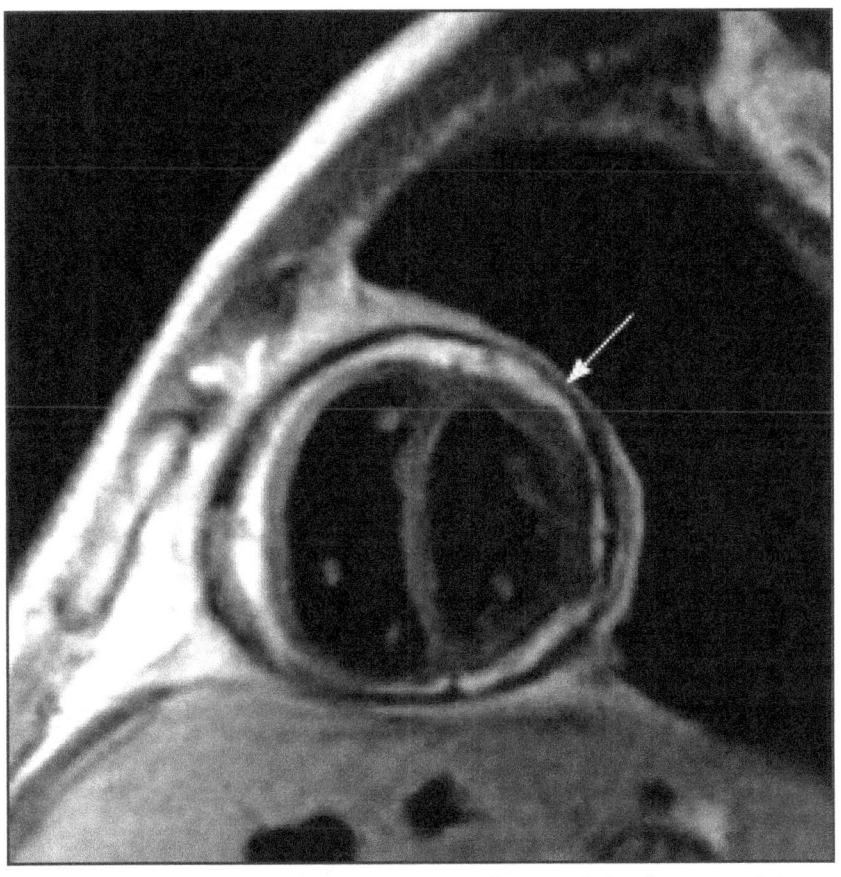

Figure above. MRI showing circumferential thickening of the pericardium (black rim between the epicardial and pericardial fat (arrow)

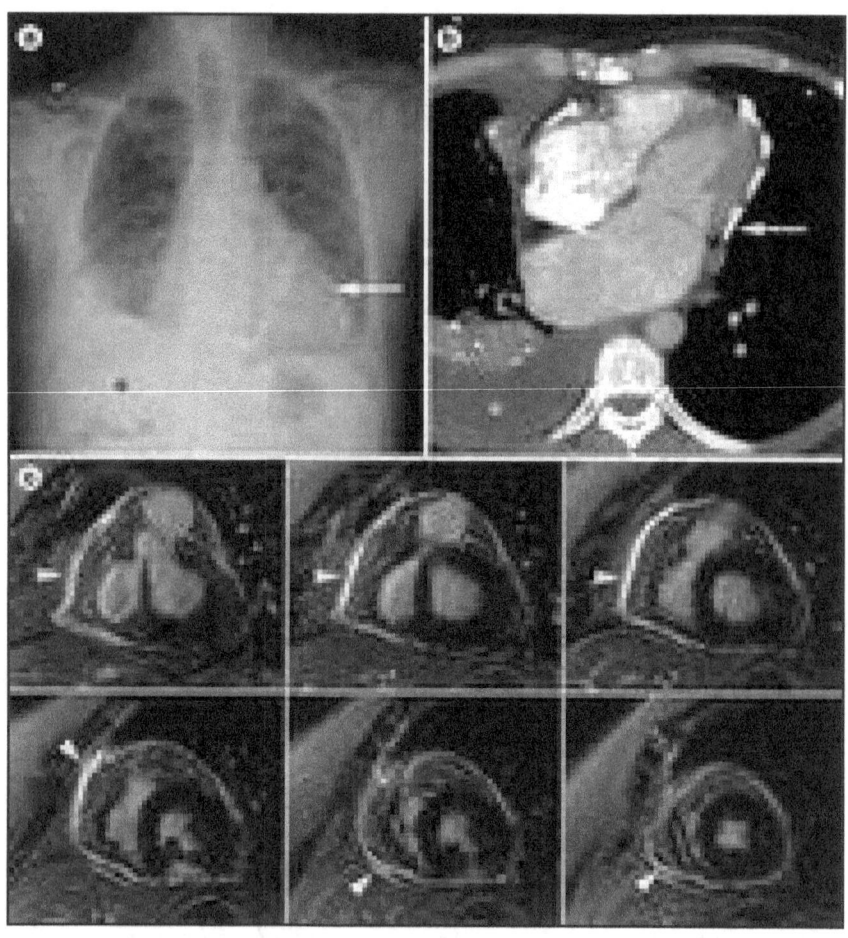

Figure above: Images of Pericardial calcification (arrows) and a right pleural effusion (*)

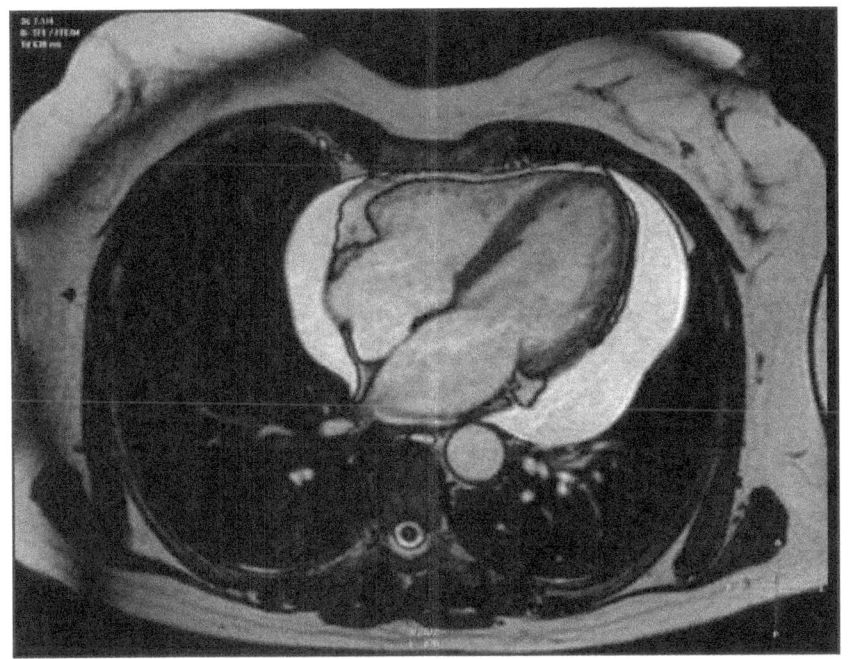

Figure above, Primary malignant pericardial mesothelioma appears as a rare cause of pericardial effusion.

PERICARDIECTOMY *(surgical removal of the covering of the heart):*

The treatment for constrictive pericarditis is to remove the thickened pericardium surgically. A picture of such an operation is shown below.

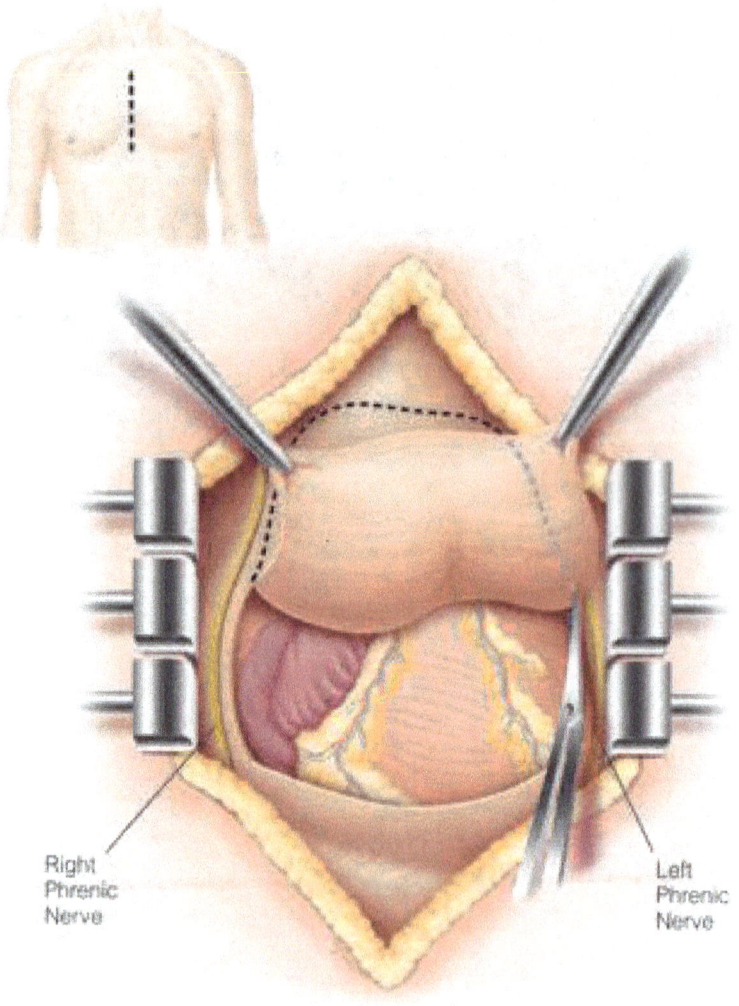

Right Phrenic Nerve

Left Phrenic Nerve

SURGICAL TECHNIQUE:

Intra-operative photographs during radical Pericardiectomy.

Description:

Median sternotomy is approached. The pericardium is freed from different structures in a step-wise fashion using cautery and sparing the phrenic nerve, finally completing the dissection of the pericardium from the diaphragm. ***Constricting layers of epicardium are removed***. Figures below).

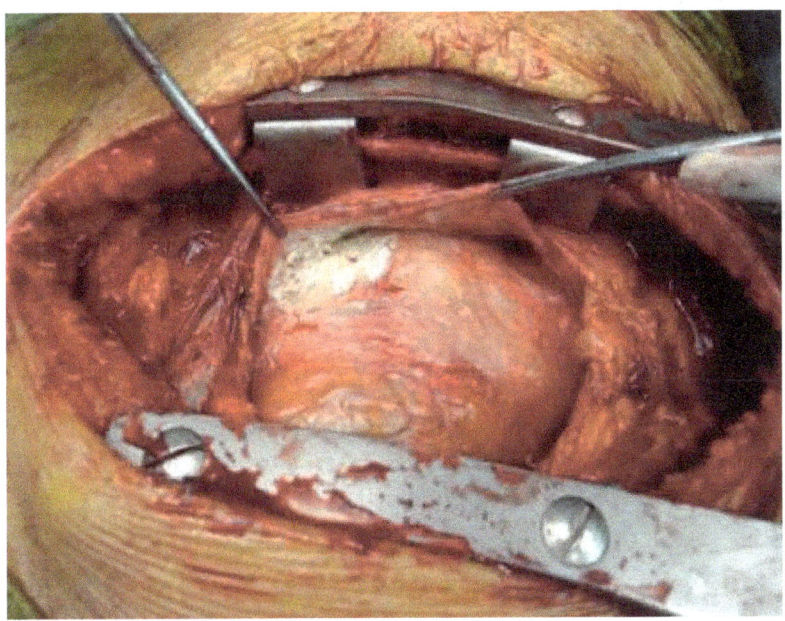

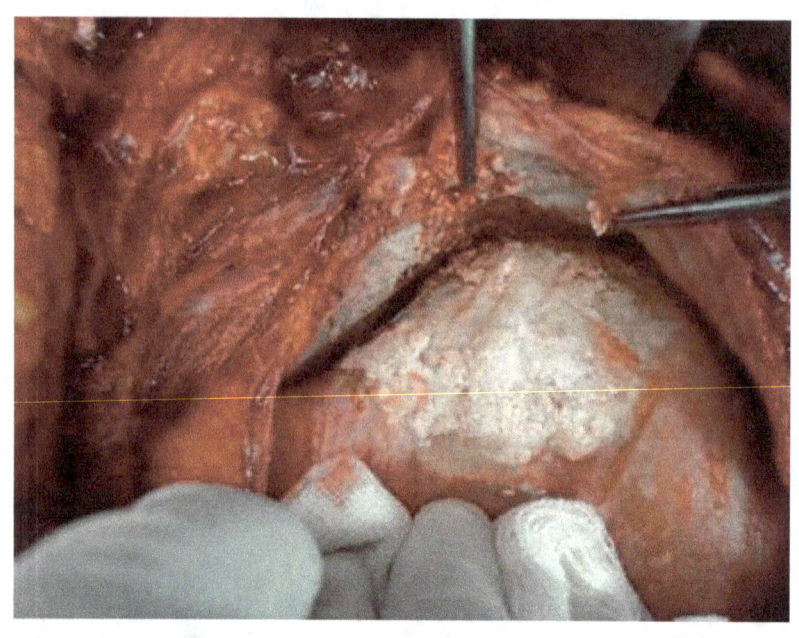

Pathological findings from a specimen (below):

Constrictive pericarditis—a curable diastolic heart failure: NATURE REVIEWS CARDIOLOGY | REVIEW <u>Faisal F. Syed</u>, <u>Hartzell V. Schaff</u> & <u>Jae K. Oh</u> **11**,530–544(2014) doi: 10.1038/nrcardio.2014.100 29 July 2014

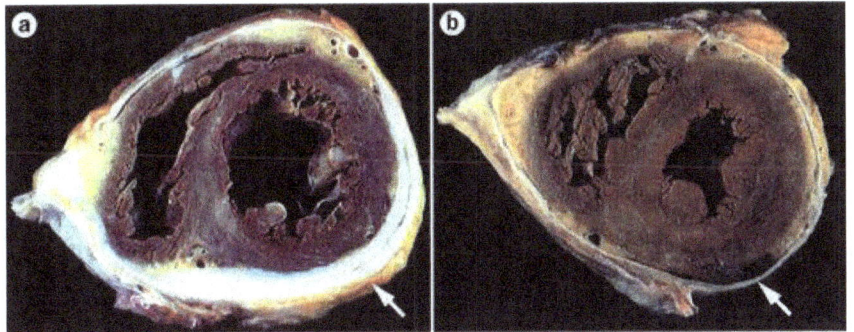

Figure above: Pathology findings in constrictive pericarditis.

a: Sample from a patient with increased pericardial thickness.

b: The pericardium in a patient with constrictive pericarditis,

but normal pericardial thickness. Arrows point to pericardium.

TREATMENT:

Acute pericarditis:

    NSAIDS

    Colchicine

Cardiac Tamponade: Fluid drainage via surgically or percutaneously.

Constrictive pericarditis: Pericardiectomy

Chapter 3
(Synopsis)
Clean, Healthy and Strong Heart

Heart is the most important organ of the body whose good health influences the whole body. Therefore, a healthy body needs a healthy, firm and strong heart. Some of the Holy verses, which may pertain to this concept, are mentioned below.

(1)

وَكُلًّا نَّقُصُّ عَلَيْكَ مِنْ اَنْبَآءِ الرُّسُلِ مَا
نُثَبِّتُ بِهٖ فُؤَادَكَ وَجَآءَكَ فِيْ هٰذِهِ الْحَقُّ
وَمَوْعِظَةٌ وَّذِكْرٰي لِلْمُؤْمِنِيْنَ

We narrate to you all such stories from the events of the messengers as We strengthen your heart therewith. And in these (stories) there has come to you the truth, a good counsel and a reminder to those who believe.

(Chapter 11, Hud: *Hud,* verse 120)

(2)

ثُمَّ اَنْزَلَ عَلَيْكُمْ مِّنْ بَعْدِ الْغَمِّ اَمَنَةً
نُّعَاسًا يَّغْشٰى طَآئِفَةً مِّنْكُمْ وَطَآئِفَةٌ قَدْ
اَهَمَّتْهُمْ اَنْفُسُهُمْ يَظُنُّوْنَ بِاللهِ غَيْرَ الْحَقِّ
ظَنَّ الْجَاهِلِيَّةِ يَقُوْلُوْنَ هَلْ لَّنَا مِنَ الْاَمْرِ
مِنْ شَيْءٍ قُلْ إِنَّ الْاَمْرَ كُلَّهٗ لِلّٰهِ يُخْفُوْنَ فِيْٓ
اَنْفُسِهِمْ مَّا لَا يُبْدُوْنَ لَكَ يَقُوْلُوْنَ لَوْ
كَانَ لَنَا مِنَ الْاَمْرِ شَيْءٌ مَّا قُتِلْنَا

هٰهُنَا قُلْ لَّوْ كُنْتُمْ فِيْ بُيُوْتِكُمْ لَبَرَزَ الَّذِيْنَ كُتِبَ عَلَيْهِمُ الْقَتْلُ اِلٰى مَضَاجِعِهِمْ وَلِيَبْتَلِيَ اللهُ مَا فِيْ صُدُوْرِكُمْ وَلِيُمَحِّصَ مَا فِيْ قُلُوْبِكُمْ وَ اللهُ عَلِيْمٌ بِذَاتِ الصُّدُوْرِ

Then, after the grief, He poured tranquility upon you - a drowsiness overtaking a group of you. Another group was worrying about their own selves, harboring thoughts about ALLAH that were untrue - thoughts of ignorance. They were saying: Is there anything in our hands? Say: The whole thing belongs to ALLAH. They conceal in their hearts what they do not disclose to you. They say, If we had any say in the matter, we would not have been killed here. Say, If you were in your homes, those destined to be killed would have come out all the way to their (final) resting-places. (All this was done) so that ALLAH may test your inner qualities and may purify what is in your hearts. ALLAH is All-Aware of what lies in the hearts.
(Chapter 3; Aale-Imran: *The Family of Imran,* verse 154)

(3)

وَّرَبَطْنَا عَلٰى قُلُوْبِهِمْ اِذْ قَامُوْا فَقَالُوْا رَبُّنَا رَبُّ السَّمٰوٰتِ وَ الْاَرْضِ لَنْ نَّدْعُوَاْ مِنْ دُوْنِهٖ اِلٰهًا لَّقَدْ قُلْنَاۤ اِذًا شَطَطًا

We made their hearts firm when they stood up and said, Our Lord is the Lord of the heavens and the earth. We shall never invoke any god other than Him, otherwise we would be saying something far from the truth.
(Chapter 18, Al-Kahf: *The Cave,* verse 14)

(4)

وَقَالَ الَّذِيْنَ كَفَرُوْا لَوْلَا نُزِّلَ عَلَيْهِ
الْقُرْاٰنُ جُمْلَةً وَّاحِدَةً ۛ كَذٰلِكَ ۛ لِنُثَبِّتَ
بِهٖ فُؤَادَكَ وَرَتَّلْنٰهُ تَرْتِيْلًا

Said those who disbelieved, Why has the Qur'an not been revealed to him all at once? (It has been sent down) in this way (i.e. in parts) so that We make your heart firm, and We reveal it little by little. (Chapter 25, Al-Furqan: *The Discrimination*, verse 32)

(5)

اِلَّا مَنْ اَتَى اللّٰهَ بِقَلْبٍ سَلِيْمٍ

Except to him who will come to ALLAH with a sound heart, (Chapter 26, *Ash-Shu'ara'*: The Poets, verse 89)

(6)

كَذٰلِكَ سَلَكْنٰهُ فِيْ قُلُوْبِ الْمُجْرِمِيْنَ

This is how We have made it pass through the hearts of the sinners. (Chapter 26, *Ash-Shu'ara'*: The Poets, verse 200)

(7)

يٰۤاَيُّهَا الَّذِيْنَ اٰمَنُوْا لَا تَدْخُلُوْا بُيُوْتَ
النَّبِيِّ اِلَّا اَنْ يُّؤْذَنَ لَكُمْ اِلٰى طَعَامٍ غَيْرَ
نٰظِرِيْنَ اِنٰىهُ ۙ وَلٰكِنْ اِذَا دُعِيْتُمْ فَادْخُلُوْا
فَاِذَا طَعِمْتُمْ فَانْتَشِرُوْا وَلَا مُسْتَأْنِسِيْنَ
لِحَدِيْثٍ ۚ اِنَّ ذٰلِكُمْ كَانَ يُؤْذِي النَّبِيَّ
فَيَسْتَحْيٖ مِنْكُمْ ۖ وَاللّٰهُ لَا يَسْتَحْيٖ مِنَ الْحَقِّ
وَاِذَا سَاَلْتُمُوْهُنَّ مَتَاعًا فَسْـَٔلُوْهُنَّ مِنْ

78

وَّرَآءِ حِجَابٍ ذٰلِكُمْ اَطْهَرُ لِقُلُوْبِكُمْ وَقُلُوْبِهِنَّ وَمَا كَانَ لَكُمْ اَنْ تُؤْذُوْا رَسُوْلَ اللهِ وَلَاۤ اَنْ تَنْكِحُوْۤا اَزْوَاجَهٗ مِنْ بَعْدِهٖۤ اَبَدًا اِنَّ ذٰلِكُمْ كَانَ عِنْدَ اللهِ عَظِيْمًا

O you who believe, do not enter the houses of the Prophet, unless you are permitted for a meal, not (so early as) to wait for its preparation. But when you are invited, go inside. Then, once you have had the meal, just disperse, and (do) not (sit for long) being keen for a chat. This (conduct of yours) hurts the Prophet, but he feels shy of (telling) you (about it), but ALLAH is not shy of the truth. And when you ask anything from them (the blessed wives of the Prophet), ask them from behind a curtain. That is better for the purity of your hearts and their hearts. It is not allowed for you that you hurt ALLAH's Messenger, nor that you ever marry his wives after him. Indeed, it would be an enormity in the sight of ALLAH.
(Chapter 33, Al-Ahzab, *The Allies,* verse 53)

(8)

اِذْ جَآءَ رَبَّهٗ بِقَلْبٍ سَلِيْمٍ

(Remember) when he came to his Lord with a pure heart,
(Chapter 37, As-Saffat: *Those Ranging in Ranks*, verse 84)

During normal circumstances, "pure" and "clean" oxygenated blood from the lungs enters into the left side of the heart. The left side of the heart (left ventricle) then pumps this pure blood to the whole body thereby enabling it to function properly. Most healthy hearts beat 60-100 times a minute and pump about 5 liters of blood per minute.

However, in order to do this enormous task throughout life, the heart muscle has to remain healthy and strong.

In cases where an "impure," "unclean," or "deoxygenated" blood is received in the left side of the heart, the same blood will be supplied to the rest of the body, including the heart muscle itself, which will obviously affect its performance and it will become weak.

Interestingly, even if it is receiving pure and oxygenated blood, if there is any blockage (stenosis) in the (coronary) arteries which feed the heart muscle (myocardium), it may cause ischemia (less blood supply) or even infarction (dead muscle) and the heart muscle will not remain healthy and strong. This will eventually affect the rest of the body.

In cases of some developmental abnormalities at birth, impure blood gets distributed throughout the body (due to right-to-left shunting), which is harmful.

Chapter 3:
Clean, Healthy and Strong Heart

A beautiful concept of a firm, healthy and strong heart may be deduced after reading some of the Holy verses. Then later, this concept will be elaborated further in the light of current medical evidence for the readers' interest. Some of the Holy verses, which may pertain to this concept, are mentioned below.

(1)

$$ وَكُـلًّا نَّـقُصُّ عَلَيْكَ مِنْ اَنْبَآءِ الـرُّسُلِ مَـا
نُـثَبِّتُ بِـهٖ فُؤَادَكَ وَجَآءَكَ فِـيْ هٰذِهِ الْـحَقُّ
وَمَـوْعِظَةٌ وَّذِكْرٰي لِـلْمُؤْمِنِيْنَ $$

We narrate to you all such stories from the events of the messengers as We strengthen your heart therewith. And in these (stories) there has come to you the truth, a good counsel and a reminder to those who believe.
(Chapter 11, Hud: *Hud,* verse 120)

(2)

$$ ثُـمَّ اَنْـزَلَ عَلَيْكُمْ مِّنْ بَعْدِ الْـغَمِّ اَمَـنَةً
نُّـعَـاسًـا يَّـغْشٰى طَآئِـفَـةً مِّنْكُمْ وَطَآئِـفَةٌ قَـدْ
اَهَمَّـتْهُمْ اَنْـفُسُهُمْ يَظُنُّوْنَ بِاللهِ غَيْـرَ الْـحَقِّ
ظَنَّ الْـجَـاهِلِيَّةِ يَقُـوْلُـوْنَ هَلْ لَّـنَا مِنَ الْأَمْرِ
مِنْ شَيْءٍ قُـلْ اِنَّ الْأَمْـرَ كُـلَّـهٗ لِلهِ يُخْفُوْنَ فِيْ
اَنْفُسِهِمْ مَّـا لَا يُـبْـدُوْنَ لَكَ يَقُـوْلُـوْنَ لَـوْ
كَـانَ لَـنَا مِنَ الْأَمْرِ شَيْءٌ مَّـا قُتِلْنَا
هٰهُنَـا قُلْ لَّـوْ كُنْـتُمْ فِيْ بُيُوْتِكُمْ لَـبَرَزَ $$

اللَّذِيْنَ كُتِبَ عَلَيْهِمُ الْقَتْلُ إِلَى مَضَاجِعِهِمُ
وَلِيَبْتَلِيَ اللهُ مَا فِيْ صُدُوْرِكُمْ وَلِيُمَحِّصَ مَا
فِيْ قُلُوْبِكُمْ وَ اللهُ عَلِيْمٌ بِذَاتِ الصُّدُوْرِ

Then, after the grief, He poured tranquility upon you - a drowsiness overtaking a group of you. Another group was worrying about their own selves, harboring thoughts about ALLAH that were untrue - thoughts of ignorance. They were saying, Is there anything in our hands? Say, the whole thing belongs to ALLAH. They conceal in their hearts what they do not disclose to you. They say, if we had any say in the matter, we would not have been killed here. Say, if you were in your homes, those destined to be killed would have come out all the way to their (final) resting -places. (All this was done) so that ALLAH may test your inner qualities and may purify what is in your hearts. ALLAH is All-Aware of what lies in the hearts.

(Chapter 3; Aale-Imran: *The Family of Imran*, verse 154)

(3)

وَّرَبَطْنَا عَلَى قُلُوْبِهِمْ إِذْ قَامُوْا فَقَالُوْا
رَبُّنَا رَبُّ السَّمٰوٰتِ وَ الْأَرْضِ لَنْ نَّدْعُوَا مِنْ
دُوْنِهِ إِلٰهًا لَّقَدْ قُلْنَآ إِذًا شَطَطًا

We made their hearts firm when they stood up and said, Our Lord is the Lord of the heavens and the earth. We shall never invoke any god other than Him, otherwise we would be saying something far from the truth.

(Chapter 18, Al-Kahf: *The Cave*, verse 14)

(4)

وَقَالَ الَّذِيْنَ كَفَرُوْا لَوْلَا نُزِّلَ عَلَيْهِ الْقُرْاٰنُ جُمْلَةً وَّاحِدَةً رِ كَذٰلِكَ رِ لِنُثَبِّتَ بِهٖ فُؤَادَكَ وَرَتَّلْنٰهُ تَرْتِيْلًا

Said those who disbelieved, Why has the Qur'an not been revealed to him all at once? (It has been sent down) in this way (i.e. in parts) so that We make your heart firm, and We reveal it little by little. (Chapter 25, Al-Furqan: *The Discrimination*, verse 32)

(5)

اِلَّا مَنْ اَتَى اللهَ بِقَلْبٍ سَلِيْمٍ

except to him who will come to ALLAH with a sound heart, (Chapter 26, *Ash-Shu'ara'*: The Poets, verse 89)

(6)

كَذٰلِكَ سَلَكْنٰهُ فِيْ قُلُوْبِ الْمُجْرِمِيْنَ

This is how We have made it pass through the hearts of the sinners. (Chapter 26, *Ash-Shu'ara'*: The Poets, verse 200)

(7)

يٰٓاَيُّهَا الَّذِيْنَ اٰمَنُوْا لَا تَدْخُلُوْا بُيُوْتَ النَّبِيِّ اِلَّآ اَنْ يُّؤْذَنَ لَكُمْ اِلٰى طَعَامٍ غَيْرَ نٰظِرِيْنَ اِنٰىهُ وَلٰكِنْ اِذَا دُعِيْتُمْ فَادْخُلُوْا فَاِذَا طَعِمْتُمْ فَانْتَشِرُوْا وَلَا مُسْتَأْنِسِيْنَ لِحَدِيْثٍ اِنَّ ذٰلِكُمْ كَانَ يُؤْذِي النَّبِيَّ فَيَسْتَحْيٖ مِنْكُمْ وَاللهُ لَا يَسْتَحْيٖ مِنَ الْحَقِّ وَاِذَا سَاَلْتُمُوْهُنَّ مَتَاعًا فَسْـَٔلُوْهُنَّ مِنْ

83

وَّرَآءِ حِجَابٍ ذٰلِكُمْ اَطْهَرُ لِقُلُوْبِكُمْ
وَقُلُوْبِهِنَّ وَمَا كَانَ لَكُمْ اَنْ تُؤْذُوْا
رَسُوْلَ اللهِ وَلَا اَنْ تَنْكِحُوْٓا اَزْوَاجَهٗ مِنْ
بَعْدِهٖٓ اَبَدًا إِنَّ ذٰلِكُمْ كَانَ عِنْدَ اللهِ
عَظِيْمًا

O you who believe, do not enter the houses of the Prophet, unless you are permitted for a meal, not (so early as) to wait for its preparation. But when you are invited, go inside. Then, once you have had the meal, just disperse, and (do) not (sit for long) being keen for a chat. This (conduct of yours) hurts the Prophet, but he feels shy of (telling) you (about it), but ALLAH is not shy of the truth. And when you ask anything from them (the blessed wives of the Prophet), ask them from behind a curtain. That is better for the purity of your hearts and their hearts. It is not allowed for you that you hurt ALLAH's Messenger, nor that you ever marry his wives after him. Indeed, it would be an enormity in the sight of ALLAH.

(Chapter 33, Al-Ahzab, *The Allies,* verse 53)

(8)

اِذْ جَآءَ رَبَّهٗ بِقَلْبٍ سَلِيْمٍ

(Remember) when he came to his Lord with a pure heart,

(Chapter 37, As-Saffat: *Those Ranging in Ranks*, verse 84)

(9)

قَالَتِ الْاَعْرَابُ اٰمَنَّا قُلْ لَّمْ تُؤْمِنُوْا
وَلٰكِنْ قُوْلُوْٓا اَسْلَمْنَا وَلَمَّا يَدْخُلِ الْاِيْمَانُ
فِيْ قُلُوْبِكُمْ وَاِنْ تُطِيْعُوا اللهَ وَرَسُوْلَهٗ لَا

يَـــلِتْكُمْ مِنْ اَعْمَالِكُمْ شَيْـــًـا ۚ اِنَّ اللّٰهَ غَفُوْرٌ رَّحِيْمٌ

The Bedouins say, we have come to believe. Say, you have not come to believe; instead, you (should) say, we have surrendered 'and the belief has not entered your hearts so far. If you obey ALLAH and His Messenger, He will not curtail (the reward of) any of your deeds in the least. Surely ALLAH is Most-Forgiving, Very-Merciful.
(Chapter 49, Al-Hujurat: *The Apartments*, verse 14)

(10)

لَا تَجِدُ قَوْمًا يُّؤْمِنُوْنَ بِاللّٰهِ وَ الْيَوْمِ الْاٰخِرِ يُوَآدُّوْنَ مَنْ حَآدَّ اللّٰهَ وَرَسُوْلَهٗ وَلَوْ كَانُوْٓا اٰبَآءَهُمْ اَوْ اَبْنَآءَهُمْ اَوْ اِخْوَانَهُمْ اَوْ عَشِيْرَتَهُمْ ۚ اُولٰٓئِكَ كَتَبَ فِيْ قُلُوْبِهِمُ الْاِيْمَانَ وَ اَيَّدَهُمْ بِرُوْحٍ مِّنْهُ ۚ وَيُدْخِلُهُمْ جَنّٰتٍ تَجْرِيْ مِنْ تَحْتِهَا الْاَنْهٰرُ خٰلِدِيْنَ فِيْهَا ۚ رَضِيَ اللّٰهُ عَنْهُمْ وَرَضُوْا عَنْهُ ۚ اُولٰٓئِكَ حِزْبُ اللّٰهِ ۚ اَلَآ اِنَّ حِزْبَ اللّٰهِ هُمُ الْمُفْلِحُوْنَ

You will not find those who believe in ALLAH and in the Hereafter having friendship with those who oppose ALLAH and His Messenger, even though they may be their fathers or their sons or their brothers or their clan. They are such that ALLAH has inscribed faith on their hearts, and has supported them with a spirit from Him. He will admit them to gardens beneath which rivers flow, in which they will live forever. ALLAH is pleased with them, and they are pleased with ALLAH. Those are the party of ALLAH. Be assured that it is (the members of) the party of ALLAH that are successful.
(Chapter 58, Al-Mujadilah: *The Pleading Woman*, verse 22)

Heart is the most important organ of the body whose good health influences upon the whole body. In other words, a healthy body needs a healthy and strong heart.

Heart is an active pump. During normal circumstances, "pure" and "clean" oxygenated blood from the lungs enters into the left side of the heart. The left side of the heart then pumps this pure blood to the whole body thereby enabling it to function properly.

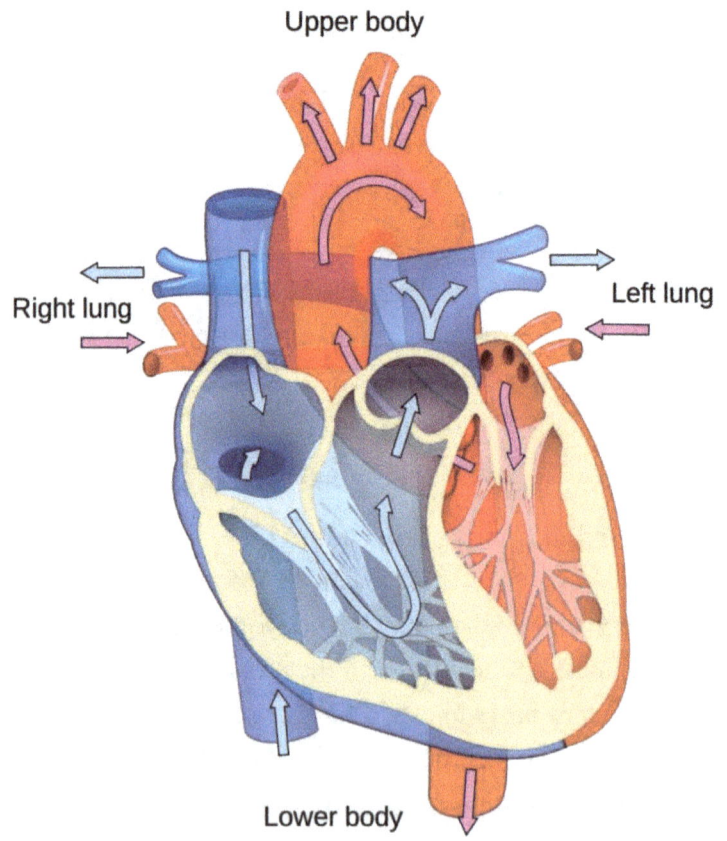

The picture above depicts the normal blood flow. The pink arrows at the top show entry of "pure or oxygenated '' blood from the right and

left lungs into the left atrium and then into the left ventricle, which then finally pumps it out to the whole body through the Aorta. The same blood, after delivering the oxygen and other nutrients to the whole body, then enters into the right atrium (blue arrows) and then to the right ventricle, from where it gets pumped into the lungs for "purification" again. This purified blood then again goes to the left side of the heart. This process goes on and on.

In cases where an "impure," "unclean," or "deoxygenated" blood is received in the left side of the heart, the same blood will be supplied to the rest of the body, including the heart muscle itself, which will obviously affect its performance.

In addition, even if it is receiving pure and oxygenated blood, if there is any stenosis or blockage in the coronary arteries, it will cause ischemia and may be infarction, and the heart muscle will not remain healthy and strong. This will ultimately affect the rest of the body.

A *cardiac shunt* is a pattern of blood flow in the heart that deviates from the normal circuit of the circulatory system. It may be described as Left-Right, Right-Left or bidirectional.

In cases of congenital right - to - left shunt anomalies, there is an abnormal blood flow from the right side to the left side in the atria, ventricles or even in great vessels. The deoxygenated or impure blood bypasses the lungs and gets distributed throughout the body, which is harmful.

A right-to-left shunt may occur:

- If there is an opening or passage between the atria, ventricles and/or great vessels; *and,*

- The right heart pressure is higher than the left heart pressure, and/or the shunt has a one-way valve-opening like a PFO (patent foramen ovale).

Causes:

Congenital:

Common causes of congenital right-to-left shunting may include:

a) Tetralogy of Fallot
b) Tricuspid atresia
c) Total anomalous pulmonary venous return
d) Transposition of great vessels
e) Persistent truncus arteriosus

Interestingly, if a left-to-right shunt remains uncorrected, it may be reversed and progresses to right-to-left shunt along with the development of pulmonary hypertension. This culminates into the supply of deoxygenated blood to the body system and cyanosis. This phenomenon is referred to as Eisenmenger syndrome and may be observed in Atrial septal defects; Ventricular septal defects, Patent ductus arteriosus and others.

Physiological Shunts:

These may be defined as the diversion of venous blood into the arterial blood circulation.

Small physiological or "normal" shunts are seen due to the return of deoxygenated blood via the bronchial artery and the Thebesian veins to the left side of the heart.

Iatrogenic R-L Shunt:

A main stem intubation with an endotracheal tube can lead to right-to-left shunting. This occurs when the tip of the endotracheal tube is placed beyond the carina. In this way, only one lung is oxygenated, and oxygen-poor blood from the non-ventilated lung dilutes the oxygen level of blood returning from the lungs in the left ventricle.

This chapter dealt with the importance of a strong and healthy heart in light of verses from the Holy Scripture. This may be just one interpretation of these Holy verses, and of course, ALLAH Almighty is the best knower of all. We pray for HIS guidance in every walk of life.

Chapter 4
(Synopsis)
The Autonomic System of the Heart and body

The heart is richly supplied with nerves.

The autonomic nervous system comprises two components:

- The Sympathetic Nervous System

- The Para-sympathetic Nervous System

Many organs are controlled primarily by either the sympathetic or the parasympathetic system. Sometimes, the two divisions have opposite effects on the same organ. For example, the sympathetic division increases heart rate, and the parasympathetic division decreases it.

The sympathetic nervous system prepares the body for an emergency situation like a "fight or flight" response during any potential danger.

The parasympathetic nervous system inhibits the body from overworking and restores the body to a calm and composed state.

We will now mention the following beautiful verses in the context of above mentioned information:

إِذْ جَآءُ وْكُمْ مِّنْ فَوْقِكُمْ وَمِنْ أَسْفَلَ مِنْكُمْ
وَإِذْ زَاغَتِ الْأَبْصَارُ وَبَلَغَتِ الْقُلُوبُ
الْحَنَاجِرَ وَتَظُنُّوْنَ بِاللهِ الظُّنُوْنَا

(Recall) when they came upon you from above you and from below you, and when the eyes were distracted, and the hearts reached the throats, and you were thinking about ALLAH all sorts of thoughts. (Chapter 33: Al-Ahzab; The Allies, Verse 10)

مُهْطِعِيْنَ مُقْنِعِيْ رُءُوْسِهِمْ لَا يَرْتَدُّ اِلَـيْهِمْ طَرْفُهُمْ ۚ وَ اَفْـِـدَتُـهُمْ هَوَآءٌ

They shall be rushing with their heads raised upward; their eyes shall not return towards them and their hearts shall be hollow." (Chapter 14: Ibrahim; *Abraham,* Verse 43)

وَ اَنْذِرْهُمْ يَوْمَ الْأزِفَةِ اِذِ الْقُلُوْبُ لَدَى الْحَـنَـاجِرِ كٰظِمِيْنَ مَا لِلظّٰلِمِيْنَ مِنْ حَمِيْمٍ وَّلَا شَفِيْعٍ يُّطَاعُ

"And warn them of the Day of approaching horror, when hearts will jump up into the throats, (and they will be) choked. There will be neither a friend for the unjust, nor an intercessor to be listened to." (Chapter 40: Ghafir, *The Forgiver,* Verse 18)

We now look at certain verses, which may appear to be pointing towards the Sympathetic and the Para-sympathetic system of the autonomic nervous system, and of course, ALLAH knows the best.

Sympathetic System:

وَاَنْزَلَ الَّذِيْنَ ظَاهَرُوْهُمْ مِّنْ اَهْلِ الْكِتٰبِ
مِنْ صَيَاصِيْهِمْ وَقَذَفَ فِيْ قُلُوْبِهِمُ الرُّعْبَ
فَرِيْقًا تَقْتُلُوْنَ وَتَأْسِرُوْنَ فَرِيْقًا

"He has brought those of the people of the Book (the Jews) who had
backed them, down from their fortresses, and cast awe into their
hearts, so as to make you kill some of them and take others as
captives."
(Chapter 33: Al-Ahzab, *The Allies:* Verse 26)

قُلُوْبٌ يَّوْمَئِذٍ وَّاجِفَةٌ

"On that day, hearts (of people) will be throbbing,."
(Chapter 79: An-Naziat, *Those Who yearn:* Verse 8)

Para- Sympathetic System:

هُوَ الَّذِيْٓ اَنْزَلَ السَّكِيْنَةَ فِيْ قُلُوْبِ
الْمُؤْمِنِيْنَ لِيَزْدَادُوٓا اِيْمَانًا مَّعَ
اِيْمَانِهِمْ وَلِلّٰهِ جُنُوْدُ السَّمٰوٰتِ وَالْاَرْضِ
وَكَانَ اللهُ عَلِيْمًا حَكِيْمًا

"He (ALLAH) is such that He sent down tranquility into the hearts of
the believers, so that they grow more in faith in addition to their
(existing) faith. And to ALLAH belong the forces of the heavens and
the earth, and ALLAH is All-Knowing, All-Wise."
(Chapter 48: Al-Fath, *The Victory:* Verse 4)

92

لَـقَـدْ رَضِيَ اللهُ عَنِ الْـمُؤْمِنِيْنَ اِذْ يُبَـايِعُوْنَكَ تَـحْتَ الـشَّجَرَةِ فَعَلِمَ مَا فِيْ قُلُوْبِـهِمْ فَاَنْـزَلَ الـسَّكِيْنَةَ عَلَيْهِمْ وَ اَثَابَـهُمْ فَتْحًا قَرِيْبًا

"ALLAH was pleased with the believers when they were pledging allegiance with you (by placing their hands in your hands) under the tree, and He knew what was in their hearts, so He sent down tranquility upon them, and rewarded them with a victory, near at hand,"
(Chapter 48: Al-Fath, *The Victory:* Verse 18)

اَلَّـذِيْـنَ اٰمَـنُوْا وَتَطْمَىِٕنُّ قُلُـوْبُـهُمْ بِذِكْرِ اللهِ اَ لَا بِـذِكْرِ اللهِ تَـطْمَىِٕنُّ الْـقُلُوْبُ

"the ones who believe and their hearts are peaceful with the remembrance of ALLAH. Listen, the hearts find peace only in the remembrance of ALLAH."
(Chapter 13: Ar-Rad, *The Thunder:* Verse 28)

An interesting phenomenon called *Takotsubo Cardiomyopathy (broken-heart syndrome) is* mentioned in the medical literature, which manifests as a weakening of the heart muscle. It is believed to be due to extreme mental anxiety.

Chapter 4:
The Autonomic System of the Heart and Body

This chapter deals with the autonomic system of the heart and its effect on daily life.

The heart is richly supplied with nerves. The autonomic nervous system comprises two components:

1. The Sympathetic Nervous System

2. The Para-sympathetic Nervous System

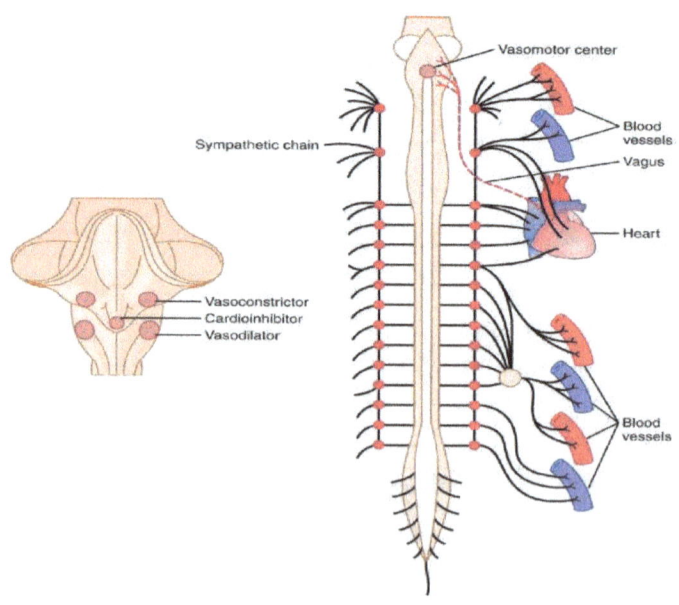

Figure above: Anatomy of the sympathetic nervous control of the circulation. Also shown by the dashed red line, a vagus nerve that carries parasympathetic signals to the heart.

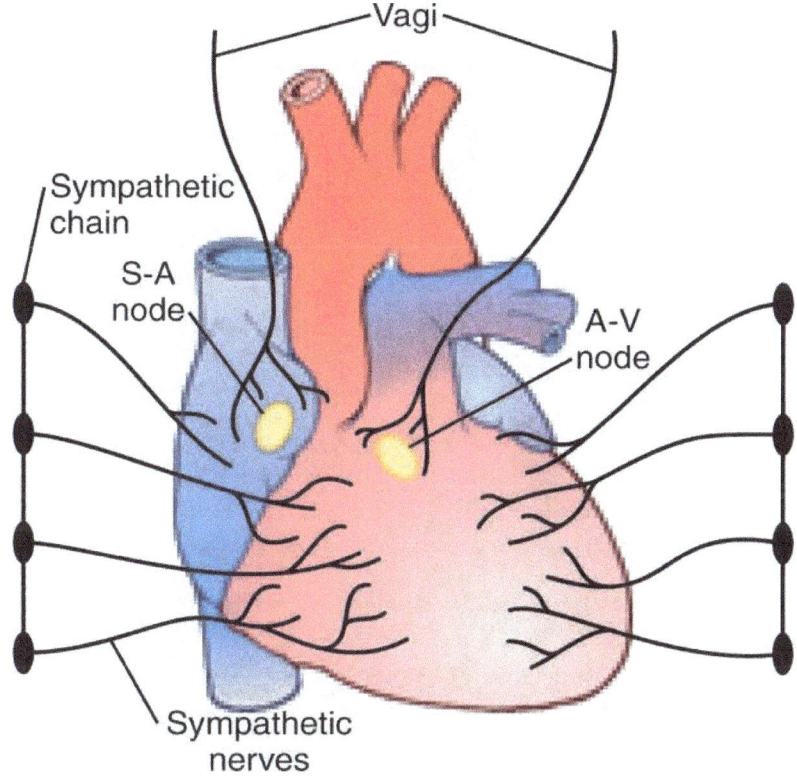

Figure above: Control of the Heart by the Sympathetic and Parasympathetic Nerves. The pumping effectiveness of the heart is also controlled by the sympathetic and parasympathetic (vagus) nerves, which abundantly supply the heart.

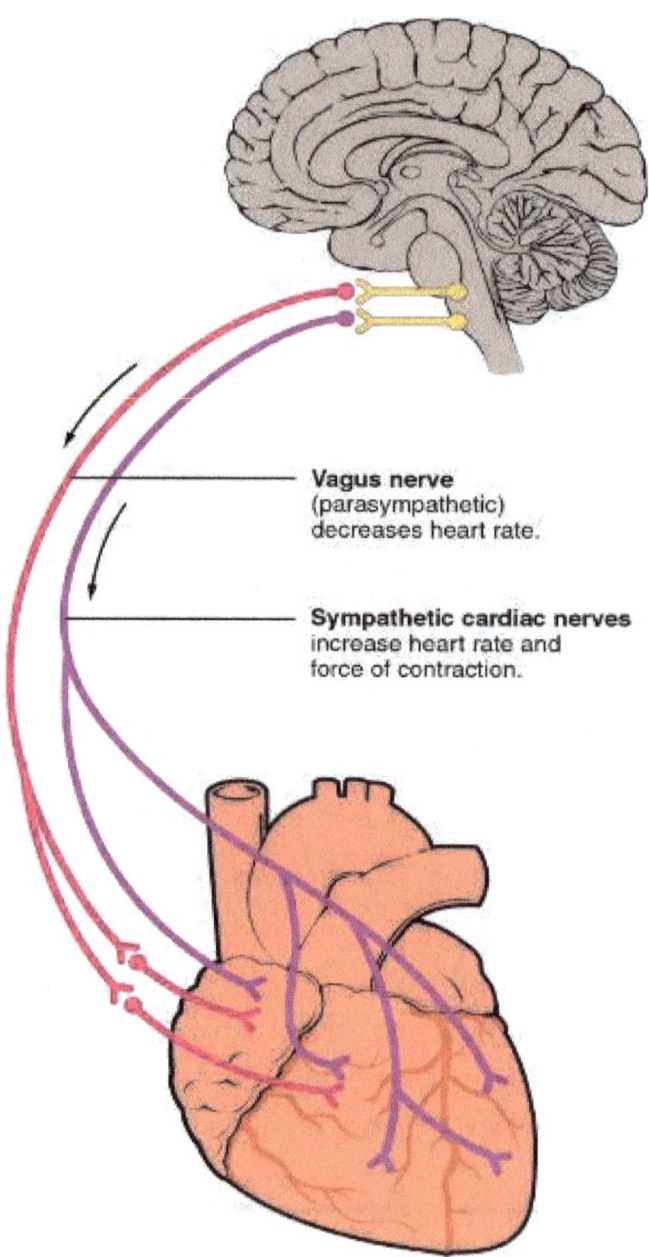

Figure above: A sketch showing autonomic innervation of the heart

Many organs are controlled primarily by either the sympathetic or the parasympathetic system. Sometimes, the two divisions have opposite effects on the same organ. For example, the sympathetic division increases heart rate, and the parasympathetic division decreases it. However, a harmonious function of these two divisions is of paramount importance to ensure that the body responds appropriately under variable circumstances.

Divisions of the Autonomic Nervous System	
Division	**Effects**
Sympathetic System	Performs the following:
	Increased heart rate and force of heart contractions.
	Increased release of energy stored in the liver
	Increased blood flow to skeletal muscle and the lungs
	Dilation of the pulmonary bronchioles through circulating epinephrine for greater alveolar oxygen exchange.
	Causes sweaty palms.
	Diverts blood flow away from less important organs such as the gastro-intestinal tract and skin via vasoconstriction in an emergency situation.
	Dilates pupils and relaxes the ciliary muscle to the lens, allowing more light to enter the eye and enhancing far vision.
	Hair to stand on end.
Parasympathetic System	Performs the following:
	Slows the heart rate
	Reduces blood pressure
	Stimulates the digestive tract to process food and eliminate wastes (in bowel movements)

The sympathetic nervous system prepares the body for the "fight or flight" response during any potential danger. The symptoms and illnesses associated with the Sympathetic Nervous System dominance may include: Hypertension, fast and rapid arrhythmias, anxiety, panic attacks, etc.

On the other hand, the parasympathetic nervous system inhibits the body from overworking and restores the body to a calm and composed state. The difference between the sympathetic and parasympathetic nervous systems are differentiated, based on the way the body responds to environmental stimuli. In health, the parasympathetic nervous system promotes the ability to rest and recover through sleep, eating and digestion, and a sense of safety.

Two neurotransmitters are normally described, which are the Acetylcholine and adrenaline for parasympathetic and sympathetic functions, respectively. A very complex mechanism occurs through which these neurotransmitters act on synaptic channels.

As mentioned above, the sympathetic nervous system deals with the so-called "emergency situation"- *the fright, flight, fear, terror, palms to sweat, hair to stand on end, and pupils to dilate,* and it does that by increasing heart rate (tachycardia), increase in the systolic blood pressure; shunting of blood supply to the vital organs like brain etc.

Now let us read the following beautiful verse in the context of above mentioned information:

إِذْ جَاۤءُوكُمْ مِّنْ فَوْقِكُمْ وَمِنْ أَسْفَلَ مِنْكُمْ
وَإِذْ زَاغَتِ الْأَبْصَارُ وَبَلَغَتِ الْقُلُوْبُ
الْحَنَاجِرَ وَتَظُنُّوْنَ بِاللهِ الظُّنُوْنَا

)Recall) when they came upon you from above you and from below you, and *when the eyes were distracted, and the hearts reached the throats*, and you were thinking about ALLAH all sorts of thoughts. (Chapter 33: Al-Ahzab; *The Allies,* Verse 10)

The above Holy verse seems to be pointing towards the activation of a sympathetic system during an emergency situation like a war scene.

Sometimes, the tachycardia or the fast heart rate can become so much that it does not "allow" the heart to relax or simply put, the heart gets "emptied," and so there is not much blood left to pump out, culminating into a situation where one starts to feel pounding in the chest, fatigue, chest pain (especially if there is an underlying coronary artery disease), dizziness or even fainting.

Look at the beautiful verses mentioned below in which the description of the mother of Prophet Moosa (May Peace Be Upon Him) was mentioned and the words explaining this as emptying of heart. In another chapter, *Ibrahim (Abraham),* a similar situation appears to be present.

وَ اَصْبَحَ فُؤَا دُ اُمِّ مُوْسٰى فٰرِغًا ۗ اِنْ كَا دَتْ لَتُبْدِيْ بِهٖ لَوْلَاۤ اَنْ رَّبَطْنَا عَلٰي قَلْبِهَا لِتَكُوْنَ مِنَ الْمُؤْمِنِيْنَ

"And the heart of the mother of Moosa became restless; indeed she was about to disclose this (the real facts about Moosa), had We not strengthened her heart to remain among those who have firm belief (in ALLAH's promise)."
(Chapter 28; Al-Qasas; *The Narrative,* Verse 10)

99

مُهْطِعِيْنَ مُقْنِعِيْ رُءُوْسِهِمْ لَا يَرْتَدُّ اِلَيْهِمْ
طَرْفُهُمْ ۚ وَ اَفْـِدَتُهُمْ هَوَآءٌ ۚ

They shall be rushing with their heads raised upward; their eyes shall
not return towards them, and their hearts shall be hollow.
(Chapter 14: Ibrahim; *Abraham,* Verse 43)

Again, this appears to show a similarity of the phenomenon wherein
extreme tachycardia due to sympathetic overdrive (in this case due to
fear) may cause "emptying of heart." Mechanistically, when there is
extreme tachycardia, the cardiac output and stroke volumes are
reduced. The stroke volume is reduced due to reduction in ventricular
filling time and decreased ventricular filling, i.e., the preload, and
surely ALLAH knows the best.

It is also thought-provoking that extreme tachycardia, due to
sympathetic overstimulation, causes the heart to move about its axis,
and this may be observed directly during an echocardiography. This
phenomenon may also be seen indirectly during a stress test where
the QRS complex of the EKG moves up and down. Now, let us review
this beautiful verse describing *"hearts coming in their throats."*

وَ اَنْذِرْهُمْ يَوْمَ الْاٰزِفَةِ اِذِ الْقُلُوْبُ لَدَى
الْحَنَاجِرِ كٰظِمِيْنَ ۚ مَا لِلظّٰلِمِيْنَ مِنْ
حَمِيْمٍ وَّلَا شَفِيْعٍ يُّطَاعُ

"And warn them of the Day of approaching horror, when hearts will
jump up into the throats, (and they will be) choked. There will be
neither a friend for the unjust, nor an intercessor to be listened to."
(Chapter 40: Ghafir, *The Forgiver,* Verse 18)

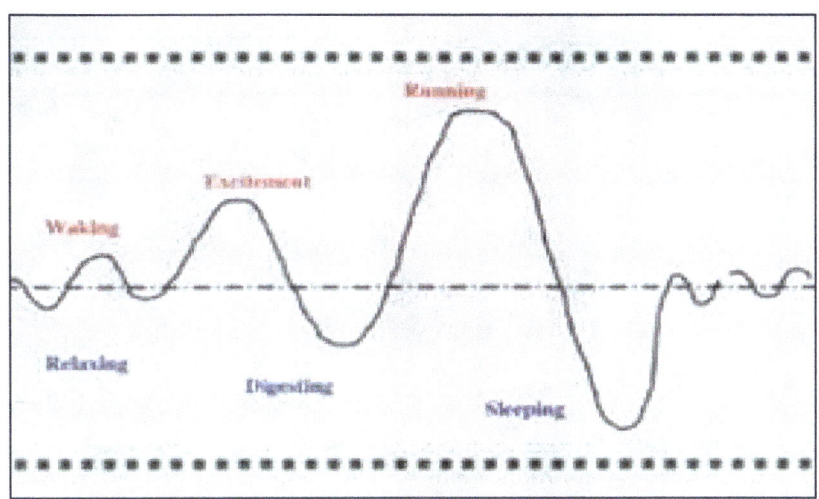

Figure above: Maintaining Homeostasis Across Activities

A healthy nervous system maintains homeostasis by balancing input from both branches of the ANS during activities ranging from relaxing, digesting and sleeping, to waking, feeling excited and running.

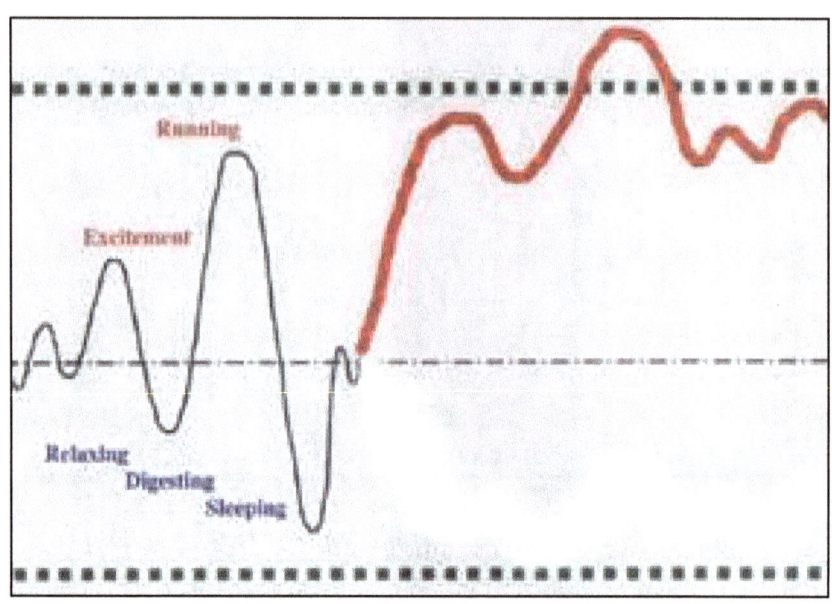

Figure above: Dominance of the Sympathetic Nervous System (SNS).

Under Normal Circumstances, the Sympathetic Nervous System promotes the ability to be active and the defense mechanism of fight or flight. It affects activities in red (above). An individual who is exposed to states of SNS dominance has an increased risk for symptoms and illnesses listed below, which have long been associated with stress.

In the heart itself, electric current is produced in the sino-atrial (SA) node, which is present in the right atrium, through which it spreads to the atrio-ventricular node (A-V node), Bundle of His and Purkinje fibers.

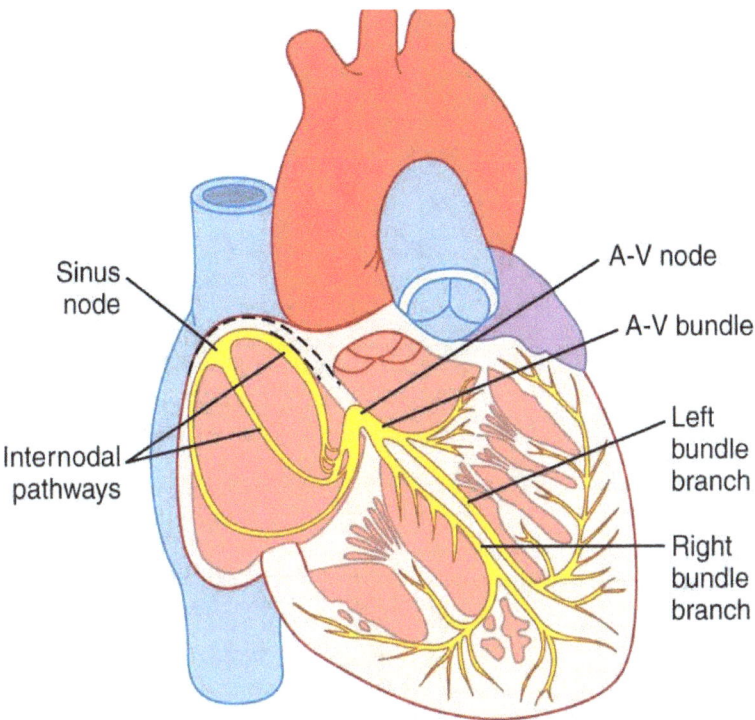

Figure above: Sinus node and the Purkinje system of the heart, showing also the A-V node, atrial internodal pathways, and ventricular bundle branches.

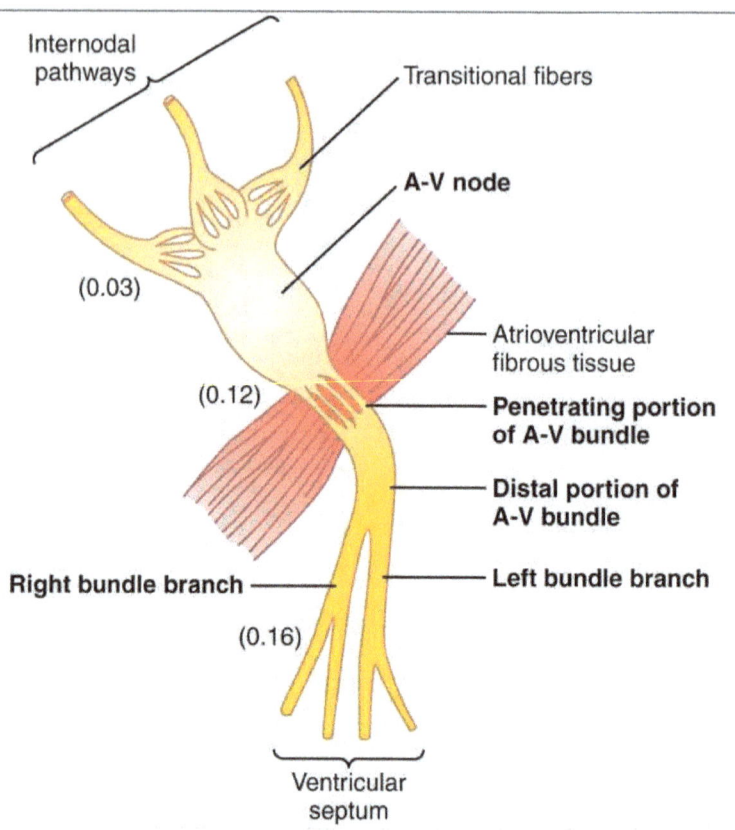

Figure above: Organization of the A-V node.

The numbers represent the interval of time from the origin of the impulse in the sinus node. The values have been extrapolated to human beings.

We now look at certain verses, which may appear to be pointing towards the Sympathetic and the Para-sympathetic component of the autonomic nervous system, and of course, ALLAH knows the best.

Sympathetic System:

الَّـذِيْنَ إِذَا ذُكِرَ اللهُ وَجِلَتْ قُلُوْبُـهُمْ
وَالصّـبِـرِيْنَ عَـلَـى مَـآ أَصَابَـهُمْ وَالْـمُقِـيْمِـي
الـصَّـلَـوةِ وَمِـمَّـا رَزَقْـنْـهُمْ يُنْفِقُـوْنَ

"those whose hearts are filled with awe when ALLAH is remembered,
and who observe patience against whatever befalls them, and who are
steadfast in Salah, and who spend (in the way of ALLAH) out of what
We have given to them".

(Chapter 22: Al-Hajj, *The Pilgrimage:* Verse 35)

سَـنُـلْقِـيْ فِيْ قُلُوْبِ الَّـذِيْنَ كَفَـرُوا الـرُّعْبَ
بِـمَـآ أَشْرَكُوْا بِـاللهِ مَـا لَـمْ يُنَـزِّلْ بِه
سُلْطٰنًـا وَمَـأوٰىهُمُ الـنَّـارُ وَبِـئْسَ مَثْـوَى
الـظّٰلِـمِـيْنَ

"We shall put awe into the hearts of those who disbelieve, since they
have associated with ALLAH something for which He has not sent
any authority. Their ultimate place is the Fire; and evil is the abode of
the unjust.

(Chapter 3: Aal-e-Imran, *The Family of Imran:* Verse 151)

مُهْطِـعِيْنَ مُقْـنِـعِيْ رُءُوْسِهِمْ لَا يَـرْتَدُّ إِلَـيْهِمْ
طَرْفُـهُمْ وَ أَفْـــئِـدَتُـهُمْ هَوَآءُ

"They shall be rushing with their heads raised upward; their eyes shall
not return towards them and their hearts shall be hollow.

(Chapter 14: Ibrahim, *Abraham:* Verse 43)

وَ الَّذِيْنَ يُؤْتُوْنَ مَآ اٰتَوْا وَّقُلُوْبُهُمْ وَجِلَةٌ اَنَّهُمْ اِلٰى رَبِّهِمْ رٰجِعُوْنَ

"And those who give whatever they give, with their hearts full of fear that to their Lord they are to return
(Chapter 23: Al-Mumenoon, *The Believers:* Verse #60)

رِجَالٌ لَّا تُلْهِيْهِمْ تِجَارَةٌ وَّلَا بَيْعٌ عَنْ ذِكْرِ اللهِ وَ إِقَامِ الصَّلٰوةِ وَ إِيْتَاءِ الزَّكٰوةِ ۚ يَخَافُوْنَ يَوْمًا تَتَقَلَّبُ فِيْهِ الْقُلُوْبُ وَ الْأَبْصَارُ

"by the men whom no trade or sale makes neglectful of the remembrance of ALLAH, nor from establishing Salah and paying Zakah ; they are fearful of a day in which the hearts and the eyes will be over-turned.
(Chapter 24: An-Noor, *The Light:* Verse 37)

وَ اَصْبَحَ فُؤَادُ أُمِّ مُوْسٰى فٰرِغًا إِنْ كَادَتْ لَتُبْدِيْ بِهٖ لَوْلَآ اَنْ رَّبَطْنَا عَلٰى قَلْبِهَا لِتَكُوْنَ مِنَ الْمُؤْمِنِيْنَ

"And the heart of the mother of Moosa became restless; indeed she was about to disclose this (the real facts about Moosa), had We not strengthened her heart to remain among those who have firm belief (in ALLAH's promise)."
(Chapter 28: Al-Qasas, *The Narrative:* Verse 10)

إِذْ جَاءُوكُمْ مِّنْ فَوْقِكُمْ وَمِنْ أَسْفَلَ مِنْكُمْ
وَ إِذْ زَاغَتِ الْأَبْصَارُ وَبَلَغَتِ الْقُلُوْبُ
الْحَــنَـاجِرَ وَتَظُنُّوْنَ بِـاللهِ الظُّنُوْنَا

"(Recall) when they came upon you from above you and from below you, and when the eyes were distracted, and the hearts reached the throats, and you were thinking about ALLAH all sorts of thoughts".
(Chapter 33: Al-Ahzab, *The Allies:* Verse 10)

وَ أَنْزَلَ الَّذِيْنَ ظَاهَرُوْهُمْ مِّنْ أَهْلِ الْكِتٰبِ
مِنْ صَيَـاصِيْهِمْ وَقَذَفَ فِيْ قُلُوْبِهِمُ الرُّعْبَ
فَرِيْقًا تَقْتُلُوْنَ وَتَأْسِرُوْنَ فَرِيْقًا

"He has brought those of the people of the Book (the Jews) who had backed them, down from their fortresses, and cast awe into their hearts, so as to make you kill some of them and take others as captives."
(Chapter 33: Al-Ahzab, *The Allies:* Verse 26)

وَ أَنْذِرْهُمْ يَوْمَ الْأزِفَةِ إِذِ الْقُلُوْبُ لَدَى
الْحَــنَـاجِرِ كٰظِمِيْنَ ۛ مَا لِلظّٰلِمِيْنَ مِنْ
حَمِيْمٍ وَّلَا شَفِيْعٍ يُّــطَاعُ

"And warn them of the Day of approaching horror, when hearts will jump up into the throats, (and they will be) choked. There will be neither a friend for the unjust, nor an intercessor to be listened to."
(Chapter 40: Ghafir, *The Forgiver:* Verse 18)

هُوَ الَّذِيّ اَخْرَجَ الَّذِيْنَ كَفَرُوْا مِنْ اَهْلِ
الْكِتٰبِ مِنْ دِيَارِهِمْ لِاَوَّلِ الْحَشْرِ نْ مَا
ظَنَنْتُمْ اَنْ يَّخْرُجُوْا وَظَنُّوْا اَنَّهُمْ مَّانِعَتُهُمْ
حُصُوْنُهُمْ مِّنَ اللهِ فَاَتٰىهُمُ اللهُ مِنْ حَيْثُ لَمْ
يَحْتَسِبُوْا آ وَقَذَفَ فِيْ قُلُوْبِهِمُ الرُّعْبَ
يُخْرِبُوْنَ بُيُوْتَهُمْ بِاَيْدِيْهِمْ وَ اَيْدِي
الْمُؤْمِنِيْنَ فَاعْتَبِرُوْا يَاۤ اُولِي الْاَبْصَارِ

"He is the One who expelled the disbelievers of the People of the Book from their homes at the time of the first gathering. You did not expect that they would leave, and they deemed that their fortresses would protect them from ALLAH. But ALLAH came to them from where they did not expect and cast fear in their hearts when they were spoiling their homes with their own hands and with the hands of the believers. So, learn a lesson, O you who have eyes to see."
(Chapter 59: Al-Hashr, *The Banishment:* Verse 2)

قُلُوْبٌ يَّوْمَىِٕذٍ وَّاجِفَةٌ

"On that day, hearts (of people) will be throbbing,,."
(Chapter 79: An-Naziat, *Those Who yearn:* Verse 8)

Para- Sympathetic System:

هُوَ الَّذِيّ اَنْزَلَ السَّكِيْنَةَ فِيْ قُلُوْبِ
الْمُؤْمِنِيْنَ لِيَزْدَادُوْۤا اِيْمَانًا مَّعَ
اِيْمَانِهِمْ وَلِلّٰهِ جُنُوْدُ السَّمٰوٰتِ وَ الْاَرْضِ
وَكَانَ اللهُ عَلِيْمًا حَكِيْمًا

"He (ALLAH) is such that He sent down tranquility into the hearts of the believers, so that they grow more in faith in addition to their (existing) faith and to ALLAH belong the forces of the heavens and the earth, and ALLAH is All-Knowing, All-Wise."

(Chapter 48: Al-Fath, *The Victory:* Verse 4)

لَـقَـدْ رَضِيَ اللهُ عَنِ الْـمُـؤْمِـنِيْنَ إِذْ يُبَايِعُوْنَكَ تَـحْتَ الـشَّجَرَةِ فَعَلِمَ مَا فِيْ قُلُـوْبِـهِمْ فَاَنْـزَلَ الـسَّكِيْـنَـةَ عَلَيْـهِمْ وَ اَثَـابَـهُمْ فَتْحًا قَـرِيْـبًا

"ALLAH was pleased with the believers when they were pledging allegiance with you (by placing their hands in your hands) under the tree, and He knew what was in their hearts, so He sent down tranquility upon them ,and rewarded them with a victory, near at hand,."

(Chapter 48: Al-Fath, *The Victory:* Verse 18)

إِذْ جَعَلَ الَّـذِيْنَ كَفَرُوْا فِيْ قُلُـوْبِـهِمُ الْـحَمِيَّةَ حَمِيَّةَ الْـجَاهِلِيَّةِ فَاَنْزَلَ اللهُ سَكِيْـنَـتَهُ عَلَـي رَسُوْلِـهِ وَعَلَـي الْـمُؤْمِنِيْنَ وَ اَلْـزَمَـهُمْ كَلِمَةَ الـتَّقْـوٰى وَكَـانُـوْا اَحَقَّ بِهَا وَ اَهْلَـهَا وَكَـانَ اللهُ بِـكُلِّ شَيْءٍ عَلِـــيْمًا

W"hen the disbelievers developed in their hearts indignation, the indignation of ignorance; then ALLAH sent down tranquility from Himself upon His Messenger and upon the believers, and made them stick to the word of piety, and they were very much entitled to it and competent for it. And ALLAH is All-Knowing about every thing."

(Chapter 48: Al-Fath, *The Victory:* Verse 26)

109

اَلَّذِيْنَ اٰمَنُوْا وَتَطْمَىِٕنُّ قُلُوْبُهُمْ بِذِكْرِ اللّٰهِ اَلَا بِذِكْرِ اللّٰهِ تَطْمَىِٕنُّ الْقُلُوْبُ

"the ones who believe and their hearts are peaceful with the remembrance of ALLAH. Listen, the hearts find peace only in the remembrance of ALLAH."

(Chapter 13: Ar-Rad, *The Thunder:* Verse 28)

اِذْ هَمَّتْ طَّاۤىِٕفَتٰنِ مِنْكُمْ اَنْ تَفْشَلَا وَاللّٰهُ وَلِيُّهُمَا وَعَلَى اللّٰهِ فَلْيَتَوَكَّلِ الْمُؤْمِنُوْنَ

"When two of your groups were about to lose heart, while ALLAH was their guardian! It is in ALLAH alone that the believers must place their trust."

(Chapter 3: Aal-e-Imran, *The Family of Imran:* Verse 122)

Both Sympathetic and Para-Sympathetic System:

اَللّٰهُ نَزَّلَ اَحْسَنَ الْحَدِيْثِ كِتٰبًا مُّتَشَابِهًا مَّثَانِيَ ڰ تَقْشَعِرُّ مِنْهُ جُلُوْدُ الَّذِيْنَ يَخْشَوْنَ رَبَّهُمْ ثُمَّ تَلِيْنُ جُلُوْدُهُمْ وَقُلُوْبُهُمْ اِلٰى ذِكْرِ اللّٰهِ ذٰلِكَ هُدَى اللّٰهِ يَهْدِيْ بِهٖ مَنْ يَّشَاۤءُ وَمَنْ يُّضْلِلِ اللّٰهُ فَمَا لَهٗ مِنْ هَادٍ

"ALLAH has sent down the best discourse, a book containing subjects resembling each other, mentioned again and again, shivered from which are the skins of those who have awe of their Lord. Then, their skins and their hearts become soft enough to tend to the remembrance of ALLAH. This is the Guidance of ALLAH with

110

which He brings to the right path whomsoever He wills. As for the one whom ALLAH lets go astray, for him, there is no one to guide." (Chapter 39: Az-Zumar, *The Companies:* Verse 23)

Takotsubo Cardiomyopathy (broken-heart syndrome)

An interesting phenomenon is the "Takatsubo cardiomyopathy," which is more common in middle-aged women who experience "ballooning" of a part of their myocardium along with a rise in cardiac Troponins (cardiac biomarkers), and the EKG showing ST elevations (a picture of true MI). It is a reversible form of ventricular dysfunction usually characterized by akinesia of the apex in the absence of obstructive coronary artery disease. In its initial phase, it may be indistinguishable from acute myocardial infarction. It has been hypothesized that severe emotional or physical stress, such as a sudden illness, the loss of a loved one or a serious accident, causes a surge in stress hormones (for example, adrenaline) and finally results into this syndrome. That's why the condition is also sometimes called *"Stress-induced cardiomyopathy."*

It is the hallmark bulging out of the apex of the heart with preserved function of the base that earned the syndrome its name, "tako-tsubo," or octopus pot in Japan. Another term for this disorder is *"Apical ballooning syndrome."*

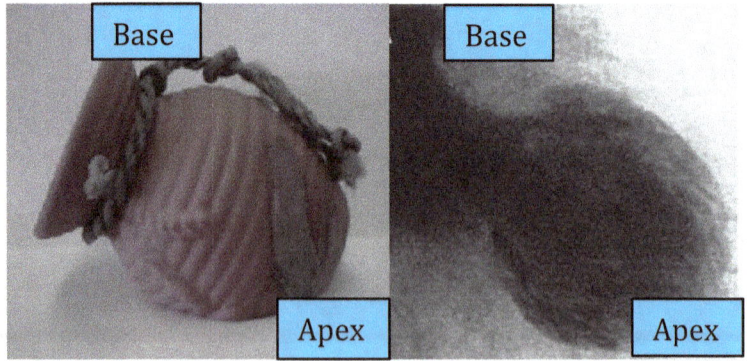

(Image above: An octopus pot on the left with a comparison to Takotsubo cardiomyopathy on the right).

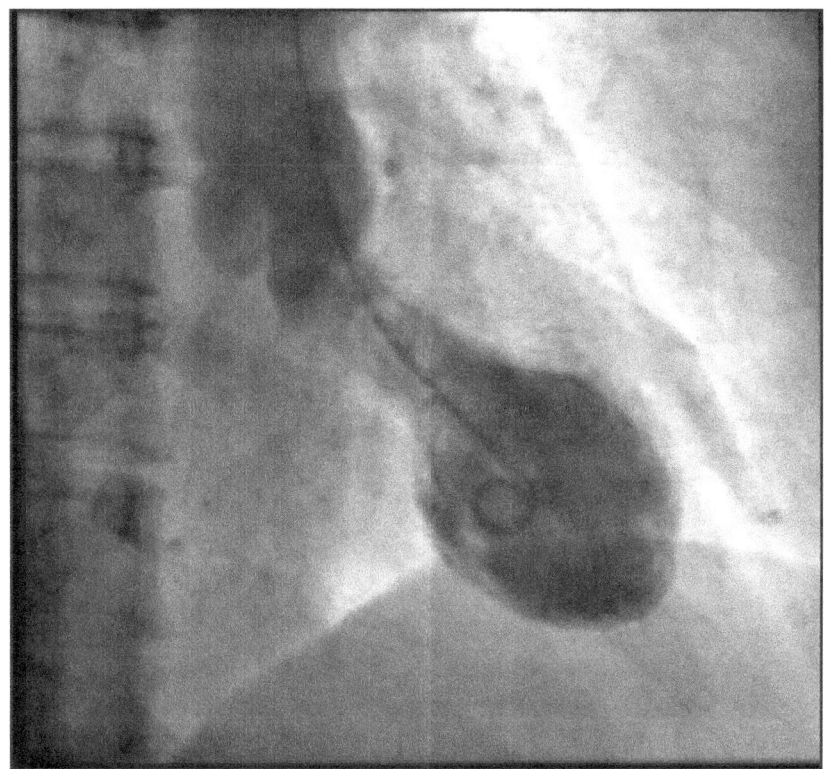

A:

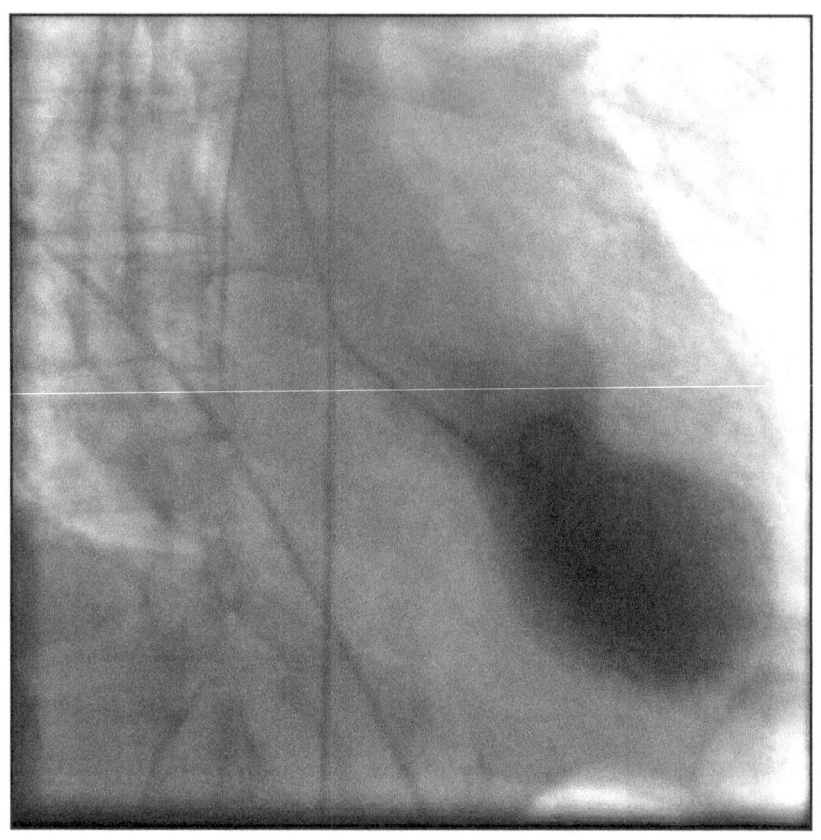

B:

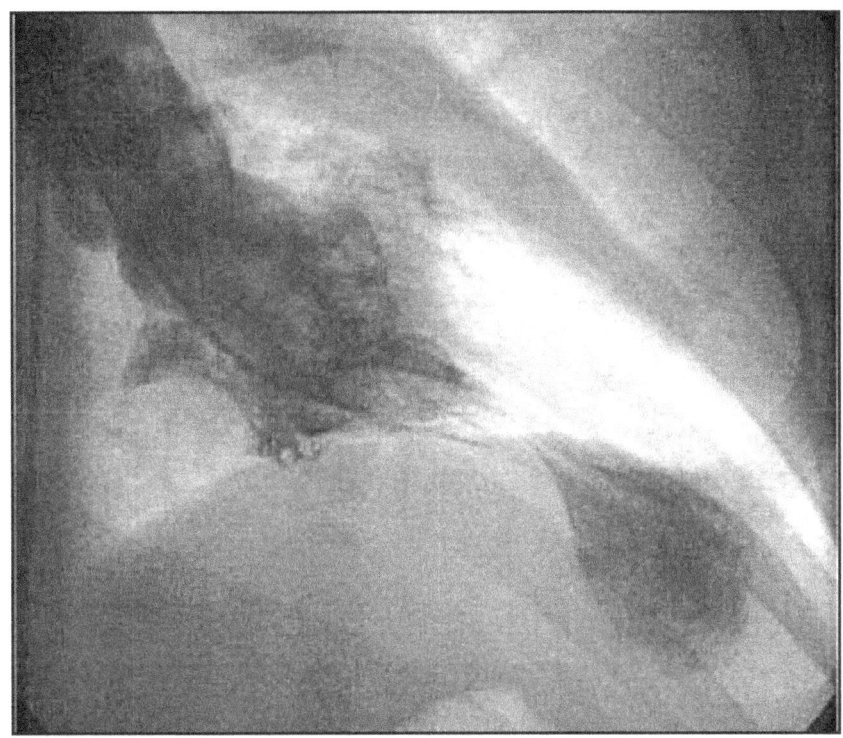

C:

Above images (A-C) of the left ventricle showing "ballooning" in Takotsubo cardiomyopathy.

An interesting association between Takotsubo Cardiomyopathy and sub-arachnoid hemorrhage has been published by our group. The abstract is mentioned below.

Acute Subarachnoid Hemorrhage and Cardiac Abnormalities: Takotsubo Cardiomyopathy or Neurogenic Stunned Myocardium? A case report: Cases Journal *2010, 3: 81 doi: 10.1186/1757-1626-3-81)*

An adult female was brought to the emergency department with somnolence. A 3 x 3 mm ruptured basilar aneurysm was found and successfully embolized. Two days later, the patient developed acute heart failure. Troponin-I was elevated to 4.2 (normal <0.4). On EKG, new symmetric T wave inversion in V3, V4, and V5 with prolonged QT were evident. Trans-thoracic echocardiogram showed severe systolic dysfunction with an ejection fraction of 20% and akinetic apex along with the distal left ventricular segments, consistent with Takotsubo cardiomyopathy. Myocardial contrast echocardiography showed a decrease in capillary blood flow and volume in the akinetic areas with delayed contrast replenishment, sparing the basal segments. A repeat study 2 weeks later showed near normalization of the perfusion parameters. The patient improved with medical management. A repeat echocardiogram, a month later revealed an ejection fraction of 45%.

Conclusion:

Our case, as well as others, reported previously, supports the diagnosis of Takotsubo cardiomyopathy in patients with Subarachnoid Hemorrhage who fulfill the clinical and imaging description of this syndrome.

ANGER- A response of Sympathetic over activity:

Anger may be defined as a feeling of strong displeasure, wrath, etc. It is very much driven by the sympathetic nervous system.

The physiological cardiovascular effects are tachycardia, a rise in blood pressure, sweating, etc.

In the medical literature, the untoward effects of anger are mentioned. There is a release of stress hormones like adrenaline during anger, which may cause the development of chest pain, culminating into either frank myocardial infarction or even dangerous arrhythmias like

116

ventricular fibrillation, especially in those suffering from an underlying coronary artery disease.

Following abstract from an interesting article is mentioned as an example:

Triggering of acute coronary occlusion by episodes of anger:

European Heart Journal: Acute Cardiovascular Care 2015 Dec; 4 (6): 493-8. doi: 10.1177/2048872615568969. Epub 2015 Feb 23. *Thomas Buckley1,2, Soon Y Soo Hoo1, Judith Fethney2, Elizabeth Shaw1,3, Peter S Hanson1,3 and Geoffrey H Tofler1,3*

Abstract:

Aims: The aim of this study was to report the association between episodes of anger and acute myocardial infarction (MI) in patients with angiographically confirmed coronary occlusion.

Methods and results: 313 participants with acute coronary occlusion (Thrombolysis in Myocardial Infarction 0 or 1 at emergency angiography) reported frequency of anger episodes in the 48 h prior to MI. In primary analysis, anger exposures within 2 h and 2–4 h prior to symptom onset were compared with subjects own usual yearly exposure to anger using case-crossover methodology. Anger level ≥ 5 (on an anger scale of 1–7) was reported by seven (2.2%) participants within 2 h of MI. Compared with usual frequency, the relative risk of onset of MI symptoms occurring within 2 h of anger level ≥ 5 (defined as very angry) was 8.5 (95% confidence interval 4.1–17.6). Anger level <5 was not associated with the onset of MI symptoms. Compared with 24–26 h pre-MI, anxiety scores >75th percentile on State-Trait Personality Inventory were associated with a relative risk of 2.0 (95% confidence interval 1.1–3.8) and in those above the 90th percentile, the relative risk of MI symptom onset was 9.5 (95% confidence interval 2.2–40.8).

Conclusion: Findings confirm that episodes of intense anger, defined as being 'very angry, body tense, clenching fists or teeth' (within 2 h) are associated with increased relative risk for acute coronary occlusion. Additionally, increased anxiety was associated with coronary occlusion. Further study, including the role of potential modifiers, may provide insight into the prevention of MI during acute emotional episodes.

The following discussion is for reference only for the reader's interest.

Anger management according to Islamic teachings:

Islam has stressed significantly upon anger management and has appreciated those who control their anger.

There are several ways of relieving one's anger mentioned in Islamic teachings. Some of these remedies may be directed towards external or bodily damage caused by the anger and some internally or the ones linked to the demerits to one's soul.

1. Seek refuge in ALLAH. Since anger is considered a satanic act, seeking ALLAH's refuge keeps the satan away, which eventually helps in relieving the anger.

This is the simplest way to control one's anger. Whenever one feels angry, it is recommended for him/her to sit down, and seek refuge in ALLAH from satan.

In Arabic, say *A'oodhu billahi minash shaytaannir rajeem (I* seek refuge with ALLAH from satan). Drinking water and avoidance of being tense is helpful.

- The Prophet (peace be upon him) said, "If a man gets angry and says, 'I seek refuge with ALLAH,' [and] his anger will go away."

- Sulayman Ibn Sard (RA) said: "I was sitting with the Prophet (peace be upon him), and two men were slandering one another. One of them was red in the face, and the veins on his neck were standing out. The Prophet (peace be upon him) said, 'I know a word which, if he were to say it, what he feels would go away. If he said, "I seek refuge with ALLAH from the shaytaan," what he feels (i.e., his anger) would go away.

2. Refrain from talking: Retaliation or talking back will only make the matter worse. In case of an argument, the better strategy would be to remain silent as anger will instigate to lose self-control, and an exchange of harsh words is possible, which may be regretful.

- The Messenger of ALLAH (peace be upon him) said: "If any of you becomes angry, let him keep silent."

3. Relaxation: It is helpful in case of anger to move away from the source of anger and change body position from standing to sitting or lying down.

The Messenger of ALLAH (peace be upon him) said: *"If one of you got angry while standing, then sit down, or if sitting down, then lay down. If anger does not go away, then do Wudu (ablution)."* [Abu Dawood]

It is also recommended to make ghusl (bath) [Abu Nuaim]

It is suggested that offering ablution with cool water causes some changes inside our bodies. Water allows the body to release heat, and therefore, ablution plays an important role in cooling the body regularly, which may be important in anger control.

To make ablution and taking a bath, deals with using water because some narrations indicate that anger is from the devil that was created from the fire, and the way to extinguish this fire is to use water, whether it is in the manner of making ablution or taking a bath. Someone's anger may go away by just making an ablution, and someone else might have to take a bath in order for the anger to subside. Human body becomes very hot during anger, so putting water on it is helpful in cooling it down through ablution or bath.

4. Analysis of situation: Speaking to the person kindly who caused the anger is helpful. Nothing good can come out of shouting at each other. It's been narrated that, "Whoever controls his anger at the time when he has the means to act upon it, ALLAH will fill his heart with contentment on the Day of Resurrection."

The cure to anger is avoiding its causes.

5. Positive thinking: It is very helpful to know and practice that those who control their anger are praised and are given high status and are praised in several noble traditions of the Holy Prophet (pbuh). The Holy Prophet (peace be upon him) said:

- "The strong man is not the one who can overpower others (in wrestling); rather, the strong man is the one who controls himself when he gets angry."

- "The strongest man is the one who, when he gets angry, and his face reddens, and his hackles rise, is able to defeat his anger."

- "The man who, when he is mistreated by another, controls his anger, has defeated his own shaytaan and the shaytaan of the one who made him angry."

6. Consideration of the consequences of anger: In extreme situations, anger can lead to <u>damages in the families</u> or someone getting seriously injured. It can be linked to mental issues or lead to health problems such as <u>high blood pressure</u> or <u>tachycardia</u>, which may subsequently cause heart attack or stroke.

7. Supplication: Supplication creates humbleness and helps in controlling the anger.

Certain supplications are mentioned below:

أَعُوذُ بِكَلِمَاتِ اللَّهِ الـتَّامَّاتِ مِنْ غَضَبِهِ وَعِقَابِهِ وَشَرِّ عِبَادِهِ وَمِنْ هَمَزَاتِ الـشَّيَاطِينِ وَ أَنْ يَـحْضُرُونِ

"I seek refuge in ALLAH's perfect words from His anger and punishment, from the evil of His slaves, and from satan's whispers and presence." (Al-Tirmizi: 3528)

لَا إِلٰهَ إِلَّا أَنْتَ سُبْحَـانَكَ إِنِّىْ كُنْتُ مِنَ الـظّٰلِمِيْنَ

"There is no God but you. May You be exalted. Indeed, I was among the wrongdoers." (Al Anbiya, verse #87)

اَللّٰهُمَّ أَذهِبْ غَيظَ قَـلـبِى

"Oh ALLAH, remove anger from my heart."

This chapter dealt with the existence of the autonomic system of the heart, its relevance in the body and the mechanism of how it controls the mind, heart and the rest of the body during various situations in someone's day to day life. For one's interest, Islamic teachings and prayers for anger control are also listed.

Chapter 5
(Synopsis)
Calcification of Arteries, Valves and Myocardium

(Hardening of heart; it's arteries, valves and muscle)

After reading the Holy scripture, a very interesting phenomenon of hardening of the heart muscle catches attention.

The blood vessels, including coronary arteries, are composed of three delicate layers *(tunica)* of tissue.

1. Tunica Intima (innermost layer)

2. Tunica Media (middle layer)

3. Tunica Adventitia (outermost layer)

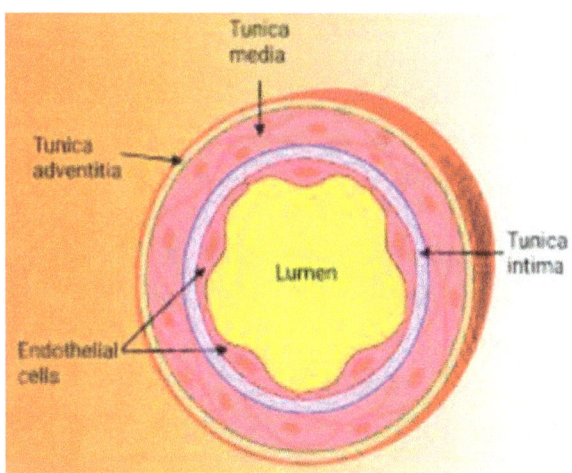

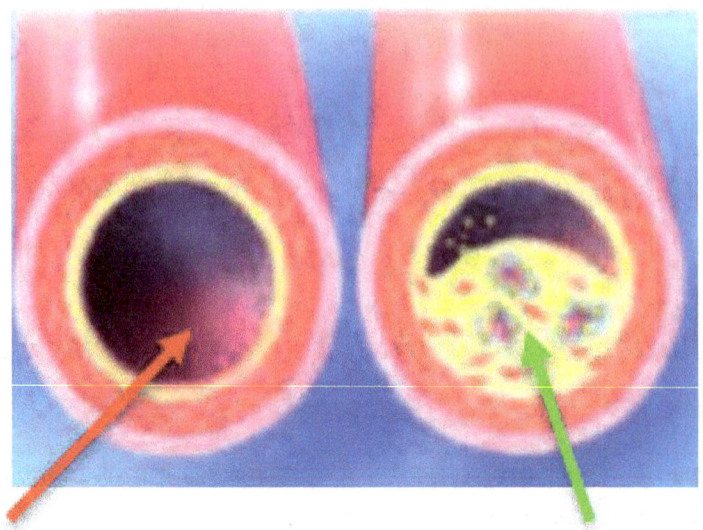

Images (above) show a sketch of a normal artery (far left). The image on the right shows a comparison of a normal artery (red arrow) and the one with atherosclerotic plaque (green arrow).

The inner most layer of intima is lined by a single layer of cells called Endothelium. In case of damage to this layer, plaques build up. This process is commonly referred to as Atherosclerosis though it is a very complex phenomenon. Plaques may be soft or hard. Calcified plaques are the hard plaques. Calcium may deposit in different cardiovascular structures, including within the coronary arteries, myocardium, and pericardium and cause hardening.

Calcium is a chemical element that is essential for living organisms. Most of the calcium within the human body is found in teeth and bone. A small amount, about one percent of total body calcium, is dissolved in the blood. Coronary calcification can begin in patients at a young age. Coronary artery calcification is a known marker for atherosclerotic coronary artery disease.

Computed tomography (CT) is a noninvasive test with high sensitivity and specificity for calcium detection and is capable of quantifying calcification.

Currently, there is no known specific treatment for coronary artery calcification. Risk factor modification is recommended and includes treating hypertension, high cholesterol, smoking cessation, and diabetes mellitus, as well as preventing the development of advanced kidney disease.

Let us now review some Holy verses with respect to the hardening and calcification of the heart and its structures:

(1)

ثُمَّ قَسَتْ قُلُوْبُكُمْ مِّنْ بَعْدِ ذٰلِكَ فَهِىَ كَالْحِجَارَةِ أَوْ أَشَدُّ قَسْوَةً وَإِنَّ مِنَ الْحِجَارَةِ لَمَا يَتَفَجَّرُ مِنْهُ الْأَنْهٰرُ وَإِنَّ مِنْهَا لَمَا يَشَّقَّقُ فَيَخْرُجُ مِنْهُ الْمَاءُ وَإِنَّ مِنْهَا لَمَا يَهْبِطُ مِنْ خَشْيَةِ اللهِ وَمَا اللهُ بِغَافِلٍ عَمَّا تَعْمَلُوْنَ

When, even after that, your *hearts were hardened*, as if they were rocks, or still worse in hardness. For surely among the rocks there are some from which rivers gush forth, and there are others that crack open and water flows from them, and there are still others that fall down in fear of ALLAH. And ALLAH is not unaware of what you do.

(Chapter 2: Al-Baqara, *The Cow:* verse 74)

125

(2)

فَلَوْلَآ إِذْ جَاءَهُمْ بَأْسُنَا تَضَرَّعُوْا وَلٰكِنْ قَسَتْ قُلُوْبُهُمْ وَزَيَّنَ لَهُمُ الشَّيْطٰنُ مَا كَانُوْا يَعْمَلُوْنَ

Why then, did they not supplicate in humility when a calamity from Us came upon them? Instead, their *hearts were hardened* and Satan adorned for them what they were doing.

(Chapter 6: Al-Anaam, *The Cattle:* verse 43)

(3)

لِّيَجْعَلَ مَا يُلْقِي الشَّيْطٰنُ فِتْنَةً لِّلَّذِيْنَ فِيْ قُلُوْبِهِمْ مَّرَضٌ وَّ الْقَاسِيَةِ قُلُوْبُهُمْ وَ اِنَّ الظّٰلِمِيْنَ لَفِيْ شِقَاقٍ بَعِيْدٍ

(All this is allowed to be done) so that He may make what Satan casts a trial for those in whose hearts there is a disease, and whose *hearts are hard*; and surely the wrongdoers are in the utmost antagonism.

(Chapter 22: Al-Hajj, *The Pilgrimage:* verse 53)

(4)

اَفَمَنْ شَرَحَ اللهُ صَدْرَهٗ لِلْإِسْلَامِ فَهُوَ عَلٰى نُوْرٍ مِّنْ رَّبِّهٖ فَوَيْلٌ لِّلْقٰسِيَةِ قُلُوْبُهُمْ مِّنْ ذِكْرِ اللهِ أُولٰٓئِكَ فِيْ ضَلٰلٍ مُّبِيْنٍ

So I ask about a person whose heart ALLAH has opened up for Islam, and consequently he proceeds in a light from his Lord. (Can he be equal to the one whose heart is hardened?) So, woe to those whose *hearts are too hard* to remember ALLAH. Those are wandering in open error.

(Chapter 39: Az-Zumar, *The Companies:* verse 22)

(5)

اَلَـمْ يَأْنِ لِلَّـذِيْـنَ اَمَـنُوٓا اَنْ تَـخْشَعَ قُـلُوْبُـهُمْ لِـذِكْرِ اللهِ وَمَـا نَـزَلَ مِنَ الْـحَقِّ وَلَا يَـكُوْنُـوْا كَـالَّـذِيْـنَ اُوْتُـوا الْـكِـتٰبَ مِنْ قَـبْلُ فَطَالَ عَلَـيْـهِمُ الْاَمَـدُ فَـقَسَتْ قُـلُوْبُـهُمْ وَكَـثِـيْـرٌ مِّـنْـهُمْ فٰـسِـقُـوْنَ

Has the time not yet come for those who believe that their hearts should be humble for the remembrance of ALLAH and for the truth that has descended (through revelation)? They must not be like those to whom the Book was given before, but a long period passed on them (in which they did not repent), therefore their *hearts became hard*, and (thus) many of them are sinners.

(Chapter 57: Al-Hadid, *Iron:* verse 16)

Following is an image of an extensive myocardial calcification on a CT scan:

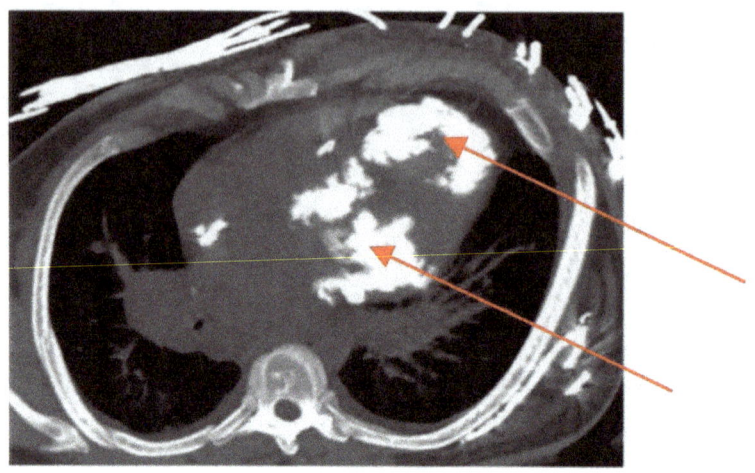

Normal aortic valve (open)

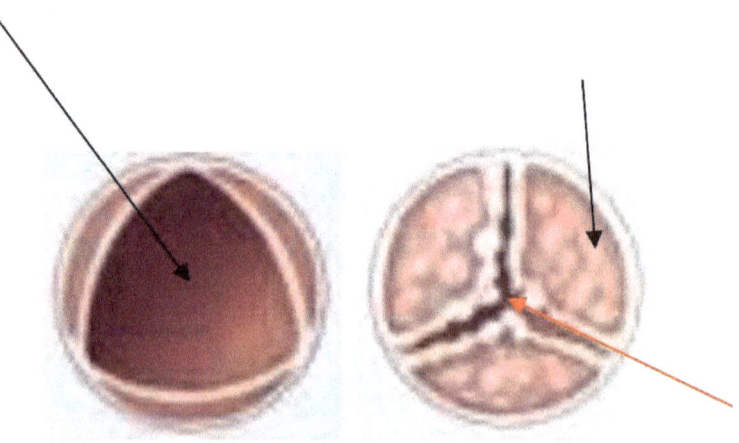

A normal (left) and a calcified aortic valve (right) are shown for comparison, which may give an idea of the disease burden with a severely reduced opening on the right (red arrow)

Chapter 5:
Calcification of Arteries, Valves And Myocardium

(Hardening of the heart; it's arteries, valves and muscle)

Calcification or hardening of the heart muscle and other vascular structures is a complex process. In the Holy scripture, we find mention of "hearts becoming hard." We now try to understand this concept in the light of modern-day medicine which is able to detect what is referred to as calcification of the heart and its structures. In order to understand it better, we begin to discuss some of the anatomical details.

The blood vessels, including coronary arteries, are composed of three delicate layers *(tunica)* of tissue.

1. Tunica Intima (innermost layer)

2. Tunica Media (middle layer)

3. Tunica Adventitia (outermost layer)

The inner most layer of intima is lined by a single layer of cells called Endothelium. In case of damage to this layer, plaques build up. This process is commonly referred to as Atherosclerosis, though it is a very complex phenomenon. Plaques may be soft or hard. Calcified plaques are the hard plaques. Calcium may deposit in different cardiovascular structures including within coronary arteries, valves, myocardium, and pericardium.

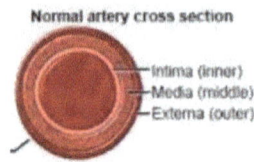

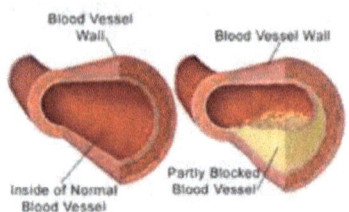

Images (above) show a sketch of a normal artery (far left). The image on the right shows a comparison of a normal artery and the one with atherosclerotic plaque.

Calcium is a chemical element that is essential for living organisms. Most of the calcium within the human body is found in teeth and bone. A small amount, about one percent of total body calcium, is dissolved in the blood. Coronary artery calcification is a known marker for atherosclerotic coronary artery disease. The calcification itself is calcium phosphate (hydroxyapatite), which is similar to that in bone.

Coronary artery calcification (CAC) is not a benign process. as it can result in reduced vascular compliance, abnormal vasomotor responses, and impaired myocardial perfusion. The presence of CAC is associated with worse outcomes in the general population and in patients undergoing revascularization (like angioplasty or open heart surgery).

Interestingly, calcium regulatory mechanisms that affect bone formation and growth also influence CAC. Alkaline phosphatase is central to early calcium deposition and has been proposed as a molecular marker of vascular calcification. Vascular smooth muscle cells (VSMCs) produce matrix vesicles, which regulate mineralization in the vascular intima and media.

Two recognized types of CAC are:

1. Intimal or Superficial calcification

2. Medial artery calcification

Calcification or hardening of the innermost layer of the arteries, *Intimal Calcification*, represents an advanced state of Atherosclerosis (plaque buildup in the inner lining of the arteries causing thickening or hardening). The risk factors may include high cholesterol, persistently elevated blood pressure, smoking, diabetes mellitus, obesity, physical inactivity, consumption of a high saturated fat diet, etc. Inflammatory mediators and elevated lipid content within atherosclerotic lesions induce osteogenic differentiation of VSMCs.

Calcification or hardening of the middle (tunica media) layer of the arteries, *Medial artery calcification,* is also known as Mönckeberg's arteriosclerosis. This condition leads to the stiffening of the elastic layer of the arterial wall, but in contrast to intimal artery calcification, it does not obstruct the arterial lumen. It is now recognized that this is not a benign process. Calcification of the vessel media is a major cause of isolated systolic hypertension in the elderly. It is also associated with higher cardiovascular mortality and risk of amputation in type 2 diabetes mellitus.

Risk Factors for Coronary Calcification

A number of risk factors are reported to contribute to the development of CAC (Table below).

Risk Factor	Intimal Calcification	Medial Calcification
Advanced age	Yes	Yes
Diabetes mellitus	Yes	Yes
Dyslipidemia	Yes	No
Hypertension	Yes	No
Male	Yes	No
Cigarette smoking	Yes	No
Renal etiology		
Dysfunction ($\downarrow$GFR)	No	Yes
Hypercalcemia	No	Yes
Hyperphosphatemia	Yes	Yes
PTH abnormalities	No	No
Duration of dialysis	No	Yes

There is also a strong genetic association with coronary arterial calcification. For example, single nucleotide polymorphisms (SNPs) in the 9p21 gene loci were strongly associated with CAC and MI. The prevalence of CAC is age- and sex-dependent, occurring in $\geq$90% of men and > 67% of women older than 70 years of age.

Computed tomography (CT) is a noninvasive test with high sensitivity and specificity for calcium detection and is capable of quantifying calcification. The density of calcium is assessed by the so-called Hounsfield scale, which measures density in Hounsfield units. The weighed score multiplied by the area of the coronary calcification provides the calcium score, commonly termed the Agatston score. The amount of calcium in the walls of the coronary arteries, assessed by the Agatston score, appears to be a better predictor of risk than standard risk factors.

A study found that the progression of coronary calcification, assessed by two scans in 2.5 years, was associated with an increased risk of cardiovascular events during a follow-up of more than seven years.

Coronary artery calcium score may be described as below:

Coronary calcium score 0: No evidence of CAD

Coronary calcium score 1-10: Minimal evidence of CAD

Coronary calcium score 11-100: Mild evidence of CAD

Coronary calcium score 101-400: Moderate evidence of CAD

Coronary calcium score > 400: Extensive evidence of CAD

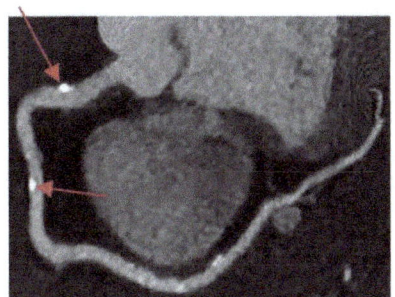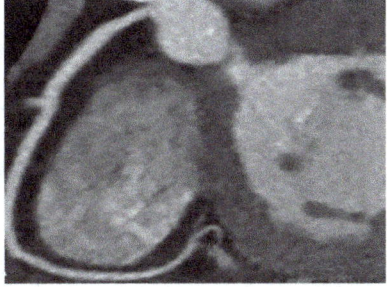

Coronary artery calcification in right coronary artery (left panel; red arrows). Absence of calcification can be noted for comparison in another right coronary artery (right panel)

Currently, there is no known specific treatment for coronary artery calcification. Risk factor modification is recommended and includes treating hypertension, dyslipidemia, and diabetes mellitus, as well as preventing the development of advanced kidney disease.

Coronary angiography has low-moderate sensitivity compared with gray-scale intravascular ultrasound (IVUS) and CT scan for detection of CAC but is very specific (high positive predictive value).

Angiographic CAC is often classified into 3 groups: none/mild, moderate, and severe.

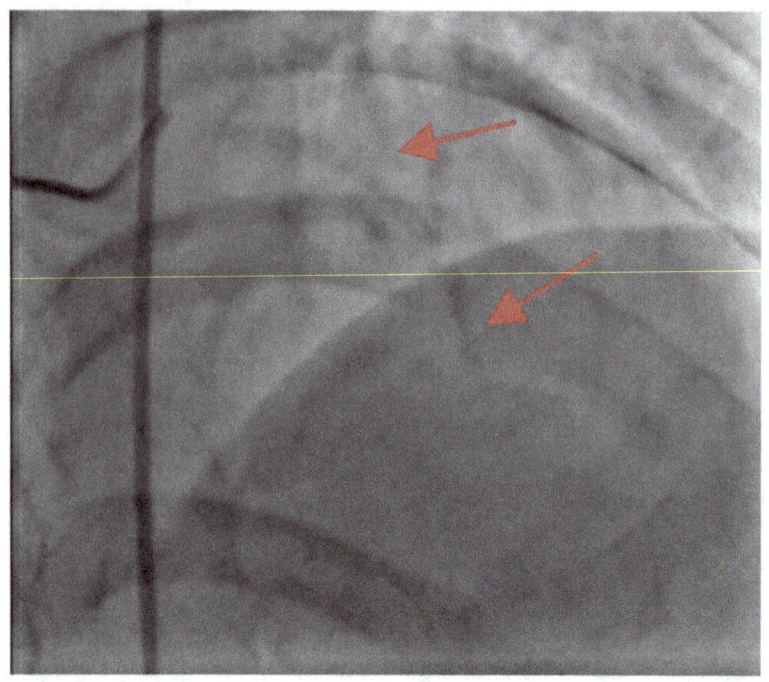

Severe calcification seen (above) in the proximal to mid LAD before contrast injection (red arrows).

Intravascular ultrasound (IVUS) is substantially more accurate in detecting CAC than cineangiography, with high sensitivity and specificity. A calcified plaque on gray-scale IVUS appears as a bright echo with acoustic shadowing. The extent of calcification can be graded by several metrics. The arc of calcium is classified as none, 1 quadrant (0 to 90), 2 quadrants (91 to 180), 3 quadrants (181 to 270), or 4 quadrants (271 to 360). Calcium location is defined as superficial if present in the intimal-luminal interface, deep if within the medial-adventitial border or closer to the adventitia than the lumen, or both superficial and deep.

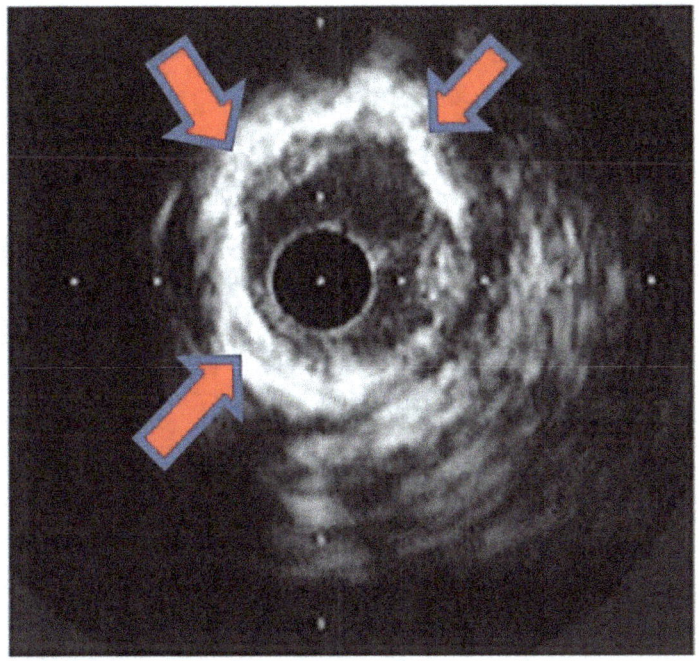

IVUS imaging showing severe calcification (arrows)

Coronary artery disease involving heavily calcified lesions has been shown to be associated with worse short- and long- term outcomes after percutaneous coronary intervention and coronary artery by-pass graft (CABG) surgery.

Let us now review some Holy verses with respect to the hardening and calcification of the heart and its structures:

(1)

ثُمَّ قَسَتْ قُلُوْبُكُمْ مِّنْ بَعْدِ ذٰلِكَ فَهِىَ كَالْـحِجَارَةِ أَوْ أَشَدُّ قَسْوَةً وَإِنَّ مِنَ الْـحِجَارَةِ لَمَا يَتَفَجَّرُ مِنْهُ الْأَنْـهٰرُ وَإِنَّ مِنْهَا لَمَا يَشَّقَّقُ فَيَخْرُجُ مِنْهُ الْـمَآءُ وَإِنَّ مِنْهَا لَمَا يَهْبِطُ مِنْ خَشْـيَةِ اللهِ وَمَا اللهُ بِغَافِلٍ عَمَّا تَعْمَلُوْنَ

When, even after that, your *hearts were hardened*, as if they were rocks, or still worse in hardness. For surely among the rocks there are some from which rivers gush forth, and there are others that crack open and water flows from them, and there are still others that fall down in fear of ALLAH. And ALLAH is not unaware of what you do.

(Chapter 2: Al-Baqara, *The Cow:* verse 74)

(2)

فَلَوْلَآ إِذْ جَآءَهُمْ بَأْسُنَا تَضَرَّعُوْا وَلٰكِنْ قَسَتْ قُلُوْبُهُمْ وَزَيَّنَ لَهُمُ الـشَّيْطٰنُ مَا كَانُوْا يَعْمَلُوْنَ

Why then, did they not supplicate in humility when a calamity from Us came upon them? Instead, their *hearts were hardened* and Satan adorned for them what they were doing.

(Chapter 6: Al-Anaam, *The Cattle:* verse 43)

(3)

لِّيَجْعَلَ مَا يُلْقِي الشَّيْطٰنُ فِتْنَةً لِّلَّذِيْنَ فِيْ قُلُوْبِهِمْ مَّرَضٌ وَّ الْقَاسِيَةِ قُلُوْبُهُمْ ۖ وَ اِنَّ الظّٰلِمِيْنَ لَفِيْ شِقَاقٍ بَعِيْدٍ

(All this is allowed to be done) so that He may make what Satan casts a trial for those in whose hearts there is a disease, and whose *hearts are hard*; and surely the wrongdoers are in the utmost antagonism.
(Chapter 22: Al-Hajj, *The Pilgrimage:* verse 53)

(4)

اَفَمَنْ شَرَحَ اللهُ صَدْرَهٗ لِلْاِسْلَامِ فَهُوَ عَلٰى نُوْرٍ مِّنْ رَّبِّهٖ ۚ فَوَيْلٌ لِّلْقٰسِيَةِ قُلُوْبُهُمْ مِّنْ ذِكْرِ اللهِ ۚ اُولٰٓئِكَ فِيْ ضَلٰلٍ مُّبِيْنٍ

So I ask about a person whose heart ALLAH has opened up for Islam, and consequently he proceeds in a light from his Lord. (Can he be equal to the one whose heart is hardened?) So, woe to those whose *hearts are too hard* to remember ALLAH. Those are wandering in open error.
(Chapter 39: Az-Zumar, *The Companies:* verse 22)

(5)

اَلَـمْ يَـاْنِ لِـلَّـذِيْـنَ اٰمَـنُوۤا اَنْ تَـخْشَعَ قُـلُـوْبُـهُمْ
لِـذِكْـرِ اللهِ وَمَـا نَـزَلَ مِنَ الْـحَقِّ وَلَا يَـكُـوْنُـوْا
كَـالَّـذِيْـنَ اُوْتُـوا الْـكِـتٰبَ مِنْ قَبْلُ فَطَالَ
عَلَـيْـهِمُ الْاَمَدُ فَقَسَتْ قُـلُـوْبُـهُمْ وَكَـثِـيْرٌ مِّـنْهُمْ
فٰـسِقُوْنَ

Has the time not yet come for those who believe that their hearts
should be humble for the remembrance of ALLAH and for the truth
that has descended (through revelation)? They must not be like those
to whom the Book was given before, but a long period passed on them
(in which they did not repent), therefore their *hearts became hard*,
and (thus) many of them are sinners.
(Chapter 57: Al-Hadid, *Iron:* verse 16)

AN INTERESTING CONCEPT:

Chapter, AL-HADID (meaning iron) and the notion of "hardening"
seem to be pointing towards it. The concept of the disease
HEMOCHROMATOSIS may be deduced from it, and the description
seems attracting in Chapter Al-Hadid (and ALLAH knows the best).

Hemochromatosis is a disease in which an excess amount of iron is
deposited in many organs of the body, especially the heart, liver and
pancreas. Hemochromatosis is frequently inherited as an autosomal
recessive disorder related to mutations in the HFE gene. The cardiac
involvement typically manifests as heart failure and arrhythmias.

An excess of iron in the liver can result in an enlarged liver, liver cancer, or cirrhosis, whereas too much iron buildup in the pancreas may ensue as diabetes.

Let us now begin discussing the calcification of coronary arteries. As we know, calcification is the marker of atherosclerosis, and the more the disease burden implies more ischemic burden. It is, therefore, when we discuss about treatment options for this particular issue, it becomes obvious that many times we need to think "out of the box" to deal with this issue. This is due to the fact that these calcified lesions sometimes do not yield easily to our routine techniques of balloon inflations only. It is also known that without a proper dilation of the lesion, stents may not be deployed properly and if any such attempt is made, it carries an inherent risk of stent thrombosis etc.

With this in mind, the contemporary mode of treatment for this issue is balloon dilation using high pressure, usage of non-compliant balloons, OPN balloons, scoring or cutting balloons and various atherectomy devices like Rotablation, Intravascular Lithotripsy or Orbital atherectomy.

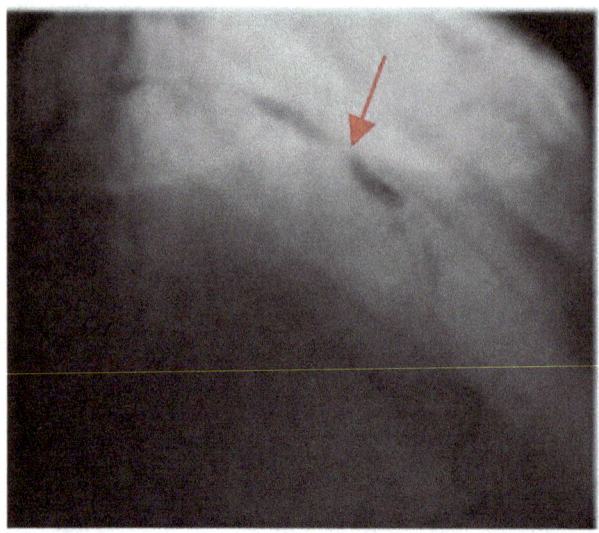

Figure above: A partially dilated balloon in LAD (red arrow) showing a severely calcified lesion and is unable to fully dilate the lesion in the middle. A rotablation (described below) may be used to appropriately dilate the lesion and deploy the stent.

ROTABLATION:

The rotablation is a procedure that is applied to very hard and calcified stenoses of the coronary arteries.

It is used when the stenoses are not distensible. To create a <u>lumen</u>, a drill head filled with fine diamond splinters, powered by compressed air, is inserted into the arterial vessels to remove the hardened <u>plaques</u>. Rotablator atherectomy has a unique mechanism of action that relies on plaque pulverization and microparticle embolization to achieve luminal enlargement.

These particles are usually small enough to pass through the capillary circulation and are subsequently removed by the reticuloendothelial system. Many studies have been conducted and did not report any significant impact on resting wall motion, myocardial perfusion, or other clinical markers of myocardial ischemia after uncomplicated Rotablator atherectomy.

The following pictures depict the structure and function of the rotablation device.

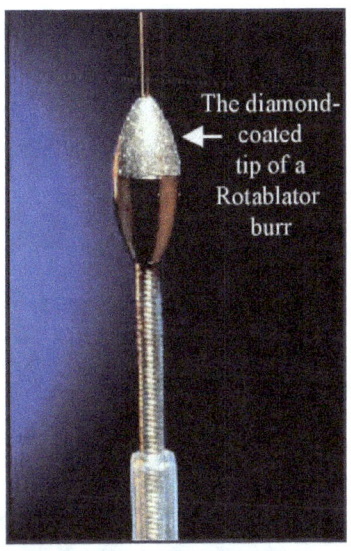

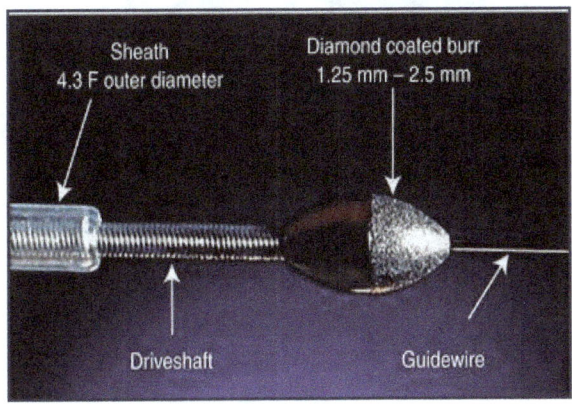

The pictures above show a rotablation device catheter.

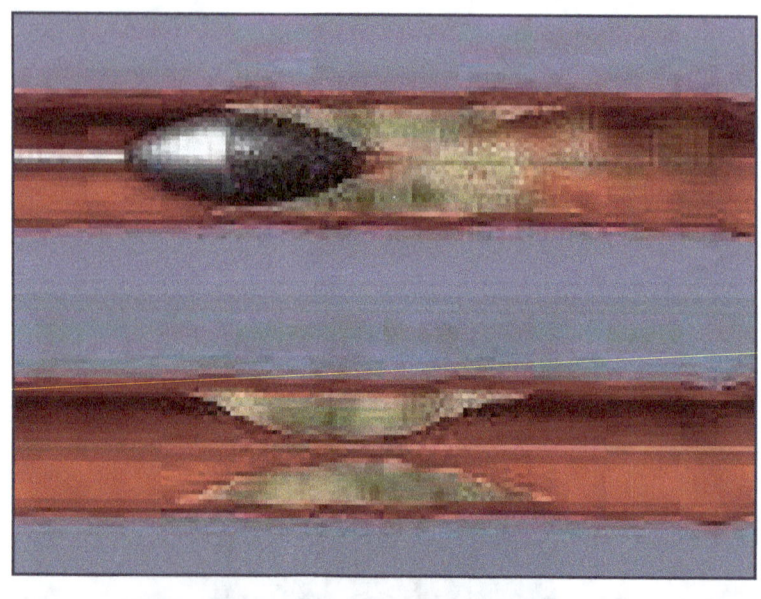

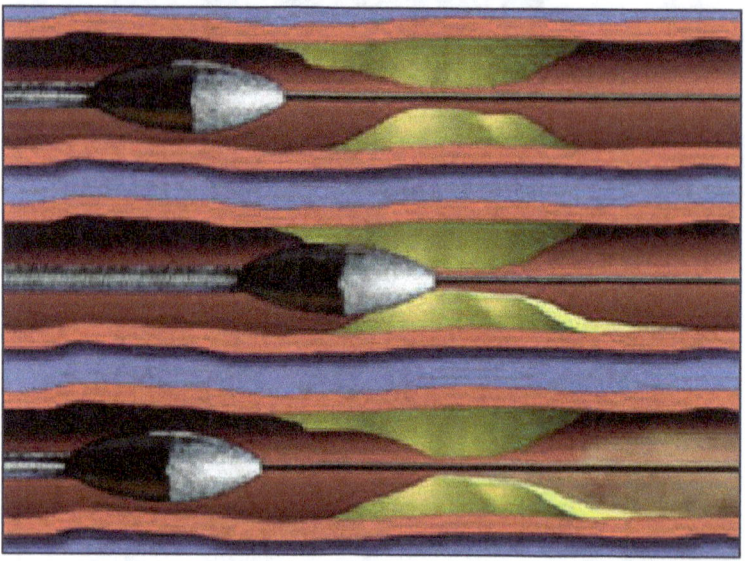

Pictures above show a rotablator passing through a calcified plaque.

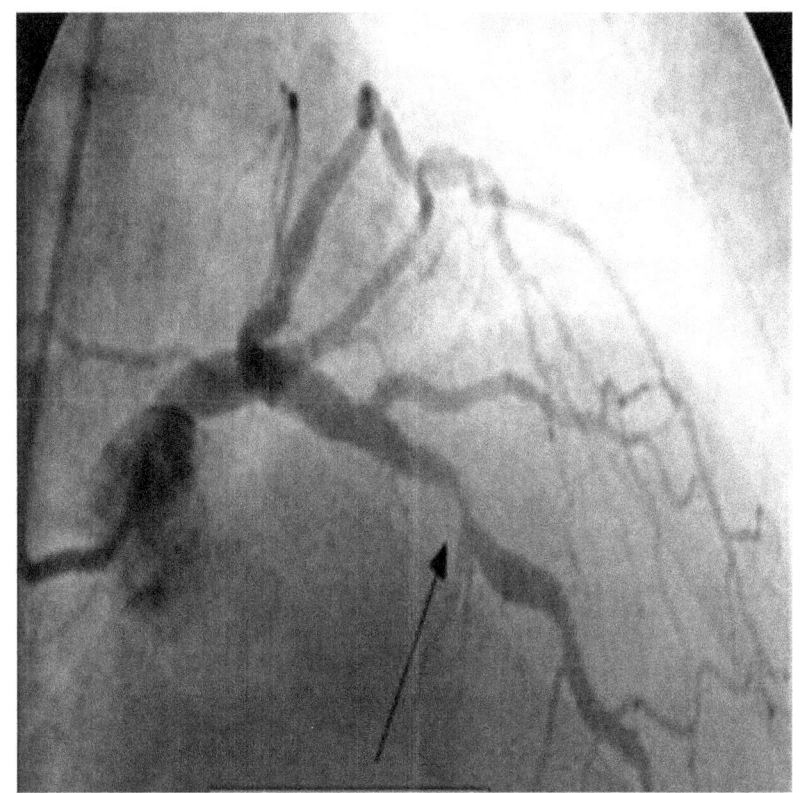

A:

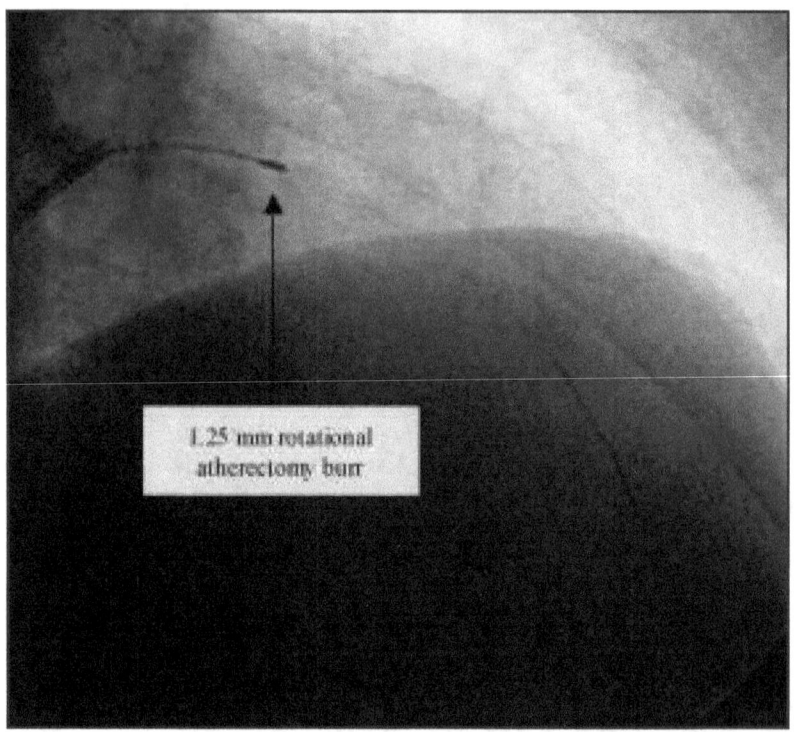

1.25 mm rotational
atherectomy burr

B:

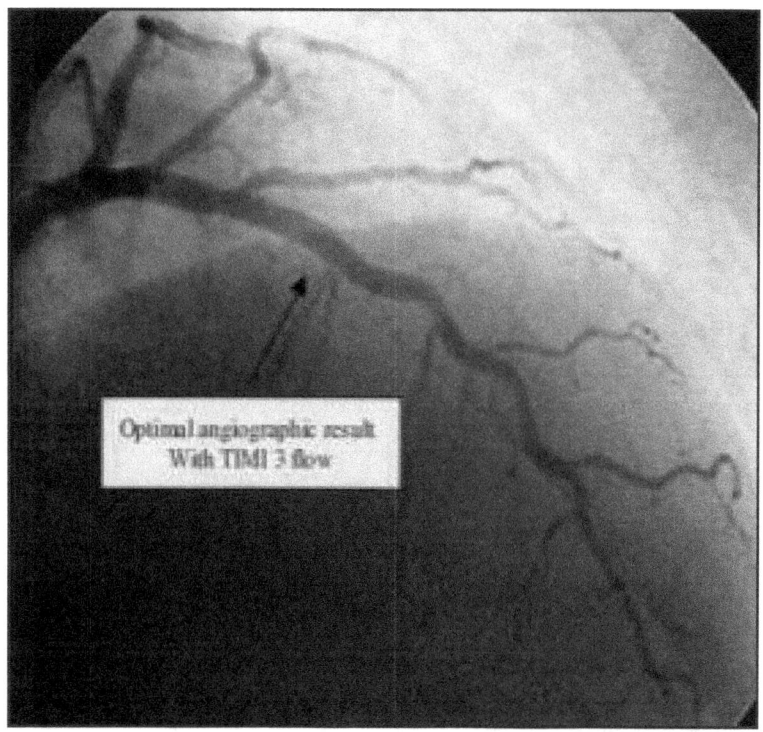

C:

The figure above depicts a severely calcified and hard stenosis in the mid-LAD (arrow in panel a), which was successfully treated with rotablation and stents. Initially, the lesion could not be fully dilated by balloon and Rotablation was performed to further dilate the vessel (arrow in panel b). This was followed by stent placement in the same lesion, which produced a satisfactory result (arrow in panel c).

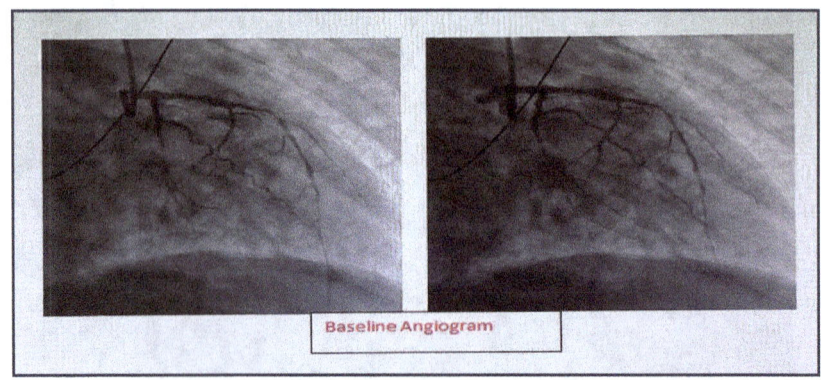

a

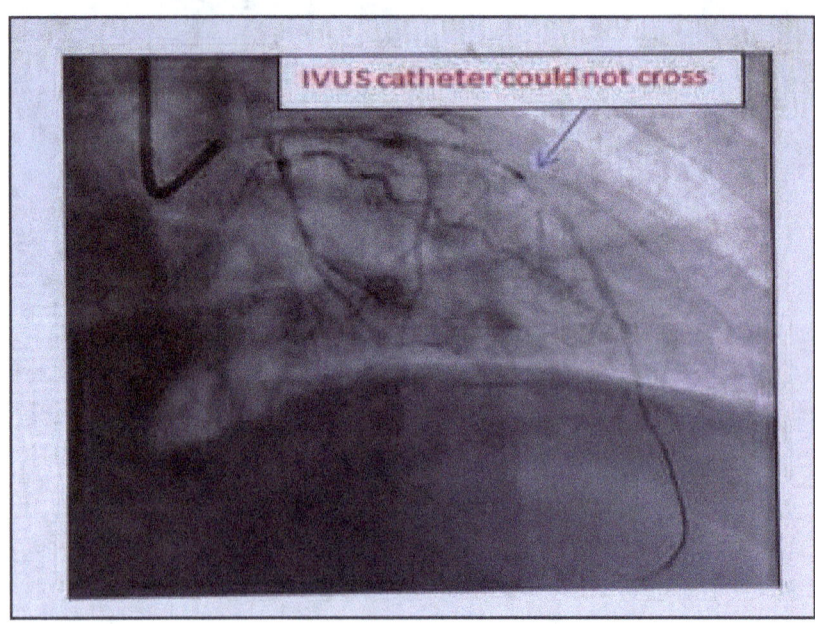

b

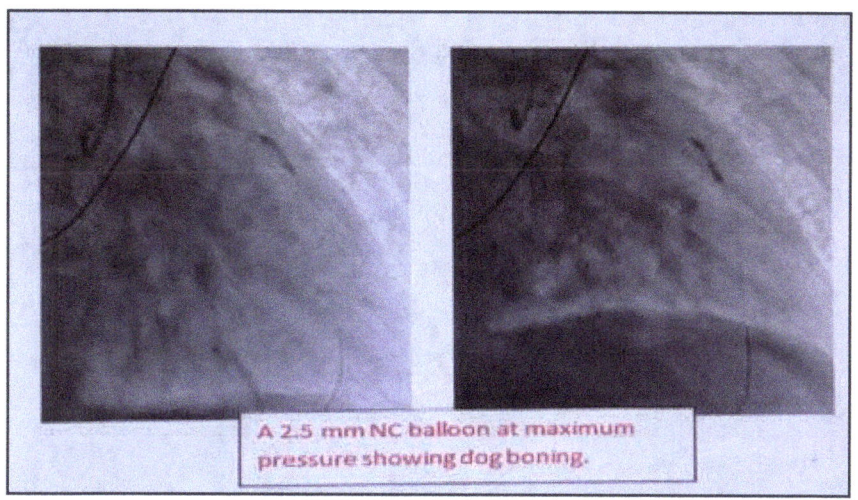

A 2.5 mm NC balloon at maximum pressure showing dog boning.

c

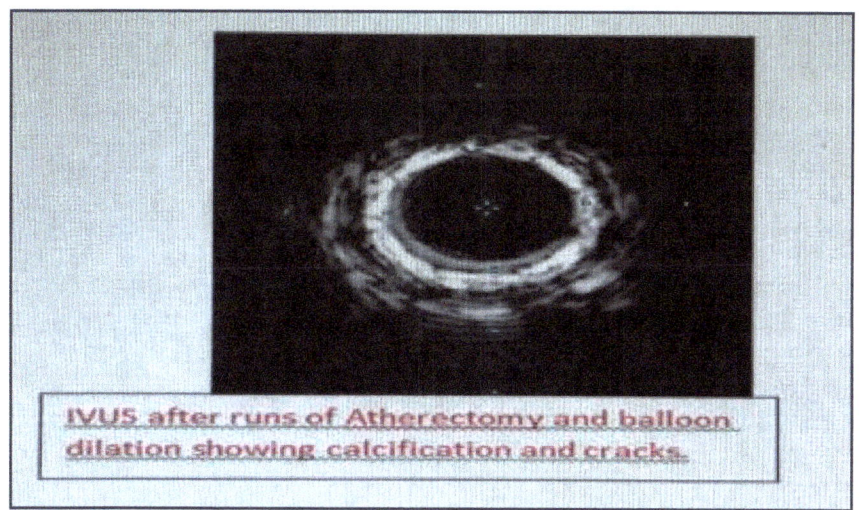

IVUS after runs of Atherectomy and balloon dilation showing calcification and cracks.

d

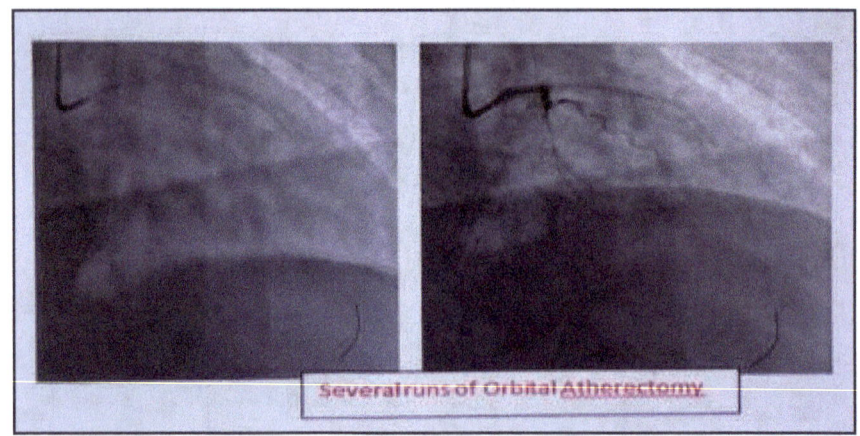

e

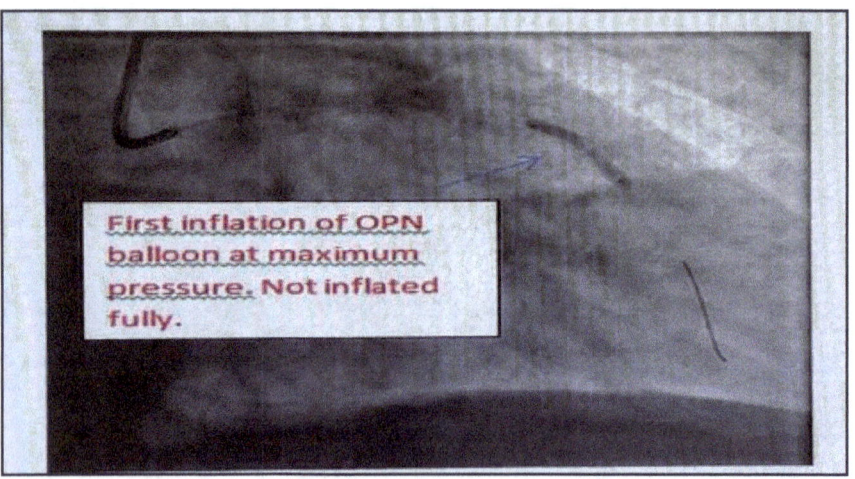

f

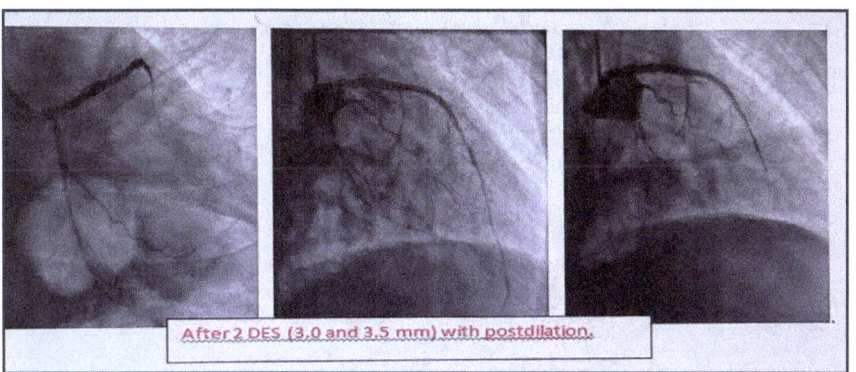

After 2 DES (3.0 and 3.5 mm) with postdilation.

g

The above images (a-g) represent one of our patients. These show a heavily calcified LAD, which was successfully treated using different devices, including orbital atherectomy and OPN balloon followed by stent placement. The lesion was so heavily calcified that the ordinary balloon would not work.

Cardiac Valve Calcification (hardening of heart valves):

Not only are the coronaries involved in the calcification process, but the valves can also be affected. The valves may become stenosed after heavy calcification, culminating in hemodynamic instability as well as syncope or even heart failure.

Following are some of the figures of stenotic cardiac valves, which may give an idea of the disease burden.

Normal tri-leaflet aortic valve (closed)

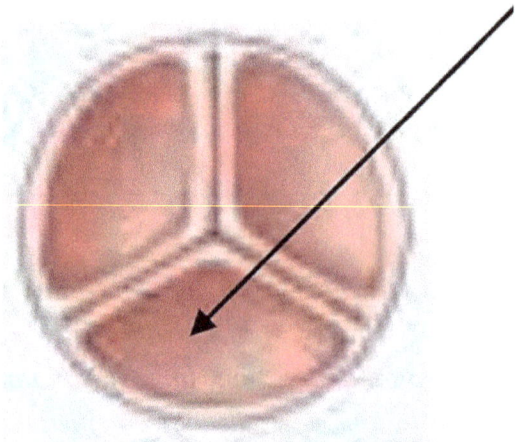

Stenotic aortic valve (closed). Calcium deposits are seen in the aortic cusps (arrows).

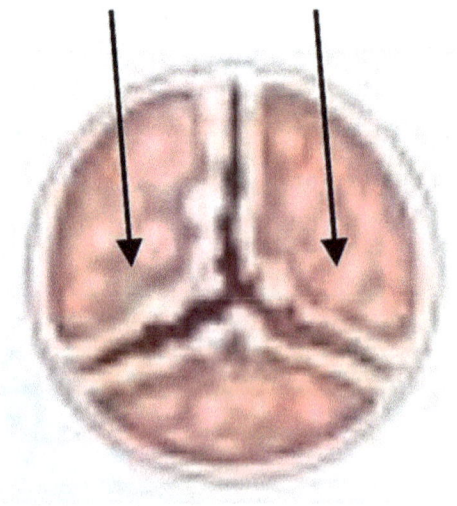

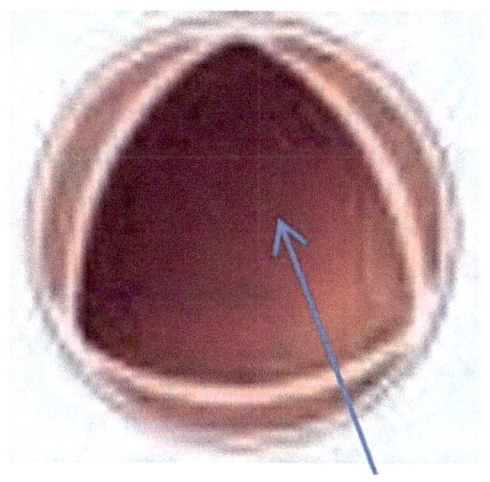

Normal aortic valve opening.

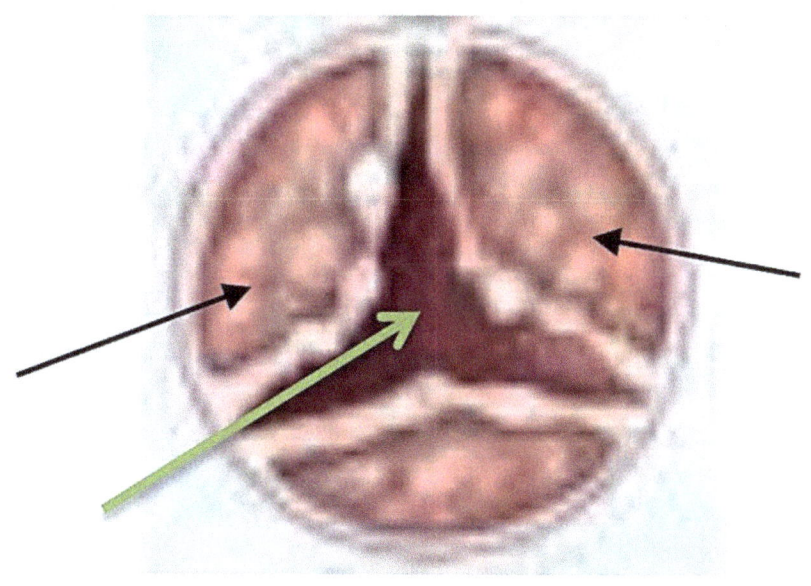

Stenotic aortic valve. Calcium deposits are seen in the aortic cusps (arrows). There is a much-reduced opening (green arrow) with the normal valve opening.

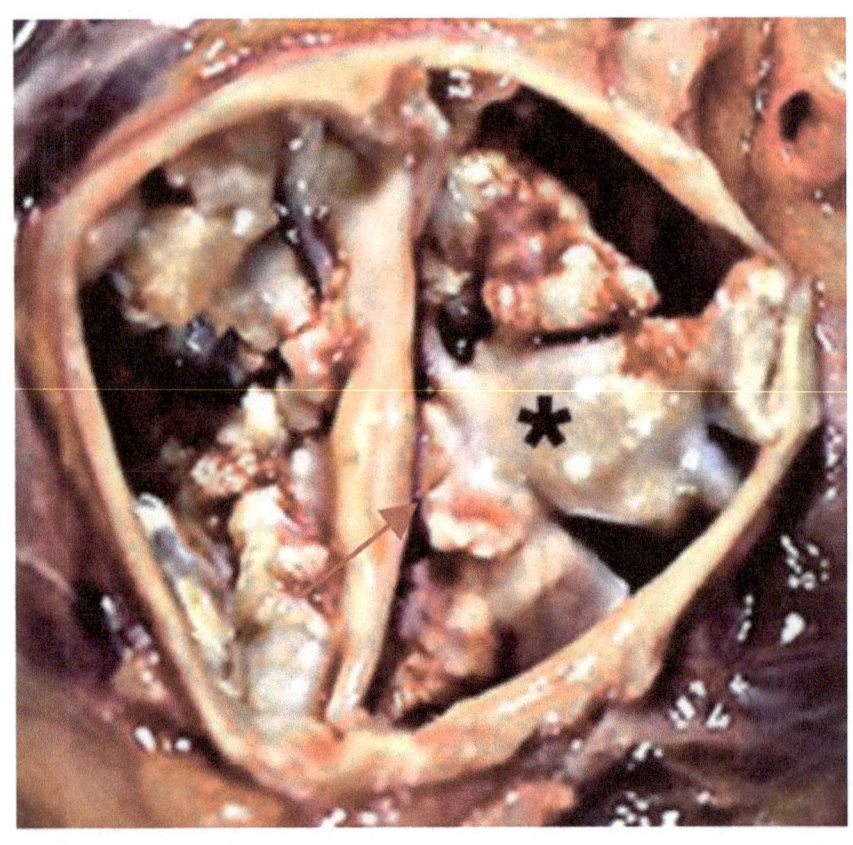

Above: Calcification of a congenital bicuspid aortic valve as seen during the surgery. The asterisk points to a large calcified area.

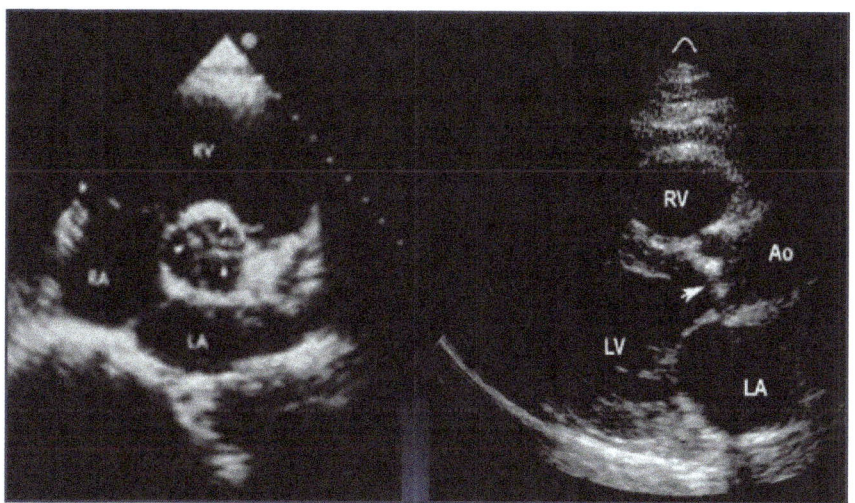

Calcified aortic valve with severe aortic stenosis in echocardiogram as shown above by arrows

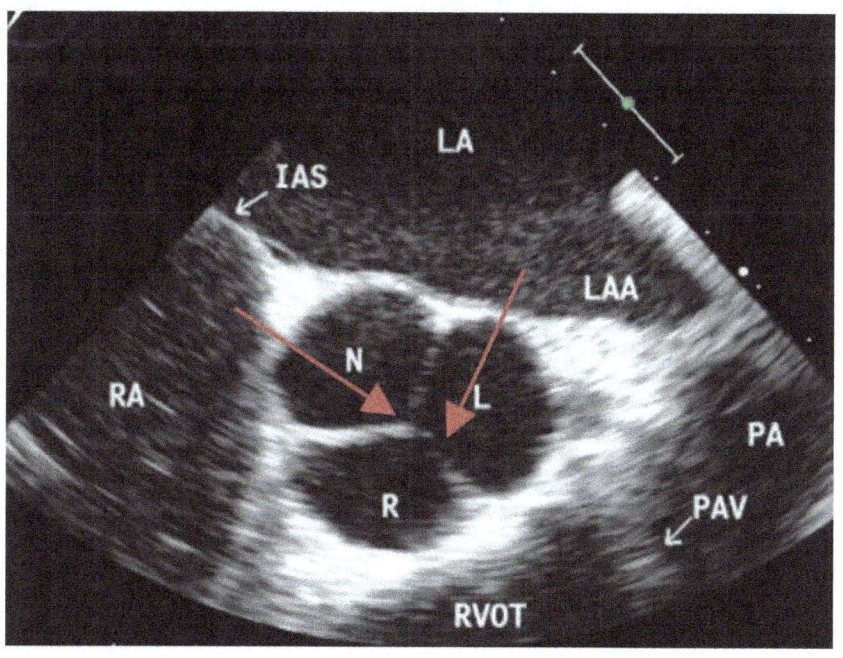

Normal aortic valve in the closed position (arrows)

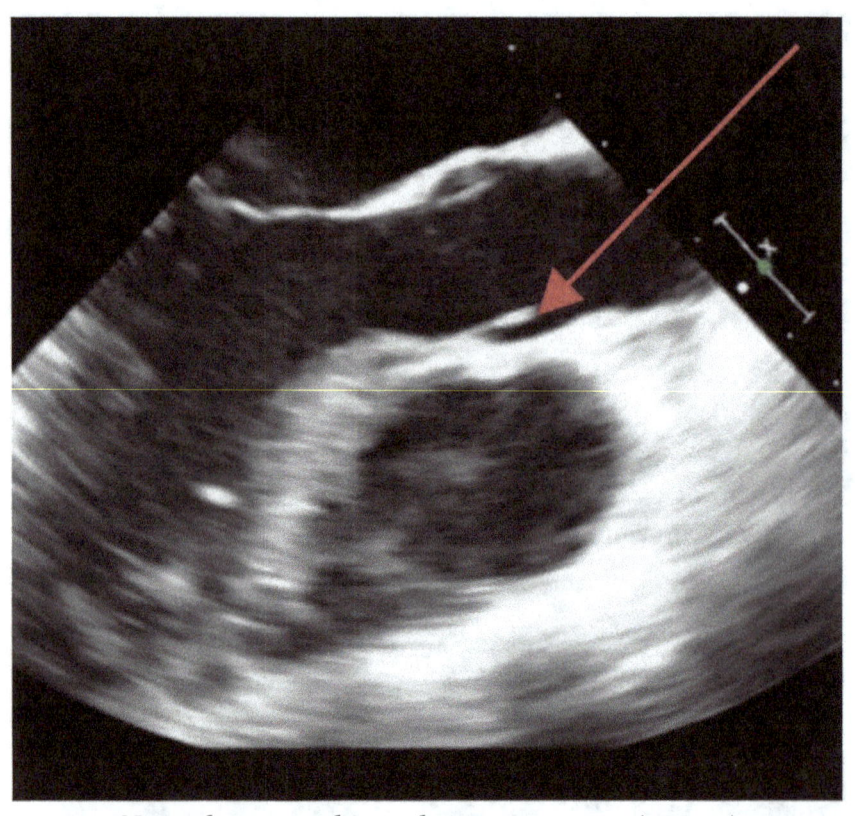

Normal aortic valve in the open position (arrows)

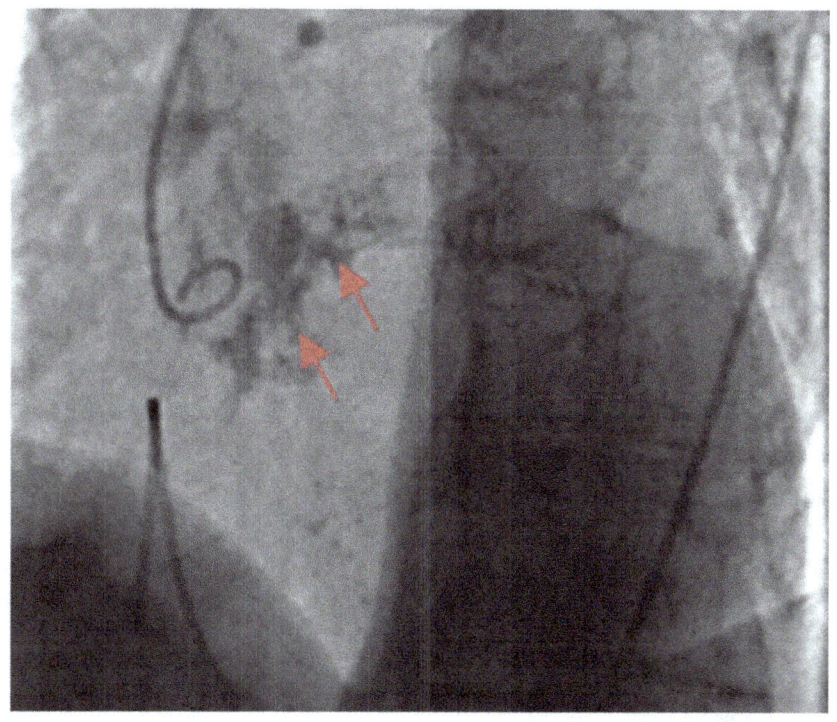

Fluoroscopy of a heavily calcified aortic valve with severe stenosis (arrows).

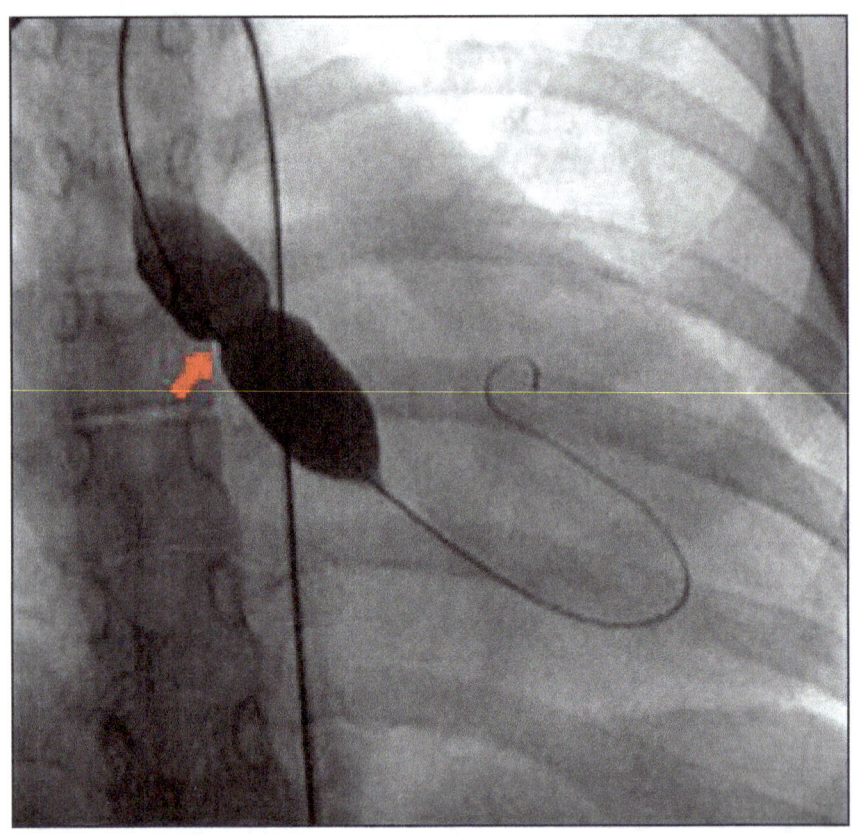

Aside from aortic valve replacement done surgically, balloon aortic valvuloplasty may also be performed in some cases, as is shown above. The constriction in the middle of the balloon corresponds to the valvular stenosis.

The above pictures clearly manifest how heavily calcified the aortic valve may become, which may be explained by the notion of ***"hearts becoming hardened."*** These valves become so heavily calcified that the normal aortic valve area of 3.0 to 4.0 cm sq. may be reduced in some cases to 0.3-0.4 cm sq., compromising effective forward flow from the left ventricle via aortic root to the whole body. When this happens, the patient may experience angina ("chest burden"), heart failure and or syncope. The chest pain symptoms may be similar in nature to what someone feels with coronary artery stenosis, as described in the chapter on chronic stable angina.

The following Holy verse now is mentioned here for better correlation.

فَمَنْ يُّرِدِ اللهُ اَنْ يَّهدِيَهُ يَشْرَحْ صَدْرَهُ لِلإِسْلَامِ وَمَنْ يُّرِدْ اَنْ يُّضِلَّهُ يَجْعَلْ صَدْرَهُ ضَيِّقًا حَرَجًا كَاَنَّمَا يَصَّعَّدُ فِي السَّمَاءِ كَذَلِكَ يَجْعَلُ اللهُ الرِّجْسَ عَلَي الَّذِيْنَ لَا يُؤْمِنُوْنَ

So, whomsoever ALLAH wills to guide, He makes his heart wide open for Islam, and whomsoever He wills to let go astray, He makes his heart strait and constricted, (and he feels embracing Islam as difficult) as if he were climbing to the sky. In this way, ALLAH lays abomination on those who do not believe.
(Chapter 6: Al-Anaam, *The Cattle: verse* 125)

If it comes to this severity, then the only treatment for aortic valve that is left over is replacement of the calcified valve with an artificial valve by surgery or percutaneously which is called *Transcatheter Aortic Valve Replacement (TAVR)*.

Let's now focus on a different valve, which is called the *Mitral valve* and its calcification.

Normal mitral valve (arrows) on echocardiogram for comparison is shown below.

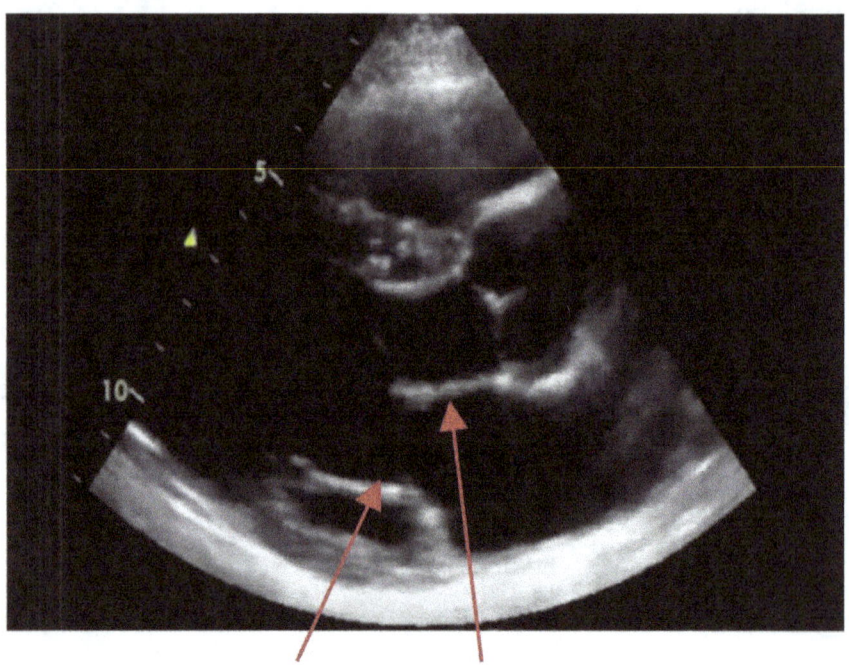

The following pictures depict a thickened and calcified mitral valve (arrows) in different views.

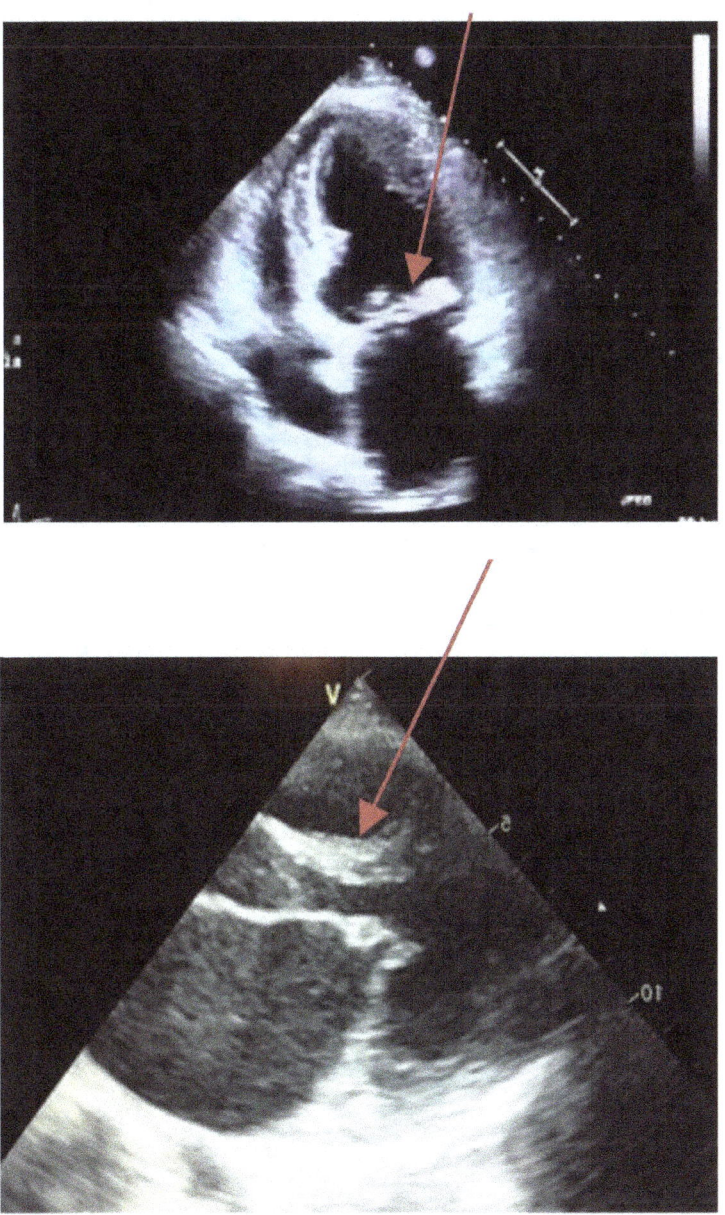

The picture below shows balloon mitral valvuloplasty. Due to severe stenosis, the balloon shows narrowing in the middle (arrow in the left panel), which finally opens up fully (arrow in the right panel) upon exerting more pressure.

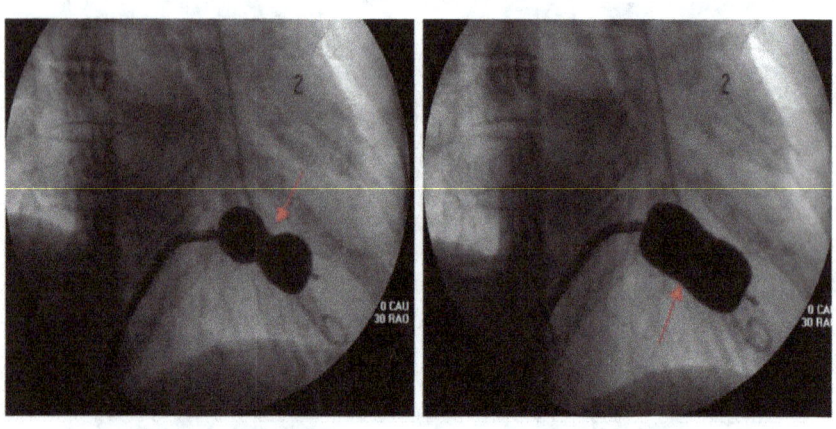

MYOCARDIAL CALCIFICATION (hardening of heart muscle):

Two of the Holy verses mentioned above are mentioned again for better comprehension of this topic.

(1)

ثُمَّ قَسَتْ قُلُوْبُكُمْ مِّنْ بَعْدِ ذَٰلِكَ فَهِىَ كَالْحِجَارَةِ أَوْ أَشَدُّ قَسْوَةً وَإِنَّ مِنَ الْحِجَارَةِ لَمَا يَتَفَجَّرُ مِنْهُ الْأَنْهَرُ وَإِنَّ مِنْهَا لَمَا يَشَّقَّقُ فَيَخْرُجُ مِنْهُ الْمَآءُ وَإِنَّ مِنْهَا لَمَا يَهْبِطُ مِنْ خَشْيَةِ اللهِ وَمَا اللهُ بِغَافِلٍ عَمَّا تَعْمَلُوْنَ

When, even after that, your *hearts were hardened*, as if they were rocks, or still worse in hardness. For surely among the rocks there are some from which rivers gush forth, and there are others that crack open and water flows from them, and there are still others that fall down in fear of ALLAH. And ALLAH is not unaware of what you do.
(Chapter 2: Al-Baqara, *The Cow:* verse 74)

(2)

فَلَوْلَآ اِذْ جَاۤءَهُمْ بَاْسُنَا تَضَرَّعُوْا وَلٰكِنْ قَسَتْ قُلُوْبُهُمْ وَزَيَّنَ لَهُمُ الـشَّيْطٰنُ مَا كَانُوْا يَـعْمَلُوْنَ

Why then, did they not supplicate in humility when a calamity from Us came upon them? Instead, their *hearts were hardened* and Satan adorned for them what they were doing.
(Chapter 6: Al-Anaam, *The Cattle:* verse 43)

MYOCARDIAL CALCIFICATION:

In addition to the above structures being affected by calcification and "hardening," the actual myocardium can, at times, also undergo this process.

The myocardial calcification may be due to local tissue damage and cellular necrosis. This process is called *Dystrophic calcification.* It is not associated with abnormalities in serum calcium levels or calcium homeostasis; however, hypercalcemia can accentuate the process.

This entity may be due to ischemia, trauma, infection or inflammation, the most common being previous myocardial infarction leading to myocyte necrosis. In this condition, calcium may accumulate in necrotized cardiac myocytes.

The other entity causing myocardial calcification is the *"Metastatic calcification."* This is due to a systemic process from hypercalcemia and/or abnormalities of calcium homeostasis. It can occur either in normal or diseased tissue. Any abnormality of calcium metabolism can lead to metastatic calcification.

Metastatic myocardial calcification is most commonly reported in patients with chronic renal failure on hemodialysis; however, it has also been reported in patients with primary hyperparathyroidism, secondary and tertiary hyperparathyroidism, oxaluria and dietary deficiency of calcium and vitamin D.

Following are some of the CT scan images of extensive myocardial calcification (arrows):

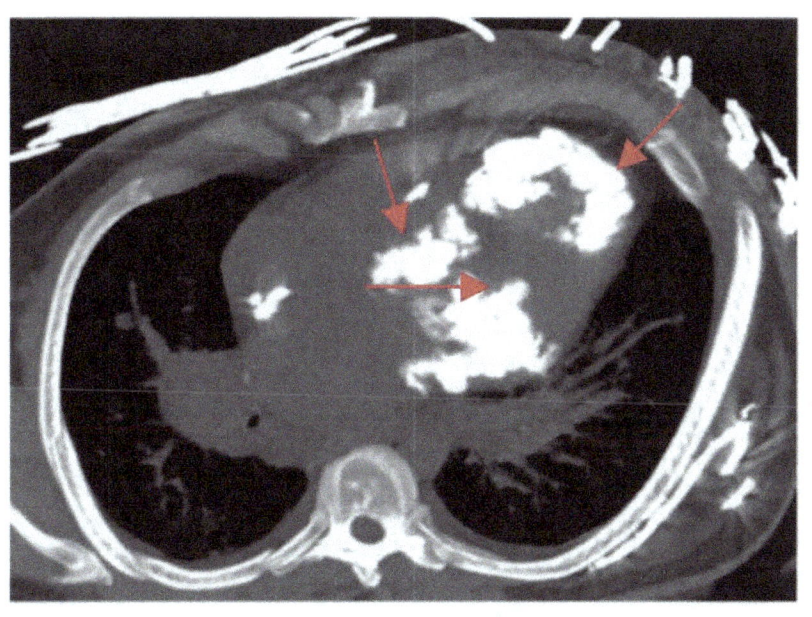

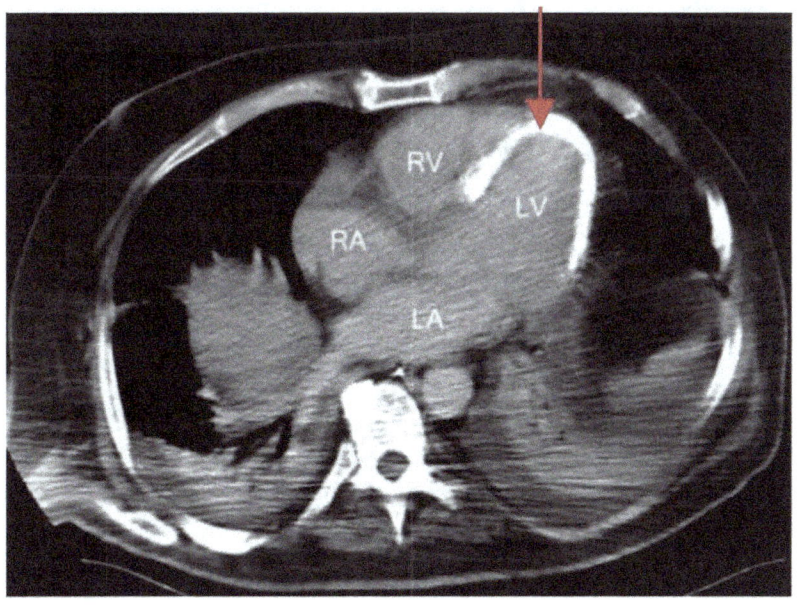

The above chapter dealt with the concept of calcification or hardening of the heart and its various structures in the light of the Holy Scripture.

References:

1. Wang L, Jerosch-Herold M, Jacobs DR Jr., et al. Coronary artery calcification and myocardial perfusion in asymptomatic adults: the MESA (Multi-Ethnic Study of Atherosclerosis). J Am Coll Cardiol 2006; 48: 1018–26.

2. Kalra SS, Shanahan CM. Vascular calcification and hypertension: cause and effect. Ann Med 2012; 44 Suppl 1: S85–92.

3. Vliegenthart R, Oudkerk M, Hofman A, et al. Coronary calcification improves cardiovascular risk prediction in the elderly. Circulation 2005; 112: 572–7.

4. Vavuranakis M, Toutouzas K, Stefanadis C, et al. Stent deployment in calcified lesions: can we overcome calcific restraint with high-pressure balloon inflations? Catheter Cardiovasc Interv 2001; 52: 164–72.

5. Demer LL, Tintut Y. Vascular calcification: pathobiology of a multifaceted disease. Circulation 2008; 117: 2938–48.

6. Johnson RC, Leopold JA, Loscalzo J. Vascular calcification: pathobiological mechanisms and clinical implications. Circ Res 2006; 99: 1044–59.

7. Abedin M, Tintut Y, Demer LL. Vascular calcification: mechanisms and clinical ramifications. Arterioscler Thromb Vasc Biol 2004; 24: 1161–70.

8. Lehto S, Niskanen L, Suhonen M, Ronnemaa T, Laakso M. Medial artery calcification: a neglected harbinger of cardiovascular complications in non-insulin-dependent diabetes mellitus. Arterioscler Thromb Vasc Biol. 1996; *16*: 978–983.

9. van Setten J, Isgum I, Smolonska J, et al. Genome-wide association study of coronary and aortic calcification implicates risk loci for coronary artery disease and myocardial infarction. Atherosclerosis 2013; 228: 400–5.

10. Hofmann Bowman MA, McNally EM. Genetic pathways of vascular calcification. Trends Cardiovasc Med 2012; 22: 93–8.

11. O'Donnell CJ, Kavousi M, Smith AV et al. Genome-wide association study for coronary artery calcification with follow-up in myocardial infarction. Circulation 2011; 124: 2855–64.

12. Greenland P, LaBree L, Azen SP, Doherty TM, Detrano RC. Coronary artery calcium score combined with Framingham score for risk prediction in asymptomatic individuals. JAMA 2004; 291: 210–5.

13. Loecker TH, Schwartz RS, Cotta CW, Hickman JR Jr. Fluoroscopic coronary artery calcification and associated coronary disease in asymptomatic young men. J Am Coll Cardiol 1992; 19: 1167–72.

14. Yamamoto H, Imazu M, Hattori Y, et al. Predicting angiographic narrowing > or 1/4 50% in diameter in each of the three major arteries by amounts of calcium detected by electron beam computed tomographic scanning in patients with chest pain. Am J Cardiol 1998; 81: 778–80.

15. Tanenbaum SR, Kondos GT, Veselik KE, et al. Detection of calcific deposits in coronary arteries by ultrafast computed tomography and correlation with angiography. Am J Cardiol 1989; 63: 870–2.

16. Greenland P, LaBree L, Azen SP, Doherty TM, Detrano RC. Coronary artery calcium score combined with Framingham score for risk prediction in asymptomatic individuals. JAMA 2004; 291: 210–5.

17. Elias-Smale SE, Proenca RV, Koller MT, et al. Coronary calcium score improves classification of coronary heart disease risk in the elderly: the Rotterdam study. J Am Coll Cardiol 2010; 56: 1407–14.

18. Erbel R, Mohlenkamp S, Moebus S, et al. Coronary risk stratification, discrimination, and reclassification improvement based on quantifi- cation of subclinical coronary atherosclerosis: the Heinz Nixdorf Recall study. J Am Coll Cardiol 2010; 56: 1397–406.

19. Polonsky TS, McClelland RL, Jorgensen NW, et al. Coronary artery calcium score and risk classification for coronary heart disease pre- diction. JAMA 2010; 303: 1610–20. Agatston AS, Janowitz WR, Hildner FJ, et al. Quantification of coronary artery calcium using ultrafast computed tomography. J Am Coll Cardiol 1990; 15: 827–32.

21. Budoff MJ, Georgiou D, Brody A, et al. Ultrafast computed to- mography as a diagnostic modality in the detection of coronary artery disease: a multicenter study. Circulation 1996; 93: 898–904.

22. Roger VL, Go AS, Lloyd-Jones DM, et al. Executive summary: heart disease and stroke statisticsd2012 update: a report from the American Heart Association. Circulation 2012; 125: e1001.

23. Nasir K, Rubin J, Blaha MJ, et al. Interplay of coronary artery calcification and traditional risk factors for the prediction of all-cause mortality in asymptomatic individuals. Circ Cardiovasc Imaging 2012; 5: 467–73.

24. Mintz GS, Popma JJ, Pichard AD, et al. Patterns of calcification in coronary artery disease. A statistical analysis of intravascular ultrasound and coronary angiography in 1155 lesions. Circulation 1995; 91: 1959–65.

25. Tuzcu EM, Berkalp B, De Franco AC, et al. The dilemma of diagnosing coronary calcification: angiography versus intravascular ultra- sound. J Am Coll Cardiol 1996; 27: 832–8.

26. Popma J, Bashore T. Qualitative and quantitative angiography. In: Topol E, editor. Textbook of Interventional Cardiology. Philadelphia, PA: WB Saunders, 1994: 1052–68.

27. Friedrich GJ, Moes NY, Muhlberger VA, et al. Detection of intralesional calcium by intracoronary ultrasound depends on the histologic pattern. Am Heart J 1994; 128: 435–41.

28. Kawasaki M, Bouma BE, Bressner J, et al. Diagnostic accuracy of optical coherence tomography and integrated backscatter intravascular ultrasound images for tissue characterization of human coronary plaques. J Am Coll Cardiol 2006; 48: 81–8.

29. Mintz GS, Nissen SE, Anderson WD, et al. American College of Cardiology Clinical Expert Consensus Document on Standards for Acquisition, Measurement and Reporting of Intravascular Ultrasound Studies (IVUS). J Am Coll Cardiol 2001; 37: 1478–92.

30. Mintz GS, Douek P, Pichard AD, et al. Target lesion calcification in coronary artery disease: an intravascular ultrasound study. J Am Coll Cardiol 1992; 20: 1149–55.

31. Hoffmann R, Mintz GS, Popma JJ, Satler LF, Kent KM, Pichard AD, Leon MB. Treatment of calcified coronary lesions with Palmaz-

Schatz stents. An intravascular ultrasound study. Eur Heart J 1998; 19: 1224e1231.

32. Moussa I, Ellis SG, Jones M, Kereiakes DJ, McMartin D, Rutherford B, Mehran R, Collins M, Leon MB, Popma JJ, Russell ME, Stone GW. Impact of coronary culprit lesion calcium in patients undergoing pacli- taxel-eluting stent implantation (a TAXUS-IV sub-study). Am J Cardiol 2005; 96: 1242e1247.

33. Bangalore S, Vlachos HA, Selzer F, Wilensky RL, Kip KE, Williams DO, Faxon DP. Percutaneous coronary intervention of moderate to severe calcified coronary lesions: insights from the National Heart, Lung, and Blood Institute Dynamic Registry. Catheter Cardiovasc Interv 2011; 77: 22e28.

34. Dietz U, Erbel R, Rupprecht H, Weidmann S, Meyer J. High-frequency rotational ablation: an alternative in treating coronary artery stenoses and occlusions. Br Heart J. 1993; 70: 327-336.

35. Ahn SS, Auth D, Marcus DR, Moore WS. Removal of focal atheromatous lesions by angioscopically guided high-speed rotary atherectomy: preliminary experimental observations. J Vasc Surg. 1988; 7: 292-300.

36. Friedman HZ, Elliott MA, Gottlieb GJ, O'Neill WW. Mechanical rotary atherectomy: the effects of microparticle embolization on myocardial blood flow and function. J Intervent Cardiol. 1989; 2: 77-83.

37. Perkins JA. Tissue Renewal, Regeneration, and Repair. In: Perkins JA, ed. Robbins and Cotran Pathologic Basis of Disease. Eighth Edition. Philadelphia: WB Saunders; 2010: 79e110.

38. Gowda RM, Boxt LM. Calcifications of the heart. Radiol Clin North Am. 2004; 42: 603e617. vi-vii.

39. Shackley BS, Nguyen TP, Shivkumar K, Finn PJ, Fishbein MC. Idiopathic massive myocardial calcification: a case report and review of the literature. Cardiovasc Path. 2011; 20: e79e83.

40. Ferguson EC, Berkowitz EA. Cardiac and pericardial calcifications on chest radiographs. Clin Radiol. 2010; 65: 685e694.

41. Zaidi AN, Ceneviva GD, Phipps LM, Dettorre MD, Mart CR, Thomas NJ. Myocardial calcification caused by secondary hyperparathyroidism due to dietary deficiency of calcium and vitamin D. Pediatr Cardiol. 2005; 26: 460e463.

42. Freeman J, Dodd JD, Ridge CA, O'Neill A, McCreery C, Quinn M. "Porcelain heart" cardiomyopathy secondary to hyperparathyroidism: radiographic, echocardiographic, and cardiac CT appearances. J Cardiovasc Comput Tomogr. 2010; 4: 402e404.

43. Vascular calcification and hypertension: Cause and effect: Annals of Medicine Volume 44, 2012 - *Issue sup1*.

44. Impact of the Severity of Coronary Artery Calcification on Clinical Events in Patients Undergoing Coronary Artery Bypass Grafting (from the Acute Catheterization and Urgent Intervention Triage Strategy Trial: Am J Cardiol 2013; 112: 1730e1737.

45. Abazid RM; Kattea MO; Sayed S; Saqqah H; Qintar M; Smettei OA: Avicenna J Med. 2015; 5(3): 83-8 (ISSN: 2231-0770)

46. Mahesh V. Madhavan BA, MadhusudhanTarigopula MD, MPH, Gary S.Mintz MD, AkikoMaehara MD, Gregg W.Stone MD·

PhilippeGénéreux MD Artery Calcification: Pathogenesis and Prognostic Implications:

47. Rob C.M. van Kruijsdijk, Joris J. van der Heijden, Ruben Uijlings and Luuk C. Otterspoor. Sepsis-Related Myocardial Calcification

48. Brit S. Shackley, Thao P. Nguyen, Kalyanam Shivkumar, Paul J. Finn, Michael C. Fishbein: Idiopathic massive myocardial calcification: a case report and review of the literature

Chapter 6
(Synopsis)
Cardiac Surgery

Cardiac surgery is performed for several indications. One of the most common being the Coronary Artery By-pass Graft (CABG; open heart or by-pass surgery)

Let us start this chapter by studying the following few Holy Verses.

اَفَمَنْ شَرَحَ اللّٰهُ صَدْرَهُ لِلْإِسْلَامِ فَهُوَ عَلَٰى نُوْرٍ مِّنْ رَّبِّهِ فَوَيْلٌ لِّلْقٰسِيَةِ قُلُوْبُهُمْ مِّنْ ذِكْرِ اللّٰهِ أُولٰٓئِكَ فِيْ ضَلٰلٍ مُّبِيْنٍ

'So I ask about a person whose heart ALLAH has opened up for Islam, and consequently he proceeds in a light from his Lord. (Can he be equal to the one whose heart is hardened?) So, woe to those whose hearts are too hard to remember ALLAH. Those are wandering in open error.
(Chapter 39: Az-Zumar, The Groups: Verse: 22)

اَلَمْ نَشْرَحْ لَكَ صَدْرَكَ

'Have We not caused your bosom to be wide open for you?"
(Chapter 94: Al-Inshirah, The Opening Forth: Verse: 1)

172

وَوَضَعْنَا عَنْكَ وِزْرَكَ

"And We removed from you your burden."
(Chapter 94: Al-Inshirah, The Opening Forth: Verse: 2)

As the name simply implies, this procedure deals with creating a "by-pass" across a severe blockage in the coronary arteries of human heart.

CABG or by-pass surgery has been recommended for the very significant blockages along with poor heart muscle function and diabetic status of the patient. In a very illuminating way, it may be inferred from the aforementioned Holy verses from the glorious Quran regarding the concept of not only by-pass surgery (opening or expanding the chest) but also pertaining to *"relieving the burden."*

In very simple words, the CABG procedure is described as opening the chest by incision, performing the "by-pass" operation and closing the chest by sutures.

The naturally existing arteries and veins in the body are used in order to complete the procedure. Usually, 2-3 veins from the legs are removed with modern technology utilizing harvesting techniques. One end of the vein is attached to the proximal aorta and the other distal to or after the severe blockage. In addition, one or more arteries from different parts of the body are used which have shown to have better patency results than the vein grafts.

The opening of the chest is not only done to perform a by-pass surgery but is also done for several other indications like replacing heart valves, etc. A more detailed discussion about this topic is mentioned below.

Chapter 6:
Cardiac Surgery

Modern-day technology has revolutionized cardiac surgery, which is performed for several indications, the most common being the Coronary Artery By-pass Graft (CABG; open heart or by-pass surgery).

Let us start this chapter by studying the following few Holy Verses.

اَفَمَنْ شَرَحَ اللهُ صَدْرَهُ لِلإِسْلَام فَهُوَ عَلَى نُوْرٍ
مِّنْ رَّبِّهٖ فَوَيْلٌ لِّلْقٰسِيَةِ قُلُوْبُهُمْ مِّنْ
ذِكْرِ اللهِ أُولٰئِكَ فِيْ ضَلٰلٍ مُّبِيْنٍ

'So I ask about a person whose heart ALLAH has opened up for Islam, and consequently he proceeds in a light from his Lord. (Can he be equal to the one whose heart is hardened?) So, woe to those whose hearts are too hard to remember ALLAH. Those are wandering in open error.
(Chapter 39: Az-Zumar, The Groups: Verse: 22)

اَلَمْ نَشْرَحْ لَكَ صَدْرَكَ

"Have We not caused your bosom to be wide open for you?"
(Chapter 94: Al-Inshirah, The Opening Forth: Verse: 1)

174

وَوَضَعْنَـا عَنْكَ وِزْرَكَ

"And We removed from you your burden."
(Chapter 94: Al-Inshirah, The Opening Forth: Verse: 2)

We will now study this interesting topic in more detail in the light of the above-mentioned Holy verses.

In order to understand CABG (open heart or by-pass surgery), we need to discuss the following:

1. Why is it done?

2. How is it done?

WHY IS IT DONE?

As the name simply implies, this procedure deals with creating a "by-pass" across a severe blockage in the coronary arteries of the human heart. Due to plaque formation or atherosclerosis in the coronary arteries, plaque building occurs, which may reach up to a critical level, culminating in severe stenosis (blockage), and the patient develops symptoms such as chest pain, shortness of breath, etc.

There are three ways to deal with these blockages:

- Medical management

- Angioplasty

- CABG or By-pass surgery

The effect of these blockages on the myocardium *(heart muscle)* varies from chest pain due to reduced blood supply to the myocardium

175

to frank myocardial infarction resulting in dead tissue. Certainly, the idea remains in protecting the integrity of the myocardium by restoring the adequate blood supply to the myocardium. In the current era, this is more commonly done by performing angioplasties. The latter has evolved tremendously from simple balloon angioplasty *(which requires opening up of the blockages by balloon inflations only)* to stent implantation *(initially, there were plain or bare metal stents, which were then advanced and improved by the introduction of drug-eluting stents)* and in the recent past by using bio-absorbable scaffolds.

For more diffuse and multiple lesions, including lesions in the Left main coronary artery, and in patients with diabetes mellitus and LV dysfunction *(poor heart muscle function)*, CABG or by-pass surgery has been recommended more traditionally.

In a very illuminating way, it may be inferred from the aforementioned Holy verses from the glorious Quran regarding the concept of not only by-pass surgery *(opening or expanding the chest)* but also pertaining to *"relieving the burden."*

This needs to be kept in mind that angina developing from coronary artery disease (or plaque building) is in itself a *"burden"* on the myocardium because the latter does not get its enough and adequate blood supply, especially when in need, like during physical activity. More so, if the myocardium *(heart muscle)* has weakened due to ischemia *(less blood supply)*, infarction *(dead heart muscle)* or cardiomyopathy *(weak heart muscle)*, the preload or the "burden" *(may also be referred to as the left ventricular end-diastolic pressure or LVEDP)* increases. And the more this pressure is the worse is the prognosis. By alleviating the underlying cause, this "burden" may be reduced significantly, and certainly, the patient tends to feel better.

This has the beneficial effects on both morbidity and mortality. Also, the patient's angina is likely to be relieved, and the quality of life improves remarkably.

HOW IS IT DONE?

During this procedure, an incision is made in the chest wall, a bypass or any other operation is performed, and the chest is closed back. In many patients, after the surgery, only a very faint scar is left which sometimes is even hard to see.

The naturally existing arteries and veins in the body are used in order to complete the procedure. Usually, 2-3 veins from the legs are removed with modern technology utilizing harvesting techniques. One end of the vein is attached to the proximal aorta, and the other end after (*distal to)* the severe blockage.

Similarly, arteries, including mammary arteries (LIMA, RIMA from the chest) and radial artery (RA) from the forearm, are commonly used. Sometimes, gastroepiploic artery (GEA) grafts are also used from the abdomen. Several studies have proved that arterial grafts, especially the LIMA once used in-situ (i.e. in its original place and not a free graft), have a 10-year patency rate of more than 90%. LIMA grafts tend to show more patency and one of the proposed reasons is that they generate more Nitric Oxide, which tends to dilate the vessel. This is in contrast with the venous grafts, which secrete less of the Nitric oxide. (Many other mechanisms are listed in the medical literature which may be beyond the scope of this manuscript).

The patency of both the right and left mammary grafts (i.e. LIMA and RIMA) are comparable, though they are not used in combination as readily due to the technical reasons along with some additional risk of infections and delayed healing, especially in diabetics. However, there is a growing interest in using bilateral mammary arteries (IMAs).

The radial and the gastroepiploic arteries have been used and studied in several trials.

A large number of clinical trials have been done to show the efficacy of CABG. The names of (using acronyms) some of the famous clinical trials are mentioned below for the reader's interest.

NOBLE

EXCEL

BARI

FREEDOM

ARTS 1-3

BARI-2D

FAME

SYNTAX

SOS

STITCH

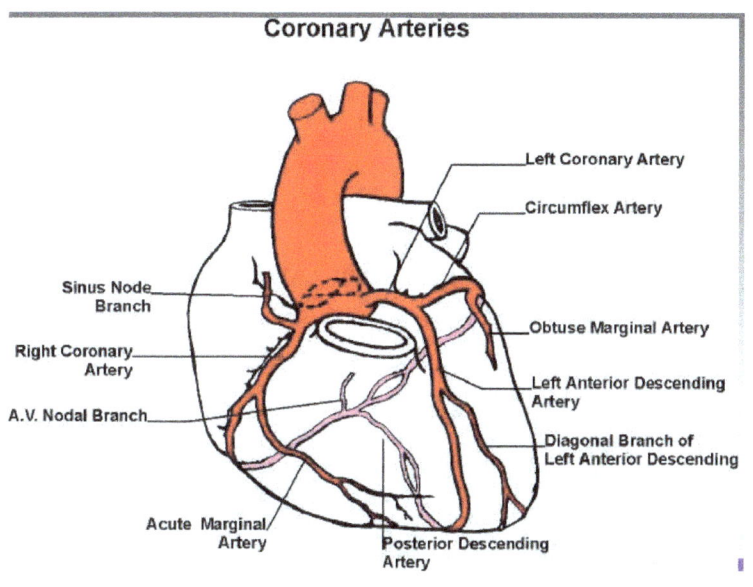

Coronary Arteries

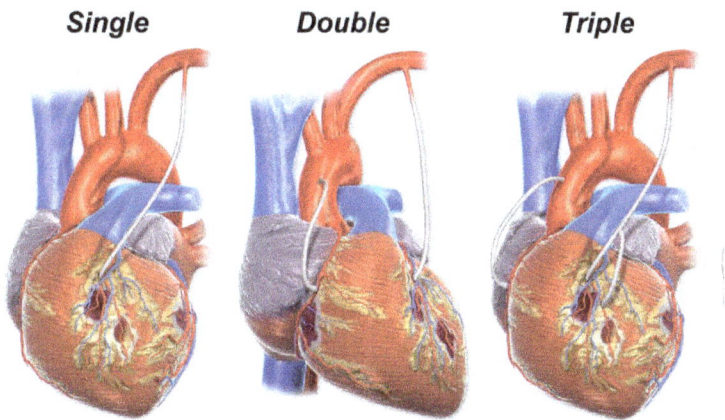

Single *Double* *Triple*

Above: Different kinds of by-pass graft surgical procedures are illustrated (By-pass grafts from the aorta or subclavian arteries are used and inserted after the stenosis or blockage).

The present-day minimally invasive surgery is also a marvelous technique (for certain patient populations) in which the surgery is performed through a small incision from the side of the chest instead of the conventional operation. Generally, an arterial (LIMA) graft is harvested on one of the arteries of the heart, most commonly, the LAD.

Below are some of the angiogram pictures showing extensive coronary artery disease in all the coronary arteries. Patients with such kinds of extensive blockages are commonly referred for by-pass surgery.

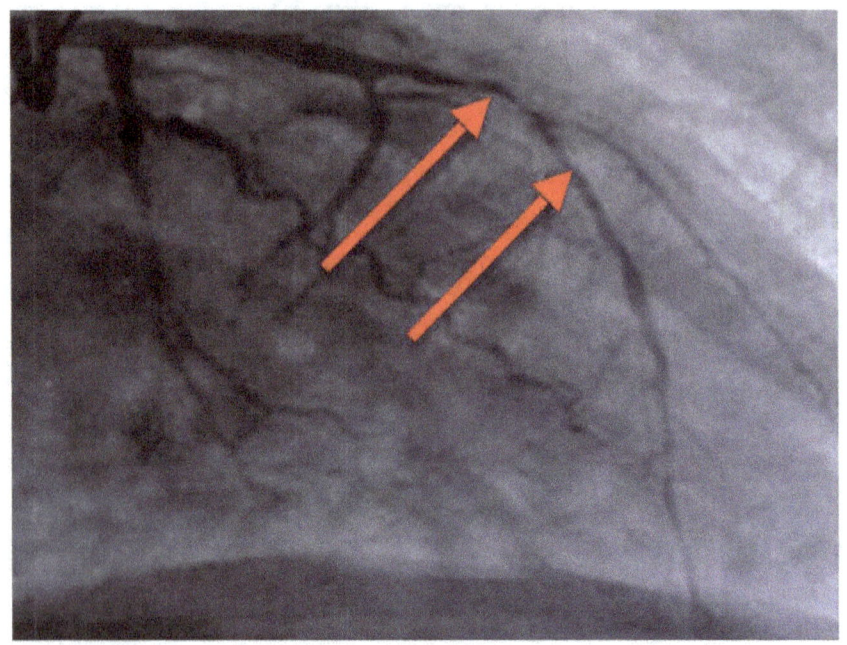

Above. Severe disease of the LAD (arrows)

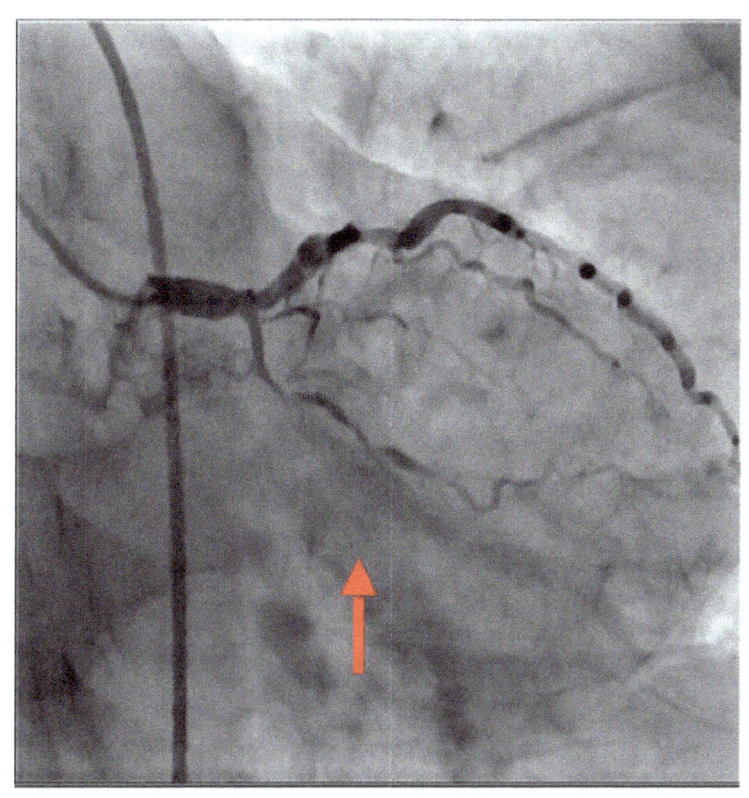

Above. Severe stenosis of the Left Circumflex Artery (arrow)

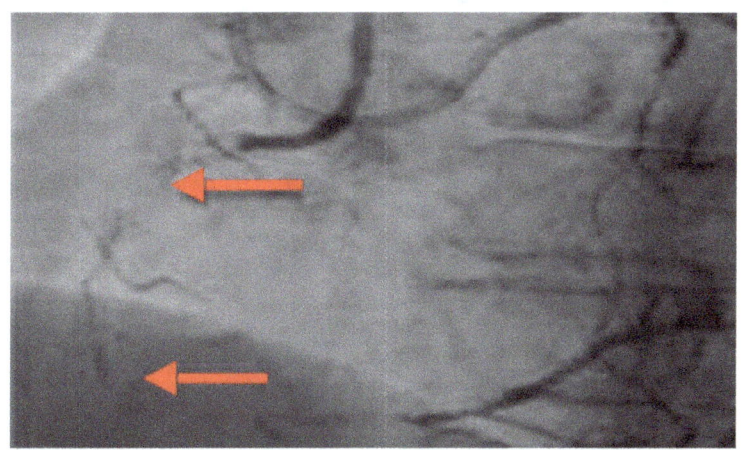

Above. Total occlusion of the right coronary artery (arrows)

The stenosis or blockages in the coronary arteries can also be treated by angioplasty, wherein a significant blockage is dilated by a balloon followed by stent deployment. A very significant stenosis (blockage) in the mid-LAD causing severe chest discomfort (burden), as shown in the figure below, with a red arrow showing severe stenosis.

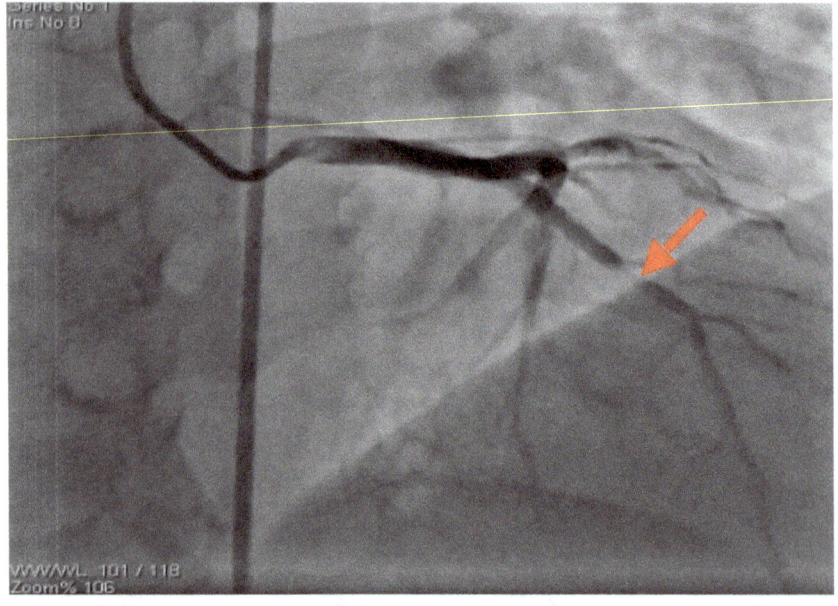

After stent deployment, the lesion is treated *(arrow in the figure below)* causing complete relief in chest discomfort or burden.

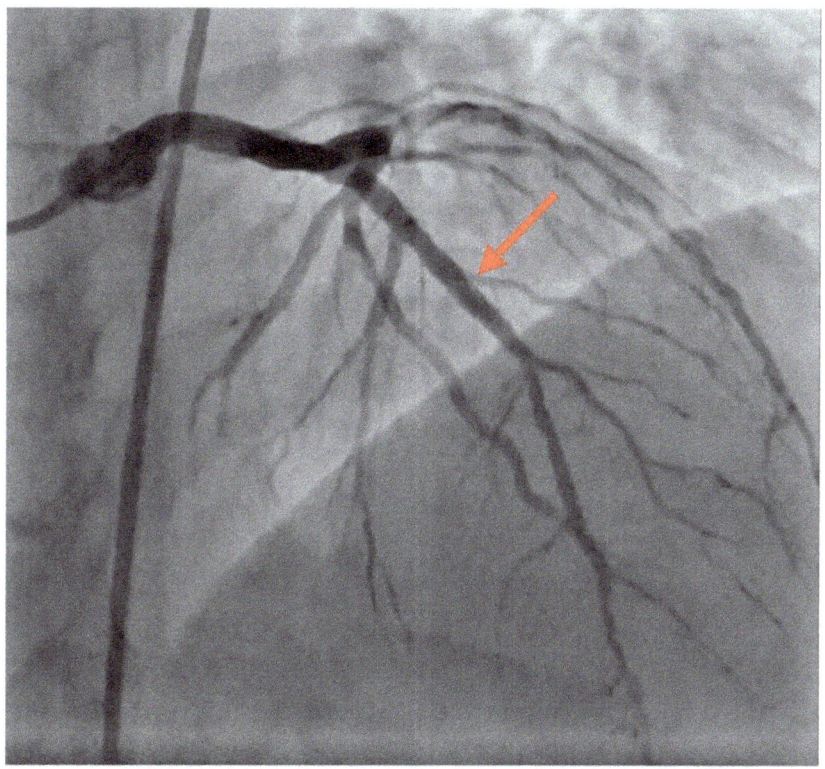

The opening of the chest is not only done to perform a by-pass surgery but is also done for several other indications.

These may include:

Valvular heart diseases
Aortic aneurysms and dissections
Pericardiectomies
Thrombectomies
Surgical myectomy in Hypertrophic Obstructive Cardiomyopathy

Cardiac surgery for Valve diseases:

There are four valves in the heart, each of which may undergo narrowing or widening. The narrowing of the valve creates difficulty for the blood to eject out and it is called *stenosis*. This carries a heavy "burden" on the myocardium and the whole body at large. The other condition (widening of the valves) is called *regurgitation*, which could be due to an abnormal widening of the valvular apparatus or infection of the valve, etc. It creates a back-flow of blood towards the main chamber and causes damage to the myocardium.

Aortic Valve Diseases:

One of the examples is depicted in the following diagram, showing a tri-leaflet normal crispy aortic valve that becomes calcified and thickened. This naturally produces great difficulty in the normal passageway of blood. Over the years, if this condition is not corrected, the myocardium becomes thickened with an extra amount of requirement of blood supply or nourishment. When this imbalance reaches to a critical level, one of the three cardinal signs of Aortic stenosis may ensue, which include syncope, congestive heart failure or angina with a very high rate of mortality if left uncorrected. Traditionally, these valves are related by tissue or mechanical valves.

Currently, for surgically inoperable cases, Transcatheter Aortic Valve Replacement (TAVR) has been introduced with acceptable results.

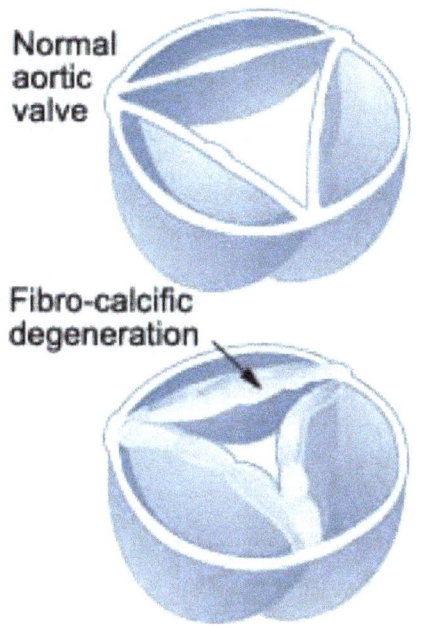

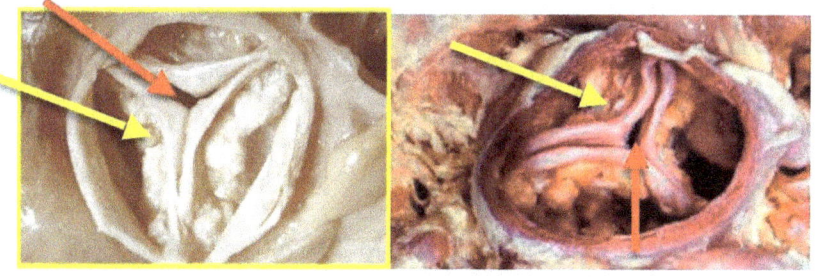

Above, Calcified Aortic valve yellow arrows) with severely reduced opening (red arrows).

The above two pictures show heavily calcified aortic valves causing severe stenosis.

Likewise, the other three valves either undergo stenosis or regurgitation causing heavy *burden* on the myocardium.

Mitral Valve Diseases:

The mitral valve can undergo stenosis (most commonly due to Rheumatic heart disease, especially in the developing world). In addition, it may also undergo leakage or regurgitation. In either case, there is a huge burden on the heart, which needs correction.

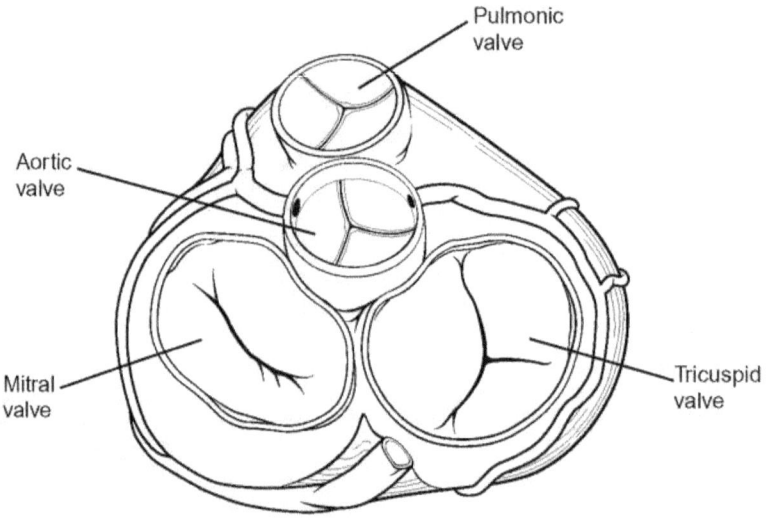

The image above shows the Mitral valve in relation to the other valves in the body.

The Mitral valve apparatus (as shown in the picture below) is composed of:

1. Left atrial wall
2. Annulus
3. Leaflets
4. Chordae Tendineae
5. Papillary Muscles
6. Left ventricular wall

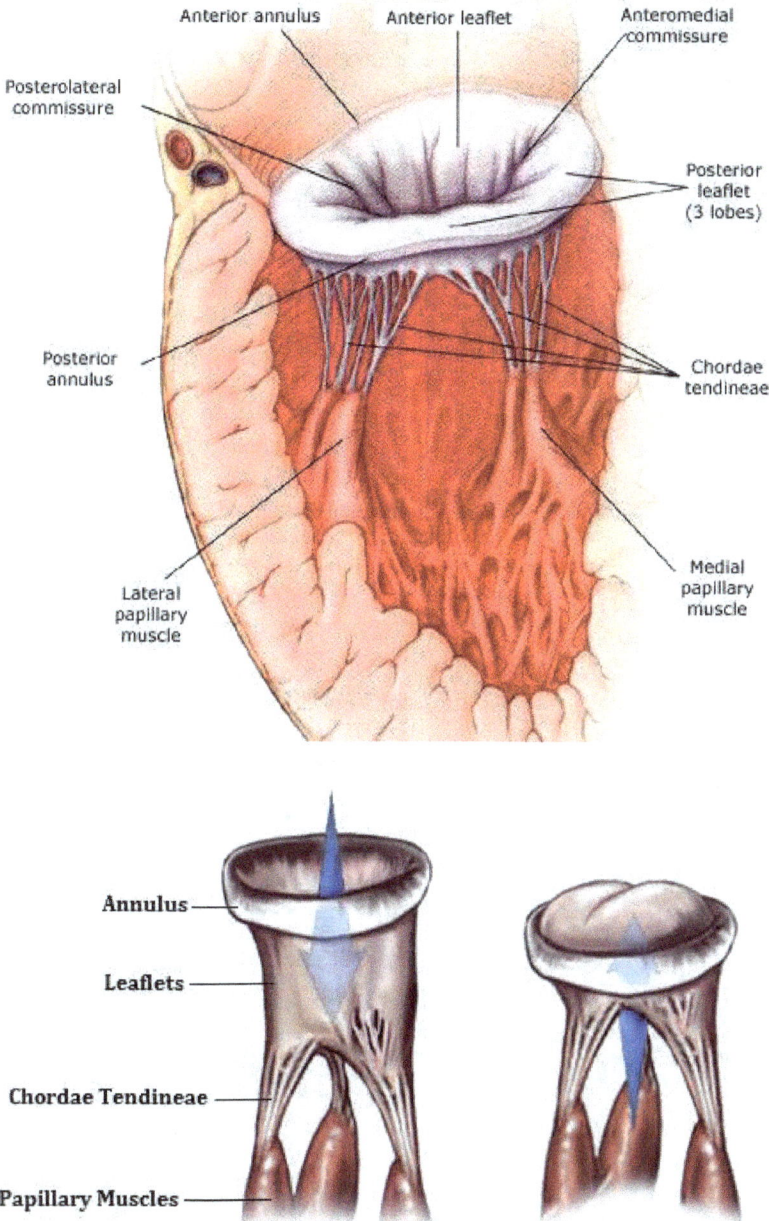

Open mitral valve   Closed mitral valve

187

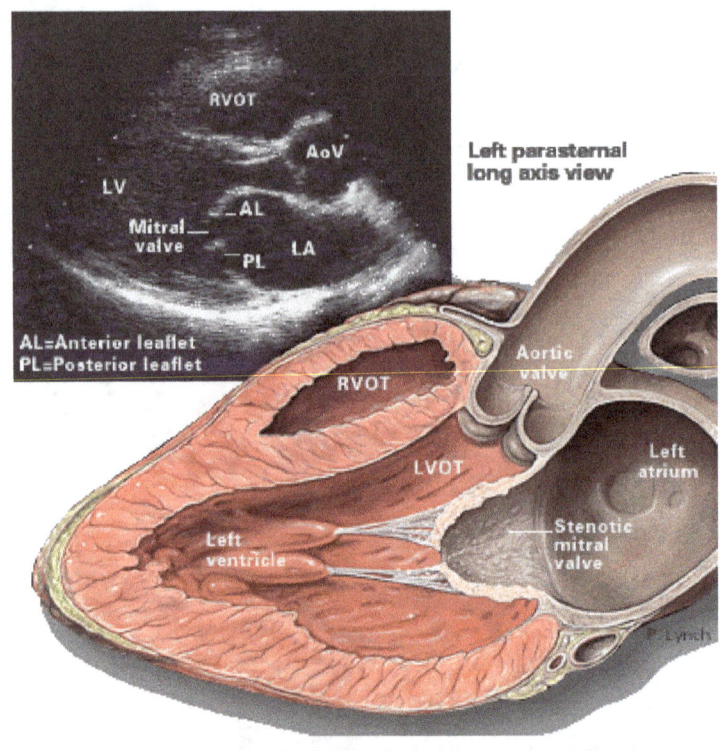

RVOT

AoV

**Left parasternal
long axis view**

LV

Mitral ___ ___ AL
valve

___ PL   LA

AL=Anterior leaflet
PL=Posterior leaflet

Aortic
valve

RVOT

LVOT

Left
atrium

Left
ventricle

Stenotic
mitral
valve

P. Lynch

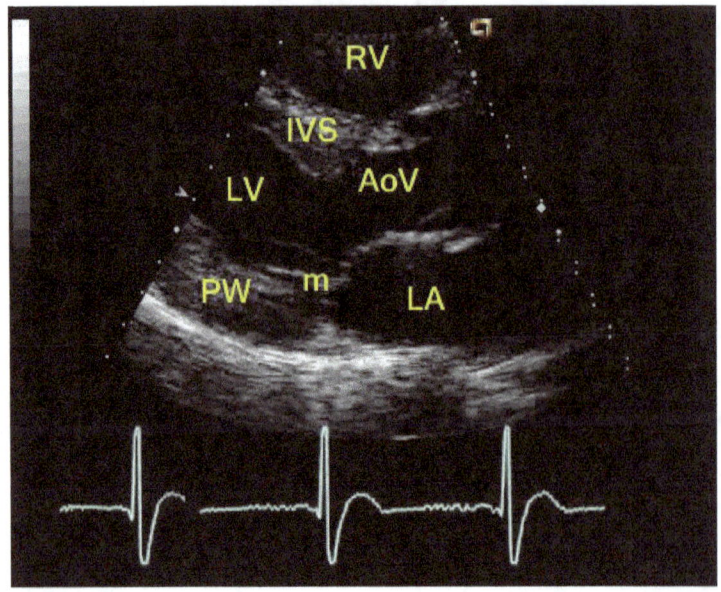

RV

IVS

LV   AoV

PW   m   LA

RV=Right ventricle

LV=Left ventricle

LA=Left atrium

PW=Posterior wall

AoV=Aortic valve

IVS=Interventricular septum

M= Mitral valve

Echocardiographic feature of mitral stenosis (MS) 2D images

In mitral stenosis, there is thickening and fusion of the mitral valve commissural edges and chordae, which will result in a *"doming" appearance of the mitral valve* opening.

Stiffening and calcification of the mitral apparatus are variable and result in further narrowing of the mitral orifice.

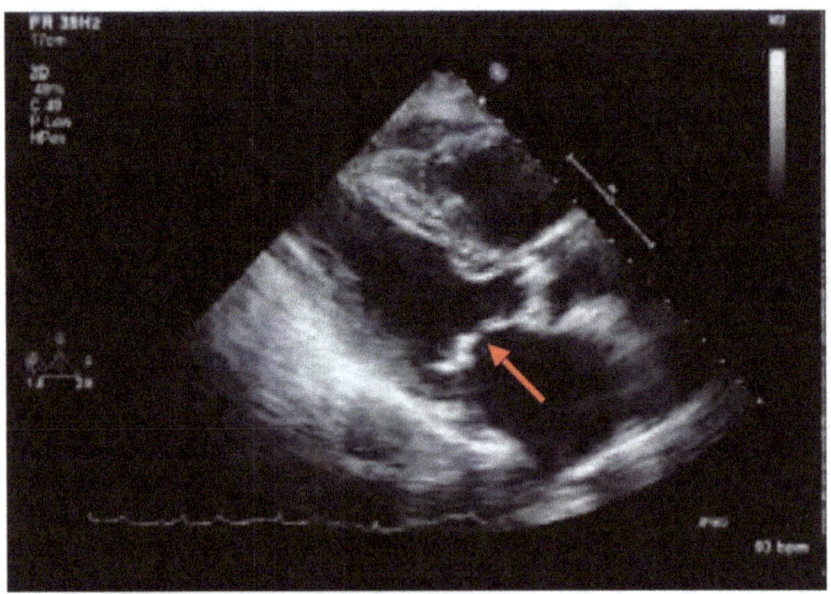

Image above, showing the calcified Anterior mitral valve leaflet (arrow).

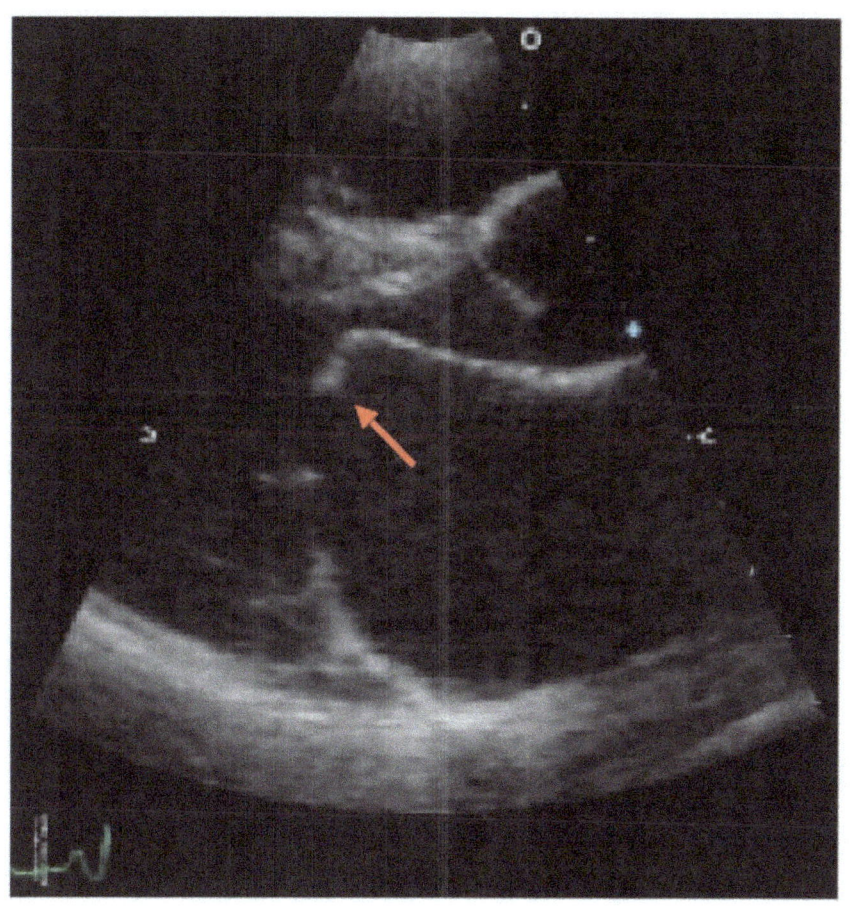

Hockey stick appearance in Mitral stenosis shown (above) in an Echocardiogram (arrow)

Hockey sticks for comparison (above)

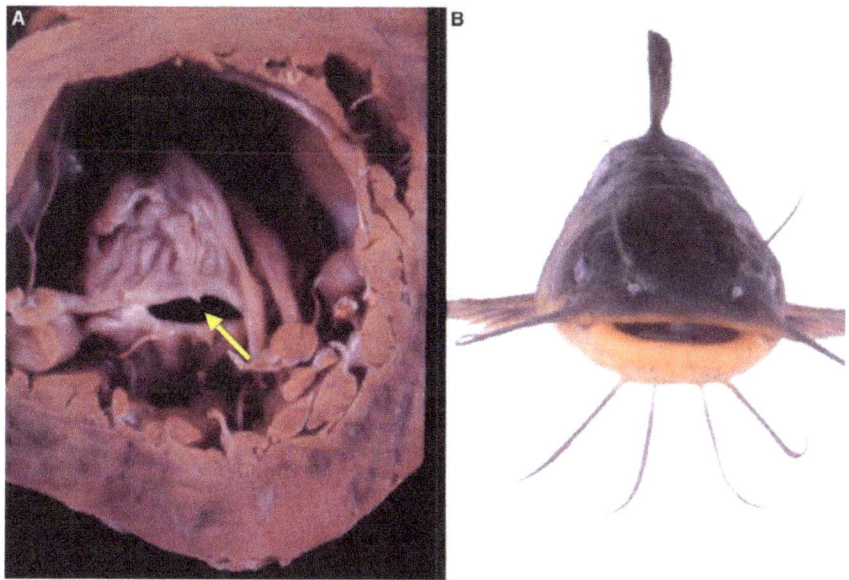

Another picture (above) from a different angle of severe mitral stenosis (arrow) which mimics a "fish-mouth."

The treatment for severe mitral stenosis may include percutaneous mitral balloon valvuloplasty, surgical commissurotomy or mitral valve replacement.

For severe mitral regurgitation, mitral valve replacement has been the standard but now new data is emerging regarding percutaneous repair and or replacement.

Pulmonary Valve Diseases:

This disease pertains to the narrowing of a right-sided valve *(which may be assumed to be a counterpart of the left-sided Aortic valve).* This valve prevents the back-flow of blood from the pulmonary arteries into the right ventricle. If this valve gets thickened, calcified and narrowed, there is an obstruction in normally easy blood flowing from the right ventricle to the lungs via the pulmonary arteries. This obstruction is then overcome by the ventricle, which eventually gets hypertrophied (thicker or more muscular) but at the cost of "chest heaviness or burden," and if left untreated, the right ventricle may begin to fail.

The following pictures show a normal and abnormal pulmonary valve.

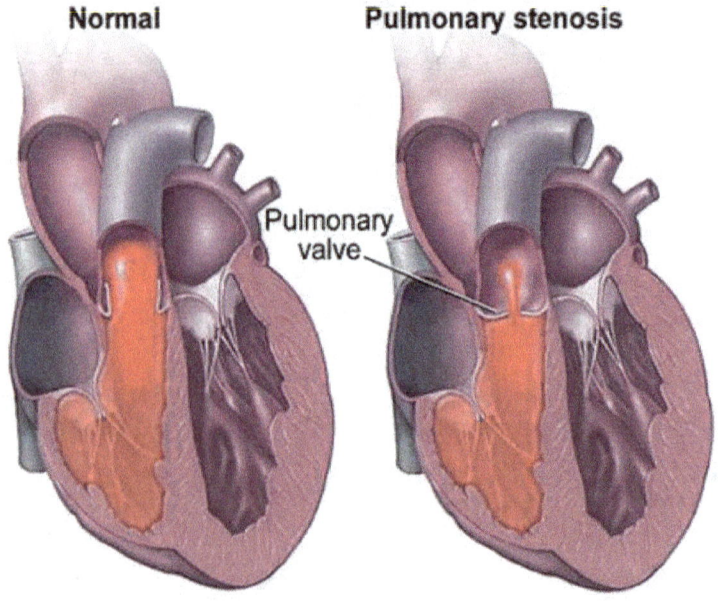

On the other hand, if the valve shows severe leakage or regurgitation, this needs treatment. In both cases, either percutaneous or surgical treatment is available depending on the indication.

Tricuspid Valve:

Similarly, the Tricuspid valve may undergo stenosis or regurgitation, requiring surgical or even percutaneous treatment.

Hypertrophic Cardiomyopathy (HCM):

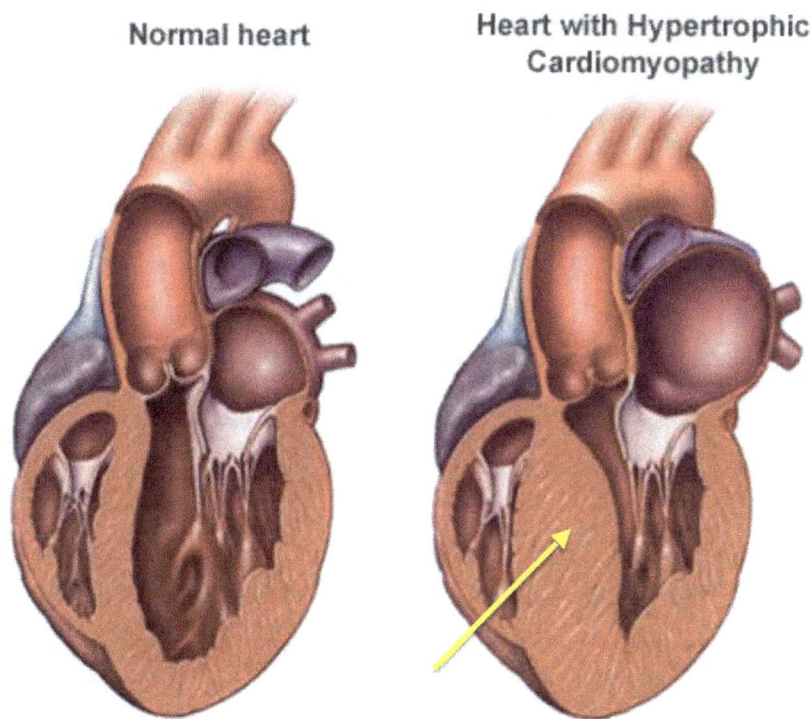

Significant thickening of the septum (arrow)

HCM is a congenital disease with a prevalence of 1/500 and is a genetic disease wherein the left ventricular walls undergo severe thickness *(hypertrophy)*. This results in the development of a significant intra-cavitary pressure gradient, which can result in chest pain *(burden or chest heaviness)*, dizziness, syncope and arrhythmias.

There are several ways of treating this condition. This includes aggressive medical management, including beta-blockers, calcium channel blockers, and recently introduced novel medicines like Mavacamten. The management also involves avoidance of after-load reducing agents and diuretics. The more invasive management includes alcohol septal ablation and myomectomy. Both treatment modalities have their own pros and cons.

The above is yet another example of "chest heaviness or burden," which can be deduced from the illustrious verses of the Holy Quran.

This concludes the chapter in which we tried to shed some light on various types of diseases causing a significant burden on the heart with the treatment options of open heart surgery in light of verses from the Holy Quran, and of course, ALLAH AL-MIGHTY is the All-Knowing.

Chapter 7
(Synopsis)
Turning or twisting of the Hearts

An interesting concept is discussed in this chapter. This relates to a phenomenon that hearts "turn," "twist," or perhaps "deviate from their axes" during their contraction. We will discuss this more in the light of the following beautiful and thought-provoking Holy verses from the Holy Quran.

Let's review some of the Holy verses:

رَبَّـنَا لَا تُـزِغْ قُلُـوْبَـنَا بَـعْدَ اِذْ هَدَيْـتَـنَا وَهَبْ لَـنَا مِنْ لَّـدُنْـكَ رَحْمَةً اِنَّكَ اَنْـتَ الْـوَهَّـابُ

"Our Lord, do not let our *hearts deviate* from the right path after You have given us guidance, and bestow upon us mercy from Your own. Surely, You, and You alone, are the One who bestows in abundance."
(Al Imran: The Family of Imran: Chapter 3; verse 8)

وَنُقَلِّبُ اَفْـــــِدَتَـهُمْ وَ اَبْصَارَهُمْ كَمَا لَـمْ يُؤْمِنُوْا بِـهٖ اَوَّلَ مَرَّةٍ وَّنَـذَرُهُمْ فِـيْ طُغْيَـانِـهِمْ يَـعْمَهُوْنَ

"We will upset their hearts and sights, as they did not believe in them at the first instance, and We will leave them wandering blindly in their rebellion."
(Al-Anaam: *The Cattle:* Chapter 6; verse 110)

197

مَنْ خَشِيَ الـرَّحْمٰنَ بِـالْـغَيْبِ وَجَاۤ ءَ بِـقَـلْبٍ
مُّنِـيْبٍ

"the one who feared Rahman (The All-Merciful ALLAH), without
seeing Him, and came up with a *heart oriented* towards Him.
(Qaaf: *Qaf:* Chapter 50; verse 33)

وَ اِذْ قَالَ مُوْسٰى لِقَوْمِهٖ يٰقَوْمِ لِمَ تُؤْذُوْنَنِيْ
وَقَـدْ تَّـعْـلَـمُوْنَ اَنِّـىْ رَسُوْلُ اللهِ اِلَـيْكُمْ فَلَمَّا
زَاغُوْۤا اَزَاغَ اللهُ قُـلُـوْبَـهُمْ وَ اللهُ لَا يَـهْدِي
الْـقَـوْمَ الْـفٰسِقِـيْنَ

"And (remember) when Musa said to his people, O my people, why
do you hurt me, while you know that I am a messenger of ALLAH
sent towards you. So, when they adopted deviation, ALLAH let their
hearts become deviate. And ALLAH does not guide the sinful
people."
(As-Saff: *The Ranks*: Chapter 61; verse 5)

It is a known fact that the heart makes rotation along its long axis and
a wringing (twisting) motion during its contraction. Several
techniques are available nowadays to study this phenomenon.

This "movement" of the heart is largely due to the orientation of
myocardial fibers. Myocardial fibers (muscle fibers of the heart
muscle) in the sub-epicardium (the outer layer) run helically in a left-
handed direction, fibers in the mid layer run circumferentially, and
fibers in the sub-endocardium (inner layer) run a right-handed
direction helically.

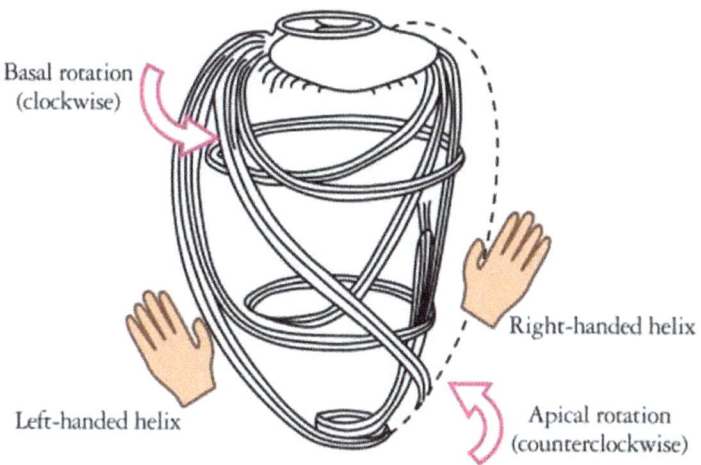

Basal rotation (clockwise)

Right-handed helix

Left-handed helix

Apical rotation (counterclockwise)

Figure above: Myocardial fiber orientation and direction of rotation

When myocardial fibers on the sub-epicardial side contract, clockwise rotational torque is produced at the base and counterclockwise rotational torque at the apex. When myocardial fibers on the sub-endocardial side contract, counterclockwise rotational torque is produced at the base and clockwise rotational torque at the apex.

There are four fundamental motions that include narrowing, shortening, lengthening, and widening.

The deviation or tilt of the heart may be explained in more than one way:

The twist may occur while there is a congenital (by birth) absence of pericardium (the layer surrounding the heart).

The embryological twist (movement or twist of the heart during its development)

Anatomical twist which could be physiological (e.g. during different phases of respiration) or pathological (e.g. in ventricular hypertrophy or thickened walls of the heart)

This interesting phenomenon is further mentioned below in more detail.

Chapter 7:
Turning or twisting of the Hearts

In this chapter, we will try to elaborate on the concept that during their contraction, hearts "turn," "twist," or perhaps "deviate from their axes," for that matter, in the light of the following beautiful and thought-provoking Holy verses from the Holy Quran. What we have endeavored in this manuscript is just another dimension to see the implications of the Holy Verses in our daily life, and of course, the real meaning is known to ALLAH alone.

Let's review some of the Holy verses.

رَبَّنَا لَا تُزِغْ قُلُوبَنَا بَعْدَ اِذْ هَدَيْتَنَا وَهَبْ لَنَا مِنْ لَّدُنْكَ رَحْمَةً اِنَّكَ اَنْتَ الْوَهَّابُ

" :Our Lord, do not let our *hearts deviate* from the right path after You have given us guidance, and bestow upon us mercy from Your own. Surely, You, and You alone, are the One who bestows in abundance."
(Al Imran: *The Family of Imran:* Chapter 3; verse 8)

وَنُقَلِّبُ اَفْـِـدَتَهُمْ وَاَبْصَارَهُمْ كَمَا لَمْ يُؤْمِنُوا بِهٖ اَوَّلَ مَرَّةٍ وَّنَذَرُهُمْ فِيْ طُغْيَانِهِمْ يَعْمَهُوْنَ

201

"We will upset their hearts and sights, as they did not believe in them at the first instance, and We will leave them wandering blindly in their rebellion."

(Al-Anaam: *The Cattle:* Chapter 6; verse 110)

مَنْ خَشِيَ الــرَّحْمٰنَ بِـالْـغَيْبِ وَجَآءَ بِـقَـلْبٍ مُّـنِـيْبٍ

"the one who feared Rahman (The All-Merciful ALLAH), without seeing Him, and came up with a *heart oriented* towards Him.
(Qaaf: *Qaf:* Chapter 50; verse 33)

وَ اِذْ قَـالَ مُـوْسٰى لِـقَـوْمِهٖ يٰـقَـوْمِ لِـمَ تُـؤْذُ وْنَـنِيْ وَقَـدْ تَّـعْـلَـمُـوْنَ اَنِّـىْ رَسُوْلُ اللهِ اِلَـيْـكُمْ فَـلَـمَّـا زَاغُوْٓا اَزَاغَ اللهُ قُـلُـوْبَـهُمْ وَ اللهُ لَا يَـهْدِي الْـقَـوْمَ الْـفٰسِقِـيْنَ

"And (remember) when Musa said to his people, O my people, why do you hurt me, while you know that I am a messenger of ALLAH sent towards you. So, when they adopted deviation, ALLAH let their *hearts become deviate*. And ALLAH does not guide the sinful people."

(As-Saff: *The Ranks*: Chapter 61; verse 5)

In view of these Holy verses, let's try to understand the rotation or deviation of the heart from its axis.

It is a known fact that the heart makes *rotation* along its long axis and a wringing (twisting) motion during its movement. Several techniques are available to study this phenomenon. These include: embedding radiopaque markers in the myocardium, observing their movements through biplane cine angiography, and making observations with sonomicrometry in animal hearts.

Other techniques may include: magnetic resonance imaging (MRI) tagging and, now more recently, a 2-dimensional speckle tracking echocardiography, which promises a high degree of accuracy.

Measurement of ventricular torsion by two-dimensional ultrasound speckle tracking imaging.

Notomi Y, Lysyansky P, Setser RM, Shiota T, Popović ZB, Martin-Miklovic MG, Weaver JA, Oryszak SJ, Greenberg NL, White RD, Thomas JD: J Am Coll Cardiol. 2005 Jun 21; 45(12): 2034-41.

Several terms, such as left ventricular rotation, twist and torsion, are used interchangeably. "Rotation" is a rotatory movement about the center of the mass in the left ventricular short-axis image.

Twist mechanics of the left ventricle: principles and application. Sengupta PP, Tajik AJ, Chandrasekaran K, Khandheria BK JACC Cardiovasc Imaging. 2008 May; 1(3): 366-76.

In the normal heart, the base rotates clockwise during systole (contraction), and the apex rotates counterclockwise, producing a wringing motion. The difference in turning angle between the base and apex is called the "net twist angle" or "net torsion angle," expressed in degrees. Looking from the apex, counterclockwise rotation is expressed with positive values and clockwise rotation with negative values, generally in units of degrees.

"Torsion" and "twist" are often used interchangeably. While the twist is sometimes used simply to mean wringing, torsion is more accurately defined as the base-to-apex gradient in rotation angle along the long axis of the left ventricle, expressed in degrees per centimeter.

Left ventricular torsion is equal in mice and humans.

Henson RE, Song SK, Pastorek JS, Ackerman JJ, Lorenz CH Am J Physiol Heart Circ Physiol. 2000 Apr; 278(4): H1117-23.

It is also interesting to know that these left ventricular twists vary from infancy to adulthood, where they increase gradually; however, with subsequent increasing age in adult life, sub-endocardial function may gradually attenuate, and LV twist increases further.

This "movement" of the heart is largely due to the orientation of myocardial fibers. As it was discussed in the chapter, "One (Helical) Heart" and in the figure below, it should be noted that myocardial fibers in the sub-epicardium run helically in a left-handed direction, fibers in the mid layer run circumferentially, and fibers in the sub-endocardium run helically in a right-handed direction.

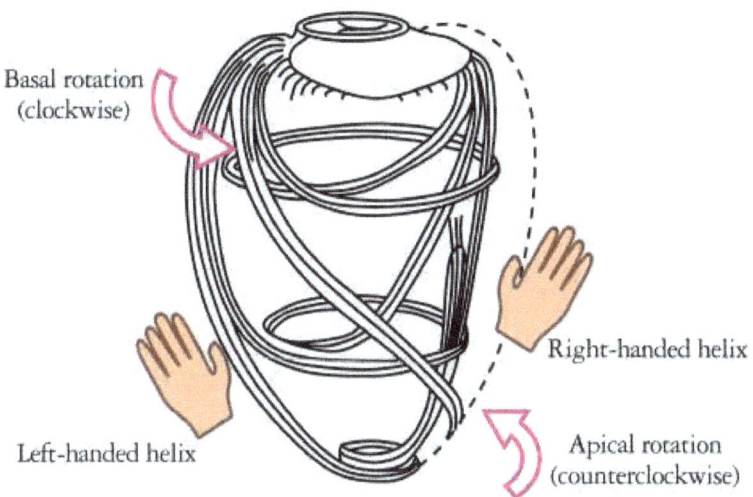

Figure above: Myocardial fiber orientation and direction of rotation

Left Ventricular Rotation and Twist: Why Should We Learn? Satoshi Nakatani, MD, PhD

When myocardial fibers on the sub-epicardial side contract, clockwise rotational torque is produced at the base and counterclockwise rotational torque at the apex. When myocardial fibers on the sub-endocardial side contract, counterclockwise rotational torque is produced at the base and clockwise rotational torque at the apex, as mentioned below in the figure.

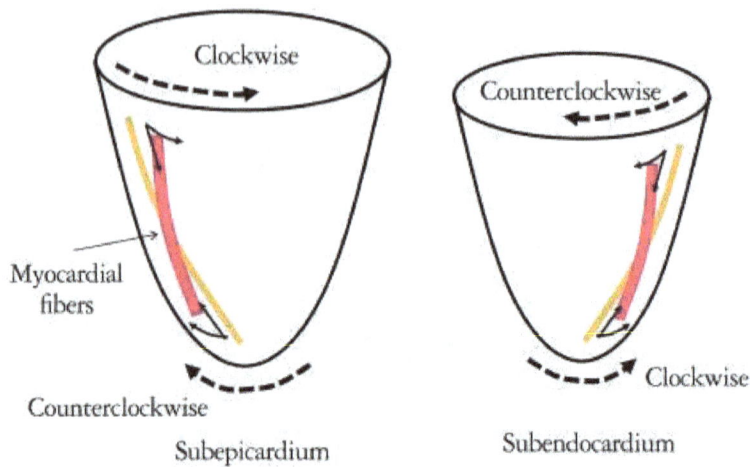

Figure above: Myocardial contraction and rotation

This orientation and the peculiar movement result in an opposite rotation at the base and apex.

This LV twist may be significantly altered in diseases like dilated cardiomyopathy, valvular heart diseases and myocardial ischemia.

Buckberg et al. mentioned that the predominant motion of the heart is not constricting and dilating but rather shortening and narrowing. There are four fundamental motions that include narrowing, shortening, lengthening, and widening which are discussed in detail in a separate chapter.

The deviation or twist of the heart may be explained in more than one way.

- The twist interplays with the presence or absence of the pericardium.

- The embryological twist

- Anatomical twist, which could be *physiological,* e.g. during different phases of respiration or *pathological,* e.g. in Left ventricular hypertrophy etc.

TWIST DUE TO DEFECTED PERICARDIUM:

The rotation and twist of the heart were found to be decreased in patients with congenital pericardial defects without any change in regional myocardial strains, as studied by Tanaka et al.

Contribution of the pericardium to left ventricular torsion and regional myocardial function in patients with total absence of the left pericardium.

Tanaka H, Oishi Y, Mizuguchi Y, Miyoshi H, Ishimoto T, Nagase N, Yamada H, Oki T. J Am Soc Echocardiogr. 2008; 21: 268–274.

In an animal study by Chang et al., the twist angle before and after incision of the pericardium, was measured and also after the pericardium was re-sutured. They found that the twist was reduced as a result of pericardiotomy and increased again as a result of re-suturing of the pericardium. This was attributed to changes in left ventricular shape that occurred as a result of pericardiotomy.

Role of pericardium in the maintenance of left ventricular twist. Chang SA, Kim HK, Kim YJ, Cho GY, Oh S, Sohn DW. Heart. 2010; 96: 785–790.

THE EMBRYOLOGICAL TWIST:

Before we discuss the abnormal blood circulation as a result of an embryological "twist," let's discuss what is the normal mechanism of blood flow in the body.

Pure and oxygenated blood comes from the lungs via pulmonary veins into the left atrium, which then goes to the left ventricle, and the latter ejects it to the aorta, from where it gets transported to the whole body and supplies pure oxygen and nutrients. The same blood (which is now less in oxygen) gets drained through the venous system, into the right atrium, from where it goes to the right ventricle and then goes to the lungs via pulmonary arteries for cleaning. It then comes back to the left atrium via pulmonary veins, and this cycle continues throughout the life. Therefore:

LA -> LV -> Aorta (pure, oxygenated blood to entire body) -> (via venous system to) RA -> RV -> Pulmonary arteries (impure, deoxygenated blood to lungs for purification -> (back to LA via pulmonary veins)

LA=Left atrium; LV= Left ventricle; RA= Right atrium; RV= Right ventricle

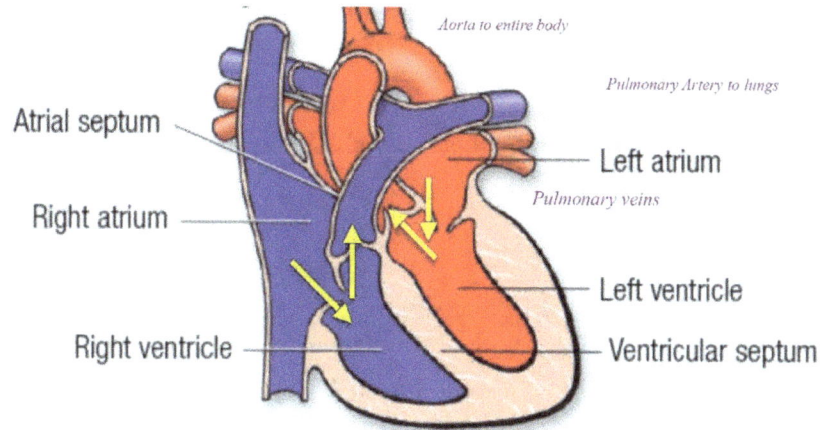

During embryological development, a "wrong twist" may result in an unnatural manifestation of the cardiac chambers.

This class of "twist" may be explained by the following examples:

Complete Transposition of the Great Arteries (Complete TGA):

The word transposition may be explained as a switch in position.

In this condition, the aorta arises from the right ventricle instead of the left ventricle and the pulmonary artery from the left ventricle instead of the right ventricle. So, the morphological right atrium is connected to the morphological right ventricle from where the aorta arises, and the morphological left atrium is connected to the morphological left ventricle from where the pulmonary trunk originates.

(In other words, there is Atrio-ventricular concordance and ventriculo-arterial discordance).

Complete TGA is a cyanotic heart defect that almost invariably results in death in infancy or early childhood if left untreated. The morphological etiology of complete TGA is an *inverted or arrested rotation of the heart outflow tract,* by which the aorta is transposed in the right ventral direction to the pulmonary trunk. It is also called d-TGA *(or Dextro-TGA).*

The result of this abnormal arrangement is that the low-oxygen systemic venous blood travels through the right heart, the aorta, the systemic circulation, and then back to the right heart. Oxygenated blood travels through the pulmonary veins, left heart, pulmonary arteries, and then back to the left heart. Thus, the systemic and pulmonary circulations run in *parallel rather than in series.*

More simplistically speaking, *the blood flow is from the atria to the correct ventricles and then from these ventricles through the wrong arteries to the body and lungs, respectively.*

i.e. Left Atrium → Left Ventricle -> Pulmonary arteries to lungs; and Right Atrium → Right Ventricle -> Aorta to the entire body

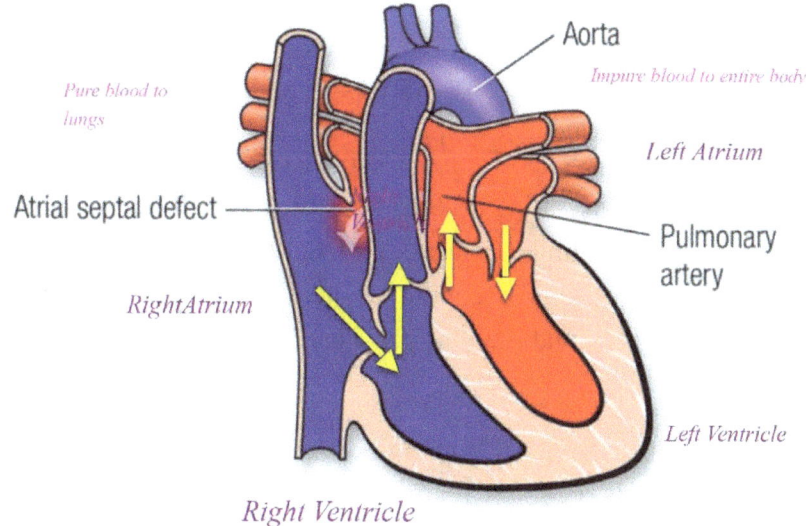

Labels within figure:
Aorta

Pure blood to lungs

Impure blood to entire body

Left Atrium

Atrial septal defect

Pulmonary artery

RightAtrium

Left Ventricle

Right Ventricle

The figure above: D-TGA with yellow arrows showing the path of blood circulation.

Unless the oxygen-rich and oxygen-poor blood can mix, at some place through the circulation, the organs of the body will not get the required oxygen. Naturally it is not compatible with life if not corrected. The survival depends on adequate mixing of the two circulations, through openings across the cardiac chambers, namely Atrial Septal Defect (ASD), Ventricular Septal Defect (VSD) or Patent Ductus Arteriosus (PDA).

Treatment:

The surgical procedure of choice is the *Arterial Switch Operation (ASO), (which results in the LV acting as the systemic ventricle).*

This surgery involves cutting off the aorta and pulmonary arteries just above the point of exiting the heart, and then they are reconnected to the proper ventricles. This procedure eventually reconstructs the heart to a normal situation, and the long-term cardiac function is expected to be excellent.

Patients with the combination of complete TGA, VSD, and Pulmonary Stenosis (PS) may require a *Rastelli procedure.*

Many adults with complete TGA have undergone an *Atrial Switch Procedure. (Mustard procedure).*

Annual follow-up with a cardiologist experienced in the management of adult congenital heart disease is recommended

Congenitally corrected Transposition of the Great Arteries (ccTGA):

Congenitally corrected transposition of the great arteries (ccTGA) is a rare heart defect in which *the heart's lower half is reversed.* It is also called L-TGA *(or levo-TGA)*

CcTGA is characterized by atrioventricular discordance and ventriculo-arterial discordance. Systemic venous blood passes from the right atrium through the mitral valve into the morphologic left ventricle to the pulmonary artery. Oxygenated blood then returns from the lungs to the left atrium through the tricuspid valve into the morphologic right ventricle and then out of the aorta.

Left Atrium→ Right Ventricle →Aorta (to whole body)

And,

Right Atrium → Left Ventricle →Pulmonary Artery (to lungs)

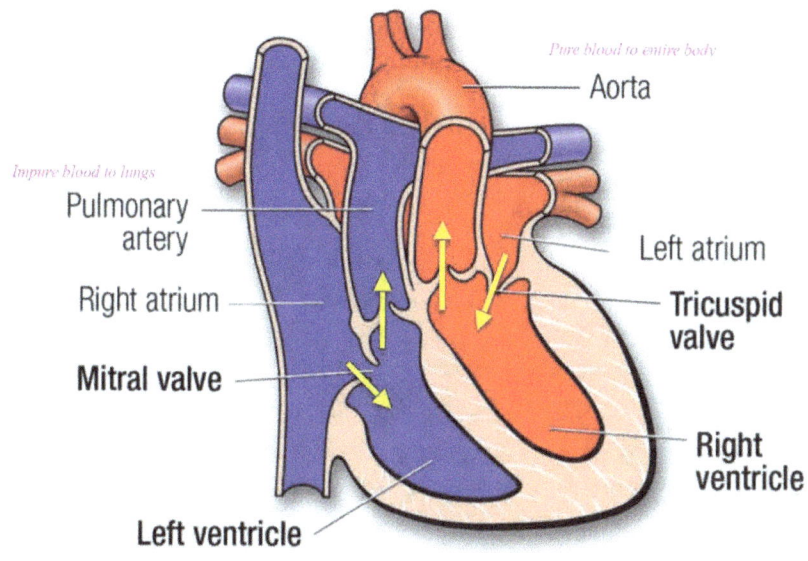

The figure above: L-TGA with yellow arrows showing the path of blood circulation.

This results in normal systemic arterial oxygenation; however, the RV is the systemic ventricle in this arrangement. This diagnosis may be made for the first time in adulthood, particularly in patients without associated lesions.

This condition is less dangerous than the d-TGA due to the reversal of the great arteries.

Many adults with congenitally corrected TGA consider themselves to be *asymptomatic*. Until the age of 45 years, 60% of patients with associated cardiac lesions and over 70% of patients without associated lesions fall into this category. However, up to two-thirds of patients with associated cardiac lesions and one-quarter of those without other associated lesions have congestive heart failure.

Surgical approaches have been developed to create an "anatomical repair," with the goal of addressing any associated defects and allowing the LV to be the systemic ventricle.

The Anatomical Twist:

The analogy of "deviation" of hearts may be explained by electrical forces during both physiological (e.g. during different phases of respiration and pathological circumstances (e.g. in Left Ventricular Hypertrophy etc.)

QRS axis:

The electrical heart axis is an average of all depolarizations in the heart. The depolarization wave begins in the right atrium and proceeds to the left and right ventricle. Because the left ventricular wall is thicker than the right ventricular wall and makes up most of the heart muscle under normal circumstances, the arrow indicating the direction of the depolarization wave is directed to the left, as mentioned in the figure on the next page.

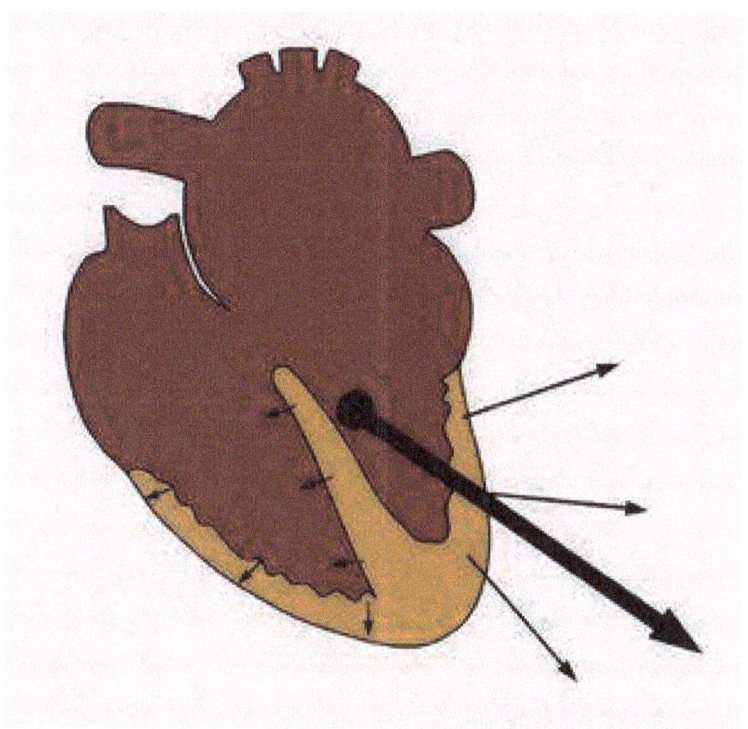

The heart axis indicates the average direction of the depolarization wave. A normal heart axis, as shown in the image above, is between -30 and +90 degrees. In this example, the heart axis is +45 degrees.

Electrical Axis Classification

There are five main electrical axis classifications:

- Normal axis *(A normal heart axis is between -30 and +90 degrees)*

- Left axis deviation; LAD. (A *left heart axis* is present when the QRS axis is between -30 and -90 degrees)

- Right axis deviation; RAD. (A *right heart axis* is present when the QRS axis is between +90 and +180)

- Extreme axis deviation. (An *extreme heart axis* is present when the axis is between +180 and -90 degrees)

- Indeterminate axis (*If the QRS complex is isoelectric or equiphasic in all leads with no dominant QRS deflection*).

Lévy S. Diagnostic approach to cardiac arrhythmias. J Cardiovasc Pharmacol. 1991; 17 Suppl 6: S24-31.

Abnormal heart axis

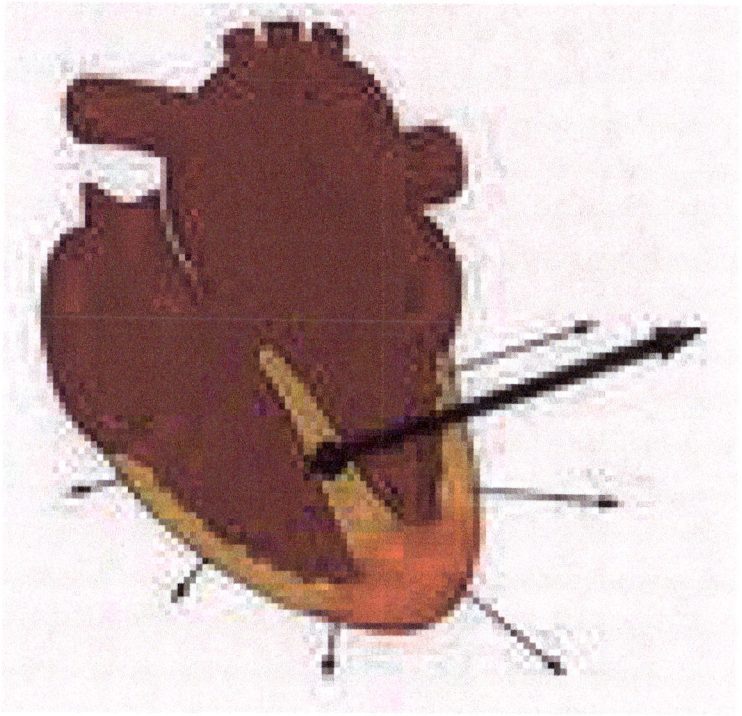

Heart axis deviation to the left in case of an inferior infarct. Left anterior fascicular block is also a common cause. A left axis is between -30 and -90 degrees. In this case, the axis is -30 degrees.

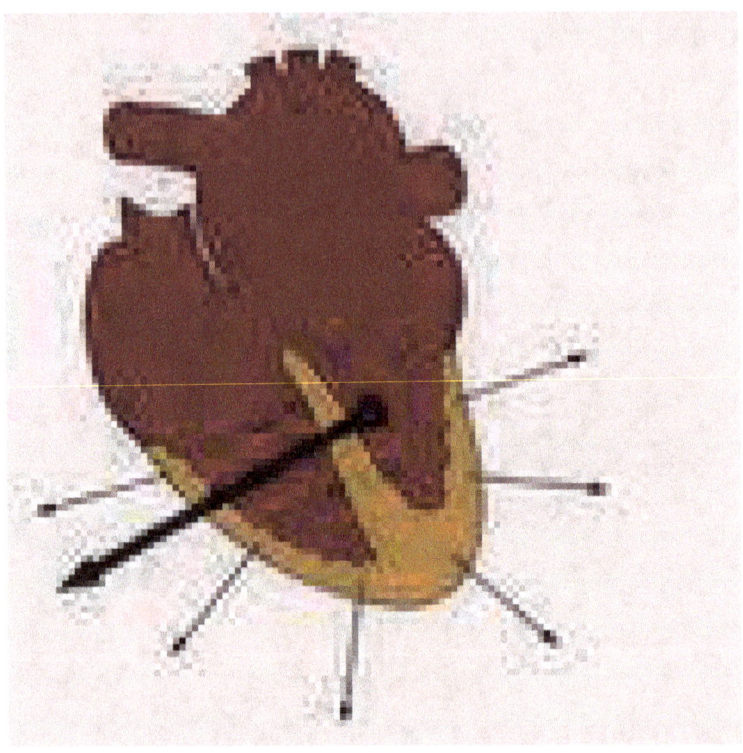

Heart axis deviation to the right in right ventricular load, as in COPD or pulmonary embolism. A right axis is between +90 and +180 degrees. In this case, the axis is +135 degrees.

The direction of the vector can change under different circumstances:

- When the heart itself is *rotated* (right ventricular overload), obviously, the axis turns with it.

- In the case of ventricular hypertrophy, the axis will deviate toward the greater electrical activity, and the vector will turn toward the hypertrophied tissue.

- Infarcted tissue is electrically dead. No electrical activity is registered, and the QRS vector turns away from the infarcted tissue.

Left axis deviation

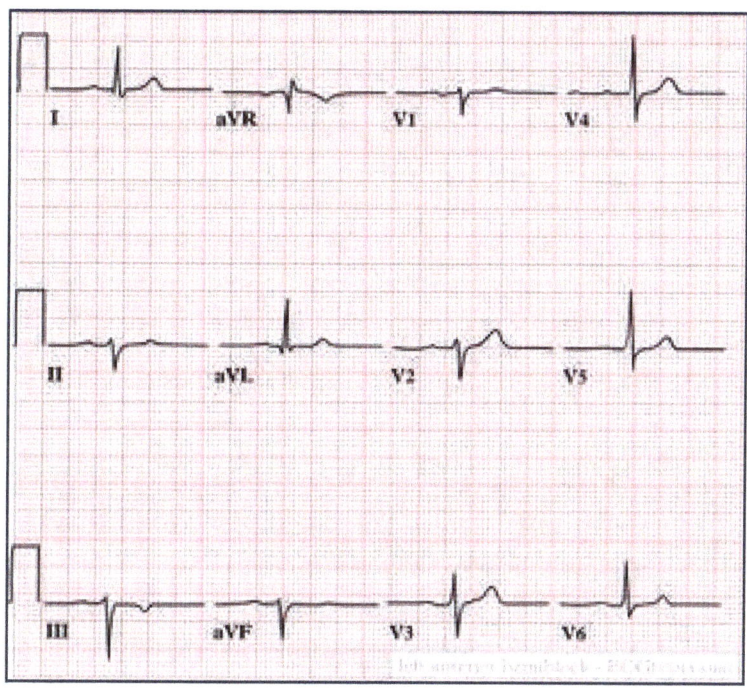

Causes of left axis deviation include:

1. Normal variation (physiologic, often with age)

2. Mechanical shifts, such as expiration, high diaphragm (pregnancy, ascites, abdominal tumor)

3. Conduction defects: left bundle branch block, left anterior fascicular block

4. Congenital heart disease (e.g. Primum atrial septal defect; Endocardial cushion defect)

5. Ventricular ectopic rhythm

6. Pacemaker rhythm

Right axis deviation

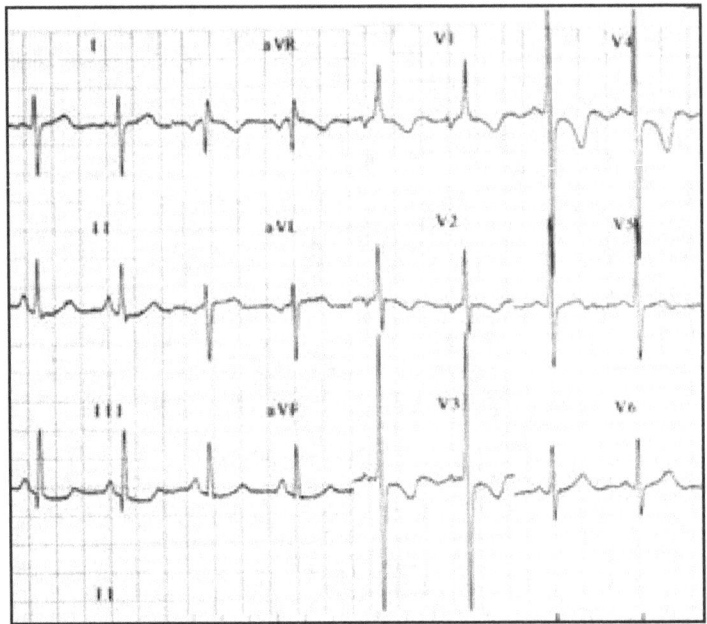

Causes of right axis deviation include:

- Normal variation (vertical heart with an axis of 90°)
- Mechanical shifts, such as inspiration and emphysema
- Conduction defects: left posterior fascicular block, right bundle branch block
- Dextrocardia
- Ventricular ectopic rhythms
- Limb-lead reversal (left- and right-arm electrodes)
- Lateral wall myocardial infarction
- Right ventricular load, for example, pulmonary embolism or cor pulmonale (as in COPD)

QRS Axis in the Frontal Plane (ÅQRSF):

The normal QRS complex is very variable in the frontal leads and quite uniform in the horizontal leads.

In the frontal leads, the direction of the QRS vector depends on body weight, body position and age. *Generally, the mean QRS axis undergoes a rotation from right to left during aging.* The reason is probably the increasing electric preponderance of the left ventricle compared to the right.

Location of the QRS axis at different ages:

The figure on the next page demonstrates the location of the QRS axis at different ages. At birth, the axis is considerably to the right, averaging +90 to +110 and even, occasionally, lies even further to the right. As the child grows and the body shape and heart shape both changes, the axis moves leftward until about 6 to 8 months of age, at which time the normal adult position of the axis is usually established. Occasionally, some right axis deviation persists into later years. It is also evident in the *figure below* that some degree of left-axis deviation is seen in normal individuals, reading -30 at times.

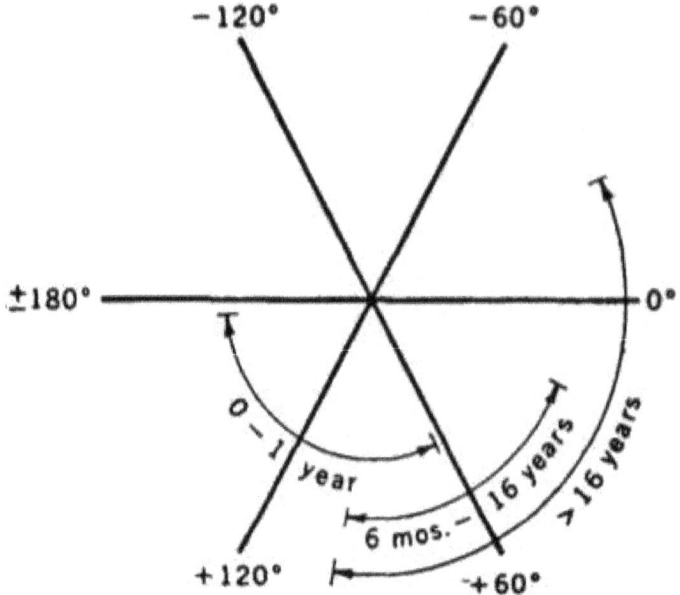

The table below shows the common ÅQRSF axis (found in about 70% of normal individuals) in relation to age.

Table below: Age-related change in QRS axis in the frontal plane (ÅQRSF):

Years	*ÅQRSF*
0–2	+ 120°
2–10	+ 90°
10–25	+ 70°
25–40	+ 60°
40–70	+20°
70–90	– 20°

The most spectacular alterations of the QRS axis without heart disease are seen in people with thoracic deformation or after resection of one lung.

Deviations of the QRS axis away from the normal - leftward or rightward - need not necessarily imply any ventricular hypertrophy of the left or right heart. Any factor which, for example, places the heart as a whole in a more horizontal position in the bony thorax will produce a deviation to the left of the electrical axis, whereas factors which place the cardiac mass in a more vertical position in the thorax will produce a deviation of the electrical axis to the right.

Non-cardiac conditions, which illustrate the horizontal position, are obesity or intestinal obstruction with rise in the diaphragm and a rising diaphragm due to pregnancy, ascites or diaphragmatic paralysis.

Examples of the vertical position are loss of body weight with a drop in diaphragmatic level, the normal, tall, thin, narrow body habitus with low diaphragm and, most important of all, lowering of the diaphragm in such conditions as emphysema or certain chest deformities. The cardiac mass is pulled out cephalo-caudally into a more tubular or vertical orientation as the diaphragm goes down. Diaphragmatic position can also alter with deep breathing, and axis shifts with a deep breath or change in bodily position from lying to sitting are often seen.

Clockwise and counterclockwise rotation may be assessed only in the chest leads (V1-V6). Normally, the R wave amplitude increases from V1 to V5. Around V3 or V4, the R wave becomes larger than the S waves, and this is called the "Transitional Zone."

In *clockwise rotation* the transition occurs after V4. This condition is also called 'poor R wave progression in the precordial leads'.

Differential diagnosis: Clockwise rotation may be seen in:

Dilated cardiomyopathy

Emphysema

Acute massive pulmonary embolism

Vertical heart (thin and tall persons)

In counterclockwise rotation, the transition occurs at or before V2.

Right ventricular hypertrophy

WPW syndrome

Hypertrophic cardiomyopathy

The following diagram gives differentiating features among different types of cardiac rotation.

No rotation

Counterclockwise rotation

Clockwise rotation

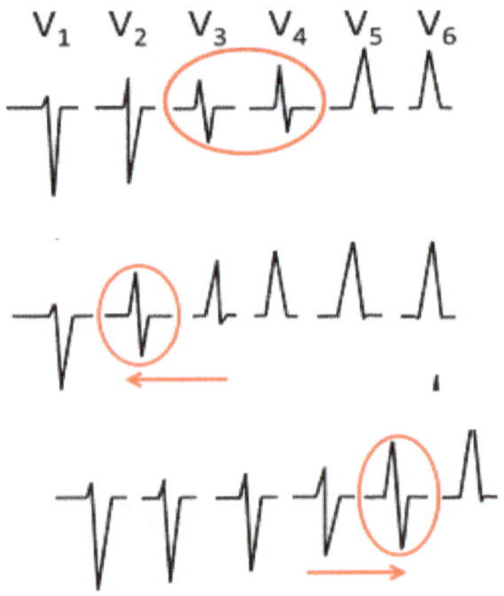

This concludes our chapter on rotation or twisting of the heart with various examples in the light of the Holy Quran; however, ALLAH Al-Mighty only knows the real meaning.

Acknowledgments

We had the opportunity to serve as the reviewers for this unique and thought-provoking book, "Heart in the Holy Quran", authored by Dr. M. Adnan Raufi. This work is an exceptional confluence of scientific knowledge and spiritual insight—an endeavor to understand the miraculous harmony between the physiological functions of the heart and the metaphysical references to the heart in the Holy Quran.

We were entrusted with reviewing the Quranic content, and the related Hadith references to ensure their conformity with established Islamic scholarship and found them to be correct and in line with religious jurisdiction. Our role involved critically examining the interpretations and analogies presented in the manuscript, especially where Dr. Raufi, with a deep sense of reverence, attempted to draw parallels between contemporary cardiac science and divine revelation.

What makes this project truly commendable is Dr. Raufi's humility and sincerity. He welcomed our feedback and incorporated our Shariah-based inputs with openness and respect, recognizing the sacredness of the Quranic message and the boundaries of interpretation. The reflections provided in this book do not claim definitive exegesis (tafsir) but rather serve as meditative explorations meant to inspire awe, curiosity, and spiritual awakening.

As Islamic researchers, we appreciated the author's clear distinction between scientific analysis and religious doctrine. Through this, the reader is encouraged to witness the divine signs within the human body, especially the heart, which is described in the Hadith as the central organ of righteousness and corruption.

We pray that ALLAH accepts this effort from Dr. Adnan Raufi and blesses it as a means of guidance and reflection for the whole of mankind. May this work inspire future collaborations between science and Islamic scholarship, always grounded in humility before the Word of ALLAH.

Dr. Mufti Muhammad Omer Rafique

PhD (Islamic Finance), Shariah Advisor and Assistant professor

omerrafiq1@gmail.com

Mufti Muhammad Junaid Salim

References

https://quizlet.com/29782536/middle-mediastinum-and-the-heart-flash-cards/

https://pdfcoffee.com/cor-anatomy-pdf-free.html

https://jumed14.weebly.com/uploads/5/8/7/5/58753271/anatomy-3.pdf

https://www.anyrgb.com/en-clipart-ocium

https://www.sciencedirect.com/topics/immunology-and-microbiology/systemic-circulation

https://www.researchgate.net/figure/n-the-human-heart-the-left-and-right-atria-are-filled-with-blood-returning-in-veins_fig1_269941835

https://quizlet.com/638778372/blood-supply-of-the-heart-flash-cards/

https://anatomie-fmpm.uca.ma/wp-content/uploads/2021/01/Anatomie-du-mediastin.pdf

https://theawesomeaustin.weebly.com/diagram.html

https://www.google.com/url?sa=i&url=https%3A%2F%2Fwww.svhhearthealth.com.au%2FArticleDocuments%2F989%2FCardiac_Surgery_Patient_Family.pdf.aspx&psig=AOvVaw1wUyRa_Bh6P-lg4Jk_lEMX&ust=1736460905508000&source=images&cd=vfe&opi=89978449&ved=0CBIQ3YkBahcKEwiQudjokueKAxUAAAAAHQAAAAAQBA

https://quizlet.com/ca/264385062/ischemic-heart-disease-flash-cards/

----

https://link.springer.com/chapter/10.1007/1-84628-146-6_17

https://www.semanticscholar.org/paper/Interpretation-of-SPECT-CT-myocardial-perfusion-and-Dvorak-Brown/70cd26b88b3400f8de0358275c22c35e94b74bf2

https://www.slideshare.net/slideshow/dr-liu-quit-smoking-slides-1-262013/16577757

https://quizlet.com/se/640733863/k3-cren-basgruppsfall-20-perikardit-och-perimyokardit-flash-cards/

https://www.physio-pedia.com/Anatomy_of_the_Human_Heart?veaction=edit

https://it.wikipedia.org/wiki/Pericardite#/media/File:Pericarditis.png

https://www.researchgate.net/figure/The-underlying-structure-of-the-cardiac-muscle-adapted-from-9_fig1_351511357

https://printables.assurances.gov.gh/form/its-inner-visceral-membrane-forms-part-of-the-filtration-membrane.html

https://quizlet.com/283178268/cardiac-tamponade-flash-cards/

https://www.slideshare.net/slideshow/cardiac-tamponade-44318438/44318438

https://quizlet.com/543992848/pocus-cardio-flash-cards/

https://www.researchgate.net/figure/n-the-human-heart-the-left-and-right-atria-are-filled-with-blood-returning-in-veins_fig1_269941835

https://unamsi.it/dalla-pesca-tradizionale-dei-polpi-in-giappone-alla-sindrome-del-crepacuore/

https://www.semanticscholar.org/paper/Endothelial-Dysfunction,-Inflammation-and-Coronary-Medina-Leyte-Zepeda-Garc%C3%ADa/ea6a39ba9e5d37f686abe7094bd10055d421fe84

https://www.researchgate.net/figure/Normal-coronary-artery-and-different-types-of-Atheromatous-plaque-with-or-without-spasm_fig1_325470085

https://en.m.wikipedia.org/wiki/File:Blausen_0052_Artery_Normalv Partially-BlockedVessel.png

https://www.hkccasc.com/2020/ppt/0704_ACHP_1145-1210_Frankie%20CC%20Tam.pdf

https://link.springer.com/chapter/10.1007/978-3-642-55131-4_5

https://teachmesurgery.com/cardiothoracic-surgery/cardiac/coronary-artery-disease/

https://medmalay.com/penyakit-injap-punca-dan-jenis

https://emedicine.medscape.com/article/1922899-overview

https://www.nejm.org/doi/full/10.1056/NEJMcp003331

https://vitalim.ca/awareness/conditions/cardiovascular-diseases/

https://www.andrewzurickmd.com/heart-failure

https://link.springer.com/chapter/10.1007/978-3-540-77290-3_8

https://www.researchgate.net/figure/Myocardial-contraction-and-rotation-When-myocardial-fibers-on-the-subepicardial-side_fig2_51076426

https://otosection.com/how-a-healthy-heart-works/

https://www.slideshare.net/slideshow/ecgpedia-ecg-course-conduction/383143

https://www.wikidoc.org/index.php/Aortic_regurgitation_electrocardiogram

https://www.wikidoc.org/index.php/QRS_axis_and_voltage

https://www.semanticscholar.org/paper/Left-Ventricular-Rotation-and-Twist%3A-Why-Should-We-Nakatani/94cdbc3821381c43c1bc7015df5fbfff0b230d36/figure/1